LOVE AND MONEY

CRITICAL CULTURAL COMMUNICATION
General Editors: Sarah Banet-Weiser and Kent A. Ono

Love and Money

Queers, Class, and Cultural Production

Lisa Henderson

NEW YORK UNIVERSITY PRESS
New York and London

NEW YORK UNIVERSITY PRESS
New York and London
www.nyupress.org

References to Internet Websites (URLs) were accurate at the time of writing.
Neither the author nor New York University Press is responsible for URLs that
may have expired or changed since the manuscript was prepared.

LIBRARY OF CONGRESS CATALOGING-IN-PUBLICATION DATA
Henderson, Lisa.
Love and money : queers, class, and cultural production / Lisa Henderson.
p. cm. — (Critical cultural communication)
Includes bibliographical references and index.
ISBN 978-0-8147-9057-1 (cl : alk. paper)
ISBN 978-0-8147-9058-8 (pb : alk. paper)
ISBN 978-0-8147-9059-5 (e-book)
ISBN 978-0-8147-4467-3 (e-book)
1. Gays—Social conditions. 2. Homosexuality—Social aspects. 3. Social classes. 4. Gays in
mass media. I. Title.
HQ76.25.H42 2013
306.76'6—dc23   2012031783

New York University Press books are printed on acid-free paper,
and their binding materials are chosen for strength and durability.
We strive to use environmentally responsible suppliers and materials
to the greatest extent possible in publishing our books.

Manufactured in the United States of America
c 10 9 8 7 6 5 4 3 2 1
p 10 9 8 7 6 5 4 3 2 1

To my mother, Lynn Henderson (1933–2011),
and my father, Peter Henderson (1935–2010)

CONTENTS

ACKNOWLEDGMENTS

Love and Money was long in the making. I am lucky to have patient colleagues at the University of Massachusetts Amherst who take my pace in stride and warmly receive my work as colleague, teacher, and administrator. For all its complexities, UMass is a place with a beating academic heart. The Department of Communication has been a multidisciplinary melting pot of critical practice and faculty governance, and I am fortunate—really fortunate—to have made my way there. Thanks to Deans Janet Rifkin and Bob Feldman for their support, integrity, and academic leadership, to Michael Morgan, who for nine years was our department chair and a veritable magician of ball-catching and good humor, and to my UMass friends, colleagues, and current and former graduate students, especially James Allan, Carolyn Anderson, Christopher Boulton, Briankle Chang, Lynn Comella, Vincent Doyle, Henry Geddes, Sut Jhally, Han Lee, Viera Lorençova, Erna MacLeod, Debra Madigan, Eve Ng, Scott Oberacker, Anca Romantan (1975–2008), Katherine Sender, Jacqueline Urla, and Emily West. Eve, Lynn, Viera, Liliana Herakova, and Tovar Cerulli were great research assistants for *Love and Money* from 2002 to 2011. Justin Lewis left UMass in 2000, but thankfully we never lost touch. He is a wonderful scholar and friend. Jackie Urla has been a wise friend and colleague since the week I arrived at UMass and has taken great interest in *Love and Money*. Julie Graham (1945–2010) was a beautiful colleague and friend; her work with Katherine Gibson has been transformative.

For invitations and opportunities to air and test my thoughts, thanks to hosts and audiences at the Center for Lesbian and Gay Studies at the City University of New York; the Future of American Studies Institute at Dartmouth College; the Five College Women's Studies Research Center; Indiana University; Keene State University; Lancaster University; Macalester College; Manchester University; McGill University; Université de Montréal; the *Queer Screen* plenary program at the University of Glasgow; the University of Illinois at Chicago; the University of Pennsylvania; and the University of Sydney. I am also grateful to the Marion and Jasper Whiting Foundation, whose sabbatical travel grant launched my fieldwork with Dorothy Allison and her readers, and to the College of Social and Behavioral Sciences at UMass and Five Colleges, Inc., whose travel support enabled me to join Liza Johnson's crew on *Desert Motel*.

In Massachusetts, I am blessed with friends on campus and off who read, heard, and responded, who are wickedly funny, who know how to live with the unexpected and how to treat people. I've been lucky to land softly among them in the best and worst of times. Thanks to Loretta Alper, Fidelma Culleton, Judith Frank, Elizabeth Garland, Ann Rosalind Jones, Susan Lowenstein, Carol Malthaner, James McDonald, Eugene Michaud (1946–2005), Barry O'Connell, Mary Russo, Peter Stallybrass, Martha Umphrey, and Daniel Warner.

I am also blessed as a member of the Conjunctures workshop in cultural studies. Thanks to everyone there, especially John Erni, Larry Grossberg, Carrie Rentschler, Gil Rodman, Kim Sawchuk, Greg Seigworth, Jonathan Sterne, and Will Straw. In Montreal, my hometown, Will has graced my life with brotherliness and brilliance for a long time, and Robert Schwartzwald has been both an exemplary academic and a prince of a friend. My love and thanks to both of them, and to Sean Holland (1968–2010), a dear friend whom I miss very much.

Sincere thanks to Eric Zinner at NYU Press for launching a new series that everyone in critical Communication studies appreciates. Sarah Banet-Weiser and Kent Ono, thank you for you editorial leadership and your enthusiasm for unconventional structure. Thanks to Ciara McLaughlin for swift trouble shooting and editorial hospitality, to early reviewers of the manuscript for their receptive insight, and to Despina Gimbel for well-oiled production.

A big thank-you to film director and writer Liza Johnson and her crew on *Desert Motel*, and to Dorothy Allison and her readers, for participating, for talking to me at my most awkward or starstruck, and for being willing to stay in the conversation through the arrival of this book. Everyone I interviewed for chapter 4 and was able to find several years later kindly granted permission for their commentary to appear in print. In one instance, I was not able to locate the contributor to renew permission and have therefore removed identifying details. The speakers in chapter 4, except Dorothy Allison and Michael Patrick MacDonald, are referred to by pseudonyms.

We all have teachers who continue to teach us no matter how collegial or friendly they become or how old we become. I am indebted to Steven Feld, Larry Gross, and Janice Radway for showing me the thrill of fieldwork, multidisciplinarity, and the study of culture. Larry introduced me to Scott Tucker in 1985, who I thank for his friendship, honesty, and rigorous thinking.

Richard Dyer is an incandescent friend whose every conversation, postcard, and especially whose every book opens up a new corner of the queer world. Richard introduced me to Jackie Stacey and Hilary Hinds, UK colleagues and friends of depth, creativity, and unself-conscious generosity. Richard, Jackie, and Hilary, thank you.

Other friends and colleagues have read and responded or contributed through conversation and hospitality while I was on the road, among them Marty Allor, Barry Dornfeld, Kathryn Furano (1964–2012), Joshua Gamson, Lori Ginzberg, Michael Hindery, Bette Kauffman, Terry King, Heather Love, Toby Miller, Kathy Peiss, Natalie Sacks, Irene Silverblatt, Sharon Ullman, Suzanna Walters, and Thomas Waugh.

Nan Woodruff is a wonderful scholar and sweet sister-mentor whose conversation and long friendship I am indebted to. Nan, prepare to retire together at Cranky Acres. Leola Johnson's intellectual gifts and long friendship are deep, and her style is impossible to imitate. Heather Murray is another original, an illustrious writer on families and queer life and a warm heart who has taught me a lot about the dangers of academic self-seriousness. My father's cousin Barrie Chavel became my friend, Toronto host, and fairy godmother in the early 1980s. Barrie died on October 19, 2010, but not without having grilled me several times about the topic, structure, and ETA of *Love and Money*. Everyone who knew Barrie recognized her husky-voiced and loving commitments to the people in her life and city. I am blessed to have been on the receiving end of those commitments for so long.

Several years into *Love and Money*, I fell in love with Thomas Streeter. Tom is not queer, though I am, which speaks to Tom's open heart, his knowing and world-weary respect for surprises, and his love of sweetness where we find it. He is a beautiful writer and a contrary and generous interlocutor. Friends have asked what brought me to Tom, at which point I'm relieved that I've never been a same-sex absolutist in print, and I quote Mae West: once, I was as pure as the driven snow, then I drifted. There's a place in queer scholarship for the study of drift, but that isn't my purpose. Thanks to Tom for his integrity, his Midwestern warmth and twang, his hospitality wherever we are, and especially for his love and solidarity.

Both of my parents, Lynn Henderson and Peter Henderson, died as I was completing *Love and Money*, my father on February 26, 2010, and my mother on June 13, 2011. I'm still composing the story of my relationships with my parents, who divorced in 1973 and whose responses to my queer life were distinct, sometimes harsh, fortunately never estranged. What strikes me the most, though, after their deaths, is how unimaginable the terms of my life would be without them. I take my libertinism and my commitments to the study and practice of culture from them, both actors, then broadcasters and writers, lovers all their lives of popular forms, promoters of genre, permissive parents who believed we *should* stay up to watch the Academy

Awards or a movie they especially liked (as long as we promised to sleep in the next day—what could be better?). When I hear others revile TV, I panic: without television, we'd have no group, no acute conversations about old and new series, no common object to laugh or disagree about or get us through every fun or nervous gathering. My mother became an accomplished writer after her retirement as announcer and host from the Canadian Broadcasting Corporation, though little of her work appears in print. My father, first a civil servant, then an open-line radio host and local impresario in Southern Ontario during his working years, remained an accomplished theater director in amateur and semiprofessional contexts, impressing me so brightly despite my sometimes imperious tastes. Lynn completed her BA at the age of sixty-two, at Concordia, taking one course a semester through an employment benefit with her first grandchildren down the street in Montreal. I went to Peter's BA graduation when I was ten, at what was then Sir George Williams University in Montreal (which later became a Concordia campus). He then completed an MA in Communication at Syracuse while living in a VW camper in the late 1970s. Lynn and Peter mean everything to me. They never saw this book, whose class idioms I was honestly more anxious about revealing to them than its queer idioms, but nor did they ever doubt I would finish it. Their love and respect have been extraordinary gifts.

That said, my final thank-you goes to the living: to my sister, Kate Henderson, and my brothers, Peter Henderson and Sean Henderson, to Valeria Henderson, my father's strong and venturesome wife of thirty-five years, and to our very extended family. Despite different lives, Kate, Peter, Sean, and I are tight, just how tight I didn't know until newcomers—most recently, Tom—would point it out. We grew up in various degrees of security and insecurity and sometimes went years without seeing one another. But we never lost touch. We learned from Peter and Lynn the virtues of the big tent, of fun, humor, and the living art of showing up. Through the equality of their love for us, we have inherited pleasure in one another's company. Kate, Pete, Sean, thanks for everything.

Some chapters of *Love and Money* were published previously: a shorter version of chapter 1 originally appeared in *Screen* 42, no. 3 (2001) and was reprinted in *The Queer Screen Reader*, edited by Jackie Stacey and Sarah Street (London: Routledge, 2007); a shorter version of chapter 2 appeared in *Media Queered: Visibility and Its Discontents*, edited by Kevin Barnhurst (New York: Peter Lang, 2007); chapter 3 originally appeared in the *Massachusetts Review* 49, nos. 1/2 (2008), a special queer issue edited by John Emil Vincent; a version of chapter 5 appeared in *GLQ: A Journal of Lesbian and Gay Studies* 14, no. 4 (2008).

Introduction

Love and Money, Queerness and Class

Love and Money is a book of cultural critique and exploration at the crossroads of queerness and class in the United States. Through field studies and comparative criticism, it asks what difference social class makes to queer subjectivity and representation, and what difference queerness makes to class hierarchy and value. I argue that we cannot see queer cultures clearly enough when we ignore class, nor can we see contemporary class outside the production of sexual difference. Sometimes the object of this argument is commercial popular culture, long the measure of queer defilement by radical standards. Other times, its objects are the beloved texts and expressions—in film and literature—of queer independent producers and queer community audiences across class lines. Still other times, the object is radical queer critique itself, in the spirit of articulating a new critical vocabulary less bound than the ones we now use by familiar oppositions between markets and politics and thus less driven by the taste hierarchies that surface so easily in the name of commercial refusal. *Love and Money* argues that the rich soil of cultural production offers renewal—ways to imagine and practice solidarity that have long been present but undersung amid class antagonism in queerness and sexual-political antagonism from the American left. Class is not a purely cultural form, but culture is vital to queer class solidarity.

Love and Money starts from a romantic and by-now nostalgic view: in queerness exists the chance for social attachments and forms of belonging that might otherwise be impossible. That something about the alloy of erotic energy, social shame, new interiorities, the open smudging of private and public, shifts in psychic expectation at once gradual and dramatic, and the limits of family acceptance would impel us to social creativity. That we would find affection and strength in new places, inhabit the world across old divisions, be slow to judge and curious about modes of living beyond our own. That we would pool what few resources we had and circulate them in new ways. That we would live with new ambitions—our own but also ambitions in common, held together by the idea that any resource brings greater pleasure if it enriches the collective and doesn't come at someone else's expense.

That love as we knew it could be rerooted in depths of feeling and social possibility, not zip codes, alma maters, and routine proprieties.

For me, this was not a myth of the 1960s, except as it spilled over into that period—the 1980s—when I came queerly and intellectually of age in my mid-twenties, by then close to completing a PhD at the University of Pennsylvania. My education expressed my life as a running repository of privilege and opportunity, though it often didn't feel that way. I had come from a family of mixed economic position in Canada of the 1960s and 70s: broke, bohemian, parents divorced, borderline professional. I believed early on that I could go to school and become what I wanted. It wasn't true, exactly, but it was an encouraging story whose limits I would need to discover—quite a different thing than having to reverse that old class injury that tells people school is not for them, nor are they cut out for school. I was overworked but well endowed, a *jeune leftiste* with a plan, a citizen of federal laws and provincial governments that kept health care and a university education in reach.

A lot has changed since then, especially in the United States, to undermine anyone's belief in queer and other forms of social possibility. AIDS and criminal indifference to health and survival; war and occupation as national security; the political ascent of religious fundamentalism and the right wing; the retrenchment of civil liberty, social welfare, affirmative action, and support for public education; and the demonization of public cultures save those polished and packaged for family and professional-managerial consumption—such developments do not open the world to reimagining and *florissance* but compel us to survival and self-protection. Old divisions are rediscovered and naturalized, erotic energies attenuated, psychic expectations plucked from cultural possibility and framed instead by "destiny" and "evolution." Social curiosity becomes suspicion, and resource-pooling a form of mismanagement corrected by concentration and upward distribution.

By some analyses, contemporary neoliberalism killed queerness and with it the fantasy of queer transformation. But within the same period—roughly since 1980—other, more promising challenges have been wrought in intellectual and political practice, those that demand greater accountability than is communicated by a transcendent fantasy of social change. Racially, economically, and sexually, who was included in the "we" of gayness, especially as gay power left bathrooms for boardrooms, city streets for city halls, and political boycotts for party politics? Borders had been redrawn and old strategies of political respectability redeployed to enfranchise some and excise others from new discourses of policy, rights, and access, enough to imagine a new regime of *homo*normativity formed in cooperation with heterosexual privilege (Duggan 2003; Murphy, Ruiz, and Serlin 2008). If admission to the club meant playing by the club's rules, then activism and critique meant being accountable to broader constituencies, those living on the nondominant side of gender, race, class, citizenship, ability, and sexual style.

Love and Money thus comes to the link between sexuality and social class to reinvigorate accountability to class hierarchy inside and outside of queerness. But it also seeks the idioms of a renewed affinity in hard times, a feeling of possibility rooted less in identity per se (though there are worse gestures) than in a form of recognition rooted simultaneously in social difference and shared cultural will. Such a move is both thorny and familiar. On its thorny side, any assertion of shared will raises the specter of suppression (of inequality) and the displacement of injustice onto cultural fantasies of integration. More familiarly, it speaks to a well-established but not easily practiced politics of coalition, best articulated by queer and feminist scholars of race, ethnicity, and diaspora (e.g., Ferguson 2004; Eng, Halberstram, and Muñoz 2005). As indebted as I am to those writers, I am also trying to animate new terms, and reanimate some old ones, to explore the cultural links between queerness and class, both in particular and in a way that might later be opened to other conjunctures of identification and alliance, harm and good.

Queer Cultural Production

Love and Money's empirical field is cultural production, referring to the making, circulation and reception of cultural forms and to cultural practices and processes in situ. It is in the making of culture—rather than the settled conventions of forms themselves—that contradiction and irresolution are revealed and thus where categories as dynamic, forceful, and incomplete as "queerness" and "class" can be explored as living categories, as resources and limiters in how we think and act.

Sometimes cultural production means processes whose outcomes or products are specialized and well defined. Filmmaking, popular music, and television production are easy examples, and a long history of studies in cultural production has addressed industrial contexts and professional routines to understand why films, television programs, and popular music genres are what they are. What, for example, in the organization of daytime "trash television" so reliably repeats "real-life" characters and conflicts at the very margins of taste and propriety? How are streams of otherwise average people recruited, cast, primed, and produced—by executives, creatives, and underlings—as the trash-talking, chair-throwing, gasp-inducing regulars on *The Jerry Springer Show* or the modest, thoughtful, and considered "experts" and "citizens" on *Phil Donahue* or *Oprah*? (Grindstaff 2002). What convergence, in other words, of class fantasy in the culture and the industrial character and contingency of commercial television in the United States favors limited innovation in genres and narratives and thus reduced images of race, class, and queer difference?

The emphasis in the cultural production tradition is on practice: what producers—as specialists and cultural citizens—do in the complex, regulated, uneven, routinized, and usually commercial contexts of culture-making. But culture is not only made there. It is made wherever people in groups create, adapt, and trade symbolic forms and live by the terms their practice enables. This introduces informal scenes and cultural practices at spatial, temporal, and political remove from the dominant commercial core—like underground music or 'zining—to the cultural production tradition, though historically such work has been written under the banner of subculture or the practice of everyday life.

Love and Money takes its questions about queerness and class to commercial, subcultural, and everyday contexts to ask about cultural forms and processes, but ultimately to think about the movement of cultural categories and citizens within and across sociocultural zones. I call this process "relay" (chapter 5) to clarify the mobile and uneven character of cultural production over time, space, and group, where outcomes are neither as concrete as objects nor as entrenched as systems and industries. Through fieldwork and criticism, my method is to untangle the threads of thought, action, and relation over space and time. The goals of such methods are not to hypothesize the cultural field but to map it, to gauge the cultural coordinates of power (as wealth, policy, and control, but also as autonomy, security, self-definition, and change), and thus to use criticism and cultural analysis as a way into political processes. Such an approach makes criticism itself a form of cultural production, though not the one I study in *Love and Money*, at least not formally.

Queer scholarship in cultural production takes place inside and outside the mantle of production studies, exploring corner pockets in mainstream contexts and flourishing—or surviving—subcultural scenes (see Henderson 2000). Queer cultural products are sometimes highly conventional and institutional, like series television (Gamson 1998), and other times more ephemeral, like performances (Muñoz 1999), or community-based, such as scenes and their archives of memory and affect (Cvetkovich 2003). Across such contexts questions are in play about definitions of queerness as antinormative sexual and gender variation and the production of queerness through racial, ethnic, gender, and, less frequently, class discourses and practices. Questions are also in play about subjectivity, community-making, and the viability and transformation of queer cultures, and about challenges to heteronormative business-as-usual through queer invention.

Such questions are a part of the broader approach to queer cultural production that I undertake in *Love and Money*, with an eye to cultural fields that are never only queer and to outcomes at once concrete and symbolic. Sometimes I study the independent production of queer short films (chapter 5) or readers' reception of queer fiction (chapter 4) to engage class questions, and other times I study how texts and genres frame queer, class, and race fantasy in the changing conditions of commercial television (chapter 2). In all cases, concrete practices and objects and more abstract values combine to enable and limit our everyday lives and how we can or might imagine the future. Relative concreteness or abstraction is not, in other words, a measure of whether things matter. As form and idea, culture is real in its effect.

Studies in cultural production also reveal class as a category that bears both concrete and abstract exploration. In *Love and Money*, class refers most broadly to the economic and cultural coproduction of social distinction and hierarchy. That is not a frame that will satisfy everyone, nor would I defend it as complete. But, even though class is traditionally an economic category, a lot of variation occurs within those stations of the cross of class historically defined through labor-capital analysis (in the Marxist tradition) or empirically defined by occupation, income, and formal education (in the liberal one), variation that cultural criticism can address. Workers, owners, professionals, incomes, and years in school do not evaporate in *Love and Money*, but nor is this a study of resource distribution per se, or one in which class is categorized, measured, and tested to determine what proportion of cultural variance we might attribute to independent class or socioeconomic variables. Here class categories work in vernacular and analytic ways to mark a cultural universe—ways recognized by their speakers to produce both openings and injuries. They do so anew in combination with vernacular queerness and with discourses of race as both the root and branch of class difference in the United States. *Love and Money* is, in other words, a cultural study of queer-class conjuncture, but that is an approach, not an argument for imagining class as fundamentally or primarily a cultural form. Culture is essential but partial in the definition and operation of social class, as it is in other human categories and endeavors. I thus intend *Love and Money* to be read alongside—not instead of—political economic analysis of social class.[1]

Queer Left Friendship

Love and Money begins with a story of queer class tragedy and ends with the plausibility of optimism rooted in *friendship*, a term universally familiar (if not transparent) and, with notable exceptions (e.g., Nardi 1999; Foucault

1981/1997), undersung in theory and social analysis. Friendship is a form of relating perhaps no less determined than other forms by *habitus* (Bourdieu 1984) or the deep tastes and dispositions of class fractions; no less psychically complicated than family attachments and romance; no less painful than those other forms when it ends badly or less nostalgic when it fades. But it is potentially a different kind of good than are other normative attachments, easier to come and go within, more responsive to circumstance, devoted and familiar but perhaps less burdened by obligation, trauma, sameness, the myth of fit or the deadening weight of *relationship work*, the mandate Laura Kipnis (2003) called domesticity's gulag. I work on relationships, but as a model for other social forms, friendship can buoy, de-dramatize, lighten things up.[2] Amid political heaviness, this is an affective and social virtue, which is why *Love and Money* ends with friendship's optimism. But one doesn't arrive there—at least I haven't—without hard thinking about failed relating and failed accountability, including across queer class lines.

What do such failures look like? They are the personal antagonisms of misrecognition, entitlement, and shame and the slights to subjectivity that leave us gasping. But they are also the organization of those affects and dispositions into social and political form, through cultural exclusion on a local level or political bottlenecking on the national—those occasions where questions of expendability are freely asked at the expense of outsiders or combatants without the political capital to prevail: the 2007 exclusion, for example, of transgender as a protected category in Human Rights Campaign efforts to pass the Employment Non-Discrimination Act, or political distancing from sex workers and undocumented immigrants in the formation of professional gay and lesbian lobbying organizations and national coalitions.[3]

Many radical observers would also include the gay and lesbian marriage-rights agenda as a class affront, since marriage assumes a normative social form and reserves for married people a range of essential resources, like health care, better distributed without regard to marriage or employment. Health care shouldn't depend on marriage. But any legal or policy measure that enables even partial redistributions in the present will count for people who don't have what they need, including where those measures may double back and limit future opportunities. Better to work for single-payer health care than marriage rights in the name of limited health provision (which only works if at least one spouse is employed, entitled to employee health benefits, and further entitled to spousal or family coverage, usually at great and increasing cost). But these are not either/or equations, and disgust with marriage activism as a homonormative and class sellout suppresses distributive urgency in many cases. A new political problem arises, however, when distributive urgency (such as marriage as the route to health care or legal entry as immigrant) is dressed in the language of God and romance, money is poured into marriage rights, and health-care activism is left to health-care activists, few (but not none) of them working for queer health.

To follow the literature and engage the politics of queer activism is to recognize these antagonisms, sometimes dismissively or with bewilderment, other times with the wish and energy to reorganize. And there is no guarantee that knowledge born of collective work across queer and class lines will mean the end of more personal or subjective antagonisms at other levels of ideology and cultural disposition. These are cultural levels less consciously acquired and practiced and the ones *Love and Money* addresses. Throughout, and especially in the penultimate chapter on optimism, I explore the relation of feeling and cultural form to social and political possibility, moved by the work of Lauren Berlant in *The Female Complaint* (2008).

Berlant is a cultural critic whose left, feminist, multiracial, and queer analyses cohabit and recombine in a sustained theorization of public culture and its political possibilities. This distinguishes her work in a Left intellectual field where, historically, queerness has been a brake on class thinking, a challenge to a Left intellectual history that is stymied by—and as often hostile to—the question of queer significance in class formation. Queerness, some have argued (Field; Morton), imagines continuities where none exist, since its distribution across class difference and conflict means that there is no meaningful possibility of queer recognition or collective interest. Where class interest is present, it will prevail, making the empathies and communities of queer sexual practice and exclusion the root of false consciousness, not social transformation.

In my experience as critic and citizen, however, wherever class primacy can be demonstrated it can also be undone, and wherever cultural identifications take root in everyday life, they will matter and will combine to overdetermine the effects of related structures and differences. In any general sense, one cannot prove the lesser social, individual, or subjective significance of queer in contrast to class harm or value, except in the abstract. This does not dismiss abstraction after all, since we quickly understand its material significance in such domains as law and policy, even when they bear only indirectly on community fortune. But the more familiar abstraction emerges not from policy or other forms of social enactment outside theorization. It emerges from intellectual history, from Left traditions of thought and politics committed to a foundational analysis of class rooted in economic production and distribution, even as the society in which it is written roots itself in consumption, including the consumer practices of critics and theorists.

For better and worse, this is a Left intellectual history and politics that I share. But it is possible to do so without the analytic chauvinism that treats other axes of social differentiation—like gender and sexuality—as satellites to economism or, worse, as expressions of self-interest and bad faith among reviled but otherwise privileged queers. *Love and Money* moves instead from the recognition that when social revulsion and privilege (rather than poverty) co-occur, they are strange bedfellows. Oscar Wilde and his heirs come to mind, though show trials and jail time are hard to swallow as evidence of privilege, and thus Wilde better illustrates a convergence of subculture, elite formation, and official degradation, where class privilege is withdrawn, not enhanced, by queerness. There are privileged queers, myself among them, but we are not to be confused with queer privilege outside the limited domain of subcultural capital.

In putting queerness and class together in this way, however, I am skating close to the edge of an old Left stereotype that imagines and distrusts queerness as itself an expression of elite derangement (or Nazi eroticism, or female double agency, or fascist impulse manifest in old-school sexual dominance and the mechanical invariance of disco music). As, in other words, an engine of strange power. Happily, however, disco rhythms vary after all, as those who lived by them and their queer solidarities in the 1970s remember well (Dyer 1979). And while the socioeconomic character of queer attachment in any broad sense has yet to be interrogated, least of all comparatively, reliable data in labor economics (e.g., Badgett 2003) demonstrate that in the present and recent past, gayness and lesbianism are suppressors, not enhancers, of household income, slightly less so for women than for men, who typically earn more and thus have more to lose.[4] Queerness *is* an engine of strange power, if you do it right, but not of class supremacy or ascendancy any more than the moderate and threatened postwar expansion of the U.S. black middle class is evidence of reverse discrimination.

In the Left stereotype of queerness as class threat, what is reviled is the sex of queerness, in contrast to the hegemonic virtues of work and family that mark some revisions and public enactments of leftism, particularly those that have sought to recapture political support from evangelical and right-wing populism since the 1960s. In that rhetoric, queerness becomes a "wedge issue." During John Kerry's candidacy in the U.S. presidential election of 2004, for example, especially in light of the Supreme Judicial Court's antidiscrimination decision on same-sex marriage in the Commonwealth of Massachusetts (Kerry's and my home state), queerness became political fodder for the antigay right wing and for trouble in the heartland, and thus an abrasion in efforts to elect a hawkish and lukewarm party Democrat. Like

Ralph Nader, queerness was framed as a spoiler—the target of Left and liberal political hostility stoked by a long history of righteous enforcement of the closet. *Why now?* complained even putatively solidary, nonqueer Kerry supporters, and a few queer ones, too. It didn't matter that queers have never controlled the timing of intervention, legislation, or backlash, however hard queer activists in Massachusetts and elsewhere may try.

I, too, wanted an end to the Reagan-Bush-Clinton-Bush era in the name of peaceability and public culture and a reduction of the chasms between the elite owners of private jets, the debt financers of middle-class health care, and the uninsured earners of minimum wage, who are made to work harder (and die younger) by being paid less, not more. But it was hardly clear that Kerry would be or would provoke those conditions, and any campaign support dependent on the renunciation of the most limited expression of equality—the equality of kinship (Tucker 1997) rooted in the Massachusetts marriage decision—revealed the limits of liberal, progressive, sometimes even lesbian or gay (non)support for the political recognition of queerness. Those who refused either/or politics (gay marriage *or* an end to the war in Iraq; repealing the Defense of Marriage Act *or* Supreme Court protection of abortion rights) were, in a word that exquisitely rehearsed the old charge of gay narcissism, "selfish." The politics that had heightened my attention to social transformation were now held responsible for blocking a historic opportunity for change.

In 2008, Barack Obama's campaign, in contrast, was bracingly cautious in its recognition of some civil rights for gays and lesbians, though Obama himself was forthright in declaring that he did not support same-sex marriage (despite the contempt he expressed in 2005 for the federal Defense of Marriage Act, a contempt that has since been revealed to have more than one side in Obama's political practice, and despite his late affirmation of same-sex marriage in the run-up to the 2012 election). When Obama won in 2008 (before the midterm "shellacking" in 2010), we knew historic significance when we saw it and our exuberance was palpable. Many, though, watched the election returns torn by disappointment as Arkansas passed an initiative to prohibit unmarried cohabitants (read: queers) to foster or adopt children, and California upheld Proposition 8, the same-sex marriage ban that overruled California's State Supreme Court decision five months earlier that the prohibition against same-sex marriage was unconstitutional. Pundits were quick to declare that it was precisely those voters who elected Obama in California—70 percent of African Americans and 52 percent of Latinos—who had also passed Prop 8. The queer organizers against Prop 8, however (among them the National Center for Lesbian Rights), thanked their multi-ethnic, multi-racial, and multi-income coalition of supporters and activists and reminded the nation that the 52 percent of white voters in California who supported Prop 8 (and some seventy million Mormon dollars) went further toward putting it in place than black and Latino voters combined. The attempt to recirculate an electoral logic of black vs. gay and Latino vs. gay was especially nauseating for black and Latino gay Californians who had worked, watched, and hoped for an election outcome of multifaceted enfranchisement. The postelection task, alongside renewed opposition to the ballot initiative, would become how to oppose the "black/Latino vs. gay" split and its narrow, antigay class implications in a universe where nonwhite is likely to mean working class or poor.[5]

But I am not expert enough in the deal making or machination of the 2004 or 2008 federal elections to answer more precisely "What went wrong?" Nor is that my question. In 2008, some things went right in a constrained political universe and the future remained to be known and created.[6] (That is still true, despite frustrations and disappointments with the administration of Barack Obama, who is nothing if not a party Democrat.) I recall these occasions to frame the political stance I bring to a critique of queer/class encounter and to remind myself of the importance of not surrendering queer commitments as a demonstration of political maturity. In the queer/class case, this means not trading denunciations of queerness in class, Left or other progressive terms, nor queer denunciations of Left politics, but asking, more expansively and in the spirit of a class-conscious and multiracial queer critique, where and how queerness and class hierarchy produce each other and, better, how queer/class inversions of all kinds make culture richer. How is each category brought into the same frame of cultural articulation to imagine, limit, reconfigure, devalue, or enfranchise the other? The historical persistence of sexual practice and character as the domains of judgment and social (de)legitimacy (e.g., Warner 1999) is a transparent reminder that queerness, like other sexual and gender forms, *will encounter* changing class configurations as queers enter and navigate the slipstreams of social and cultural life. Thus, my intention in *Love and Money* is to develop a language of queer class engagement that makes itself available to other expressions of the sex–gender–class chain and other convergences in social form and possibility.

Queer Class Repair

Several linkages give this study its shape: queerness, class, and trauma; the class markers of queer worth; queerness as a question of *how to be*; class recognition in queerness; queer *relay* as a form of social creativity; and plausible optimism as political affect. From trauma to creativity, the arc they trace expresses what Eve Kosofsky Sedgwick (2003) movingly called a reparative mode of reading. Sedgwick defines reparative reading in contrast to the more familiar "paranoid" mode. Paranoid reading embodies a critic's anxiety that because there can be no bad surprises, there can be no surprises at all. Here a critic is anticipatory: she knows before she starts what bad news she'll find. A paranoid critic is mimetic: she practices what she may diagnose in the text—the rigidity and violence of categorization, say—in the spirit of not being caught unaware of precisely the violence she suspects is there. Paranoid reading is strong in everywhere finding evidence of its suppositions, and it disavows its persistently negative affect and force. In its disavowal, it offers negativity as truth and the exposure of textual or social violence as grail.

Anticipatory, mimetic, strong, negative, and exposing (Sedgwick 2003, 130): paranoid reading is near-ubiquitous in queer and cultural studies, familiar to me in my own writing and teaching. Expertise in negative detection in advance of another critic, or of being trumped, somehow, by precisely the negative effects one detects, emerges as a kind of proliferative tautology, a gesture ceaselessly reproducible in each new critique of each new bit of anticipated bad news on the social and cultural horizon. As Sedgwick points out, paranoid reading starts with the claim that "things are bad and getting worse" (142), a proposition at once irrefutable and so general as to be fallow; culture becomes a salt flat where little that is oppositional or that recognizes and enables survival can grow. Enfranchised critics working in the paranoid tradition do survive, but it is more likely that we are sustained by our enfranchisement and reparative underside than by our paranoia.

I encountered Sedgwick's essay on paranoid and reparative reading in the course of researching and writing chapter 4, on class recognition in queerness. At the time, debates were under way in social theory about recognition and redistribution as differential forms of social remedy. Some argued that recognition—the social and policy acknowledgment and inclusion of historically marginalized groups—was a value best attached to cultural identity (gender, ethnicity, sexuality) and inert in the domain of class, here imagined as not "merely cultural" (Butler 1997) but something deeper in the infrastructure. Recognition could not remedy class inequality; only the erasure or limiting of class hierarchy through economic redistribution could do that (e.g., Skeggs 2000).

The most persuasive versions of such theorizing argued for interdependency rather than opposition between recognition and redistribution.[7] In

Nancy Fraser's terms (1996), social collectivities are defined both symbolically through cultural identification and economically through resource distribution, and thus social theory and policy must work at the level of bivalence rather than embattle itself with questions of political primacy. "Recognition or redistribution?" became a descriptive question, not an ethical one.

In 1997, Judith Butler published a compelling argument about the *distributive* consequences of *cultural* misrecognition, drawing on socialist feminism's early analyses of the economic consequences of gender difference and extending feminist insight to sexuality and sexual difference. It did not come as news to queers that the economic resources of employment, inheritance, immigration, and other entitlements distributed through such family ties as marriage were withheld from them *as a class* (with variable outcomes predicted by wealth, race, and citizenship). But this was not commonplace in arguments about the primacy of redistribution as social remedy, rooted as those arguments were in older political and intellectual divisions. Butler convinced some that the misrecognition of queerness had distributive consequence after all, that identitarian collectivities like queers routinely bear the burden of maldistribution *and* misrecognition, and thus that recognition could not be sequestered and dismissed as the nuisance politics of identity, in contrast to a Left universe of rigorous class struggle.

Butler's analysis, however, left open the relevance of recognition to class difference. Were there such things as class identity and (mis)recognition and, if so, did they matter? Were class identity and attachment negative traps in the long revolution toward classlessness? As I spoke with a range of interlocutors about their class locations (including those who described themselves as class "escapees," people from working-class backgrounds who had "gotten out," but at the cost of family disavowal and paralyzing ambivalence), class identity didn't seem so distant or irrelevant, to them any more than to me, with my mix of genteel poverty, patrician bohemianism, and educational privilege born of family possibility and state enablement. Thus finding a place for the language of class recognition became a matter of social and ethical value, a reparative gesture that I had not understood in those terms as I undertook fieldwork. At that moment, and in the most fortuitous way, Sedgwick's (2003) ideas authorized a move in a new and more generous direction, one that echoed the survival value of class recognition, as those I'd interviewed told it.

Colleagues and critics in many places have distrusted that move as I have presented work on class recognition, but not persuasively enough— however richly argued—to abandon the impulse to listen or to imagine without already knowing what role class recognition might play in queer transformation. I do believe that class recognition matters, but that is not a quasi-religious belief; it is inductive, an interpretation derived from ranging and pointed conversation, including with those quoted in chapter 4. And although that belief departs from the most refined and demanding qualities of Sedgwick's (2003) account of reparative critique, it shares with Sedgwick's account a political and ethical regard for survival as the first condition of thriving. Class recognition need not be a threat to redistribution. It neither entrenches class hostility nor disables a politics of class abolition. It strikes me as dishonest, then, and politically unfair, to withhold such recognition and its value while a distant revolution is engineered.

Thus in its opening chapters, *Love and Money* moves from engagement with familiar forms of criticism that anticipate—and indeed find—bad news in the class character of queerness, especially its most visible expressions in commercial popular culture. It then turns to writer-director-actor Miranda July's 2005 film *Me and You and Everyone We Know* as a kind of boundary or liminal text, a work whose story and aesthetic suspend pronouncement long enough to imagine the everyday social calculations of vulnerable people and to reimagine queerness as a question of *how to be.* July's work is a good place to shift gears, a cultural switching system that redirects me toward softness without disavowing insights from the route taken through negative or even paranoid critique. Paranoid critique is not enough, in other words, but nor does a reparative disposition claim that social damage or threat isn't occurring all around us. Rather, it claims that stepping into the critical cycle of threat and defense disables other forms of reading, other insights, and, ultimately, other forms of living. *Love and Money* thus leads with cases where familiar ideas about class pathology structure images and narratives of queer trauma, and where class, race, and value combine to condition queer visibility in some of the harshest ways. From there it moves in a different and hopefully not naive direction, to recognition, relay, and optimism.

The Chapters

As a project that seeks to capture the multiform relationship between queerness and class, *Love and Money* offers different points of entry, an elastic method that I hope creates a mirror image of cultural development itself. The analysis is thus not linear (if A, then B; if B, then C), though it is cumulative. It is also not centripetal, all energy moving to a theoretical center. Better to read it as a faceted sphere; as you turn the sphere over to land on a new facet, the light is refracted differently. In cultural studies, this analytic form is usually called "articulation," where new social possibilities arise out of historical (not necessary) linkages between groups and ideas.

Chapter 1, "The Class Character of *Boys Don't Cry*," is my opening gambit for queer class critique. *Boys Don't Cry* (1999) is a film recognized as a narrative of transgender trauma and transphobic murder, one based on the true story of Brandon Teena. Teena was a Midwestern, transgender teenager killed alongside his friends Lisa Lambert and Phillip DeVine by John Lotter and Tom Nissen in Humboldt, Nebraska, in 1993. Teena had befriended Lotter and Nissen in his relocation to the nearby Nebraska town of Falls City. As Judith Halberstam (2005) has written, Teena's "true story" emerges in retrospect from the cultural archive of Teena's life and death, an archive that is ranging, uneven, and revealing of the interests and dispositions of those who have produced it. By "archive," Halberstam refers not simply to a collection of documents or data but to a "discursive field and a structure of thinking" (32–33), a repertoire of frames, images, narratives, and judgments, in Teena's case about gender ambiguity, rural life, and the desires of young people in scenes of need and aspiration.

Boys Don't Cry is an important signifier in the Brandon Teena archive, the one best known to those least connected to transgender scenes and to many transgender people. Popularly received as the occasion of Hilary Swank's Oscar-winning performance as Brandon, and thus as literal evidence of the performability of gender from the outside in, *Boys* was rarely addressed as a class text. But what does it tell us if we make a point of reading it that way, if we ask how its story of rural, white, working-class abjection structures transgender representation, in a world where class and gender nonconformity are rooted in hierarchy and exclusion? In *Boys Don't Cry*, class marks gender trauma, and gender variance is both the hope and denial of class transcendence—hope in Brandon and Lana's romance, denial in Brandon's exposure and murder. Such dramatic images of class failure are cautionary, not just an expression but an enactment of bourgeois white supremacy. Trace feelings of recognition may connect moments in the film to gestures and practices in everyday life, but they also attach to the shame historically embedded in the relationship between modes of living and self-defeat, a shame at the root of class injury (Sennett and Cobb 1972). In *Boys*, trauma and shame are a queer class affair, and the category of class itself is queered (Kaplan 2000), its historical certainties shaken down and reconstructed through new modes of longing and expression.

"Queer Visibility and Social Class," chapter 2, moves from the question of stakes to a structural analysis of the symbolic engines of queer/class articulation. What, I ask, are the class markers of queer worth in that other archive,

Scotty kisses Kevin, *Brothers and Sisters*, "Date Night," Season 1, Episode 5 © 2006 Touchstone Television.

both celebrated and distrusted in the 1990s and early 2000s as the "new queer visibility"?

The most forceful critics of contemporary queer media images describe the 1990s as the decade of the lesbian and gay media extravaganza (Gross 2001; Walters 2001). It is true: proportionate increases are impressive—easy, when you start from nothing—with a few regular characters and dozens of walk-ons per season of broadcast television, and designated series like *Queer as Folk* and *The L Word* arriving on cable in the new millennium. But the terms of entry have been constrained by heteronormative and consumer expectation and by cautious commercial investment, each next possibility conditioned by the fortunes of the last. It took micro-generations of commercial cultural advance and retreat to ensure a biweekly screen kiss for Kevin Walker (Matthew Rhys), for example, the gay lawyer sibling on the prime-time family melodrama *Brothers and Sisters,* which entered the program schedule in 2006.

Those chaste and sincere kisses were preceded by long histories of desexualization and the most plodding forms of positive imaging. Where boutique dramas like *NYPD Blue* could risk a nude, average, and married male backside to heighten its realist style, the sprinkling of gay characters was fully costumed, and queer kisses remained the last frontier in drama and situation comedy for almost two decades. But, since television had provoked a flagging film industry to specialize in sex and violence in the 1960s, escalating competition between cable and broadcast programming in the late 1990s and early 2000s meant strategic shifts toward a new edge in queer character-ization on broadcast television, enough so that by 2006, *not* letting healthy, well-attired, white gay male lawyers from dynastic families kiss would be a joke (how long could they go?), but in the wrong genre. Thus buried in the amber of Kevin's on-screen kisses were the fossils of television's past, recon-figured by what many describe as the most powerful and limiting appropria-tion of the fruits of gay political activism: niche marketing (see Sender 2004).

Up-marketeering, however, is not the only class story in queer visibility. Market-authored media images also borrow liberally from the class fantasies of everyday life, especially fantasies of mobility and having. Although class and consumption have been attached in different ways for a century and a half (Williams 1961), in the contemporary period it is important to untangle commercial imperatives, industry practices, and popular fantasy in account-ing for that attachment. Such an untangling exposes the continuity of queer class fantasy inside the media and out, and thus the roots of class injury as in the culture rather than in the media system as separately conceived. This requires both an examination across genres, looking to noncommercial nar-rative examples to discover whether they share anything with *Will & Grace* (they do), and whether the critical shorthand that says contemporary media queers are uniformly rich, white, healthy, and male holds up (it doesn't). The repertoire of queer characters and gestures is more varied, and the vari-ants are judged according to fairly stable premises rooted in comportment, familialism, and modes of acquisition (or how we get what we have). Across forms, genres, and nonmedia cultural practice, such premises exceed *Ellen* or *Will & Grace* by a long and wide margin.

In chapter 3, I shift gears, making criticism itself a class project (Ortner 2003) in the reparative mode. In my response to Miranda July's *Me and You and Everyone We Know* (2005) and to her story collection, *No One Belongs Here More Than You* (2007), I move away from ideological critique and the generative rules of queer/class articulation, instead to be guided by the work itself in new forms of queer reading. July's work is not obviously queer in the usual senses; it is not marked by antinormative gender variance or same-sex eroticism, though normative categories are sexually troubled by venture-some teenage girls in the film and, in one of the stories, by tensely related sis-ters. Overall, however, *Me and You and Everyone We Know* and July's stories invite a calm uncertainty about how to be, in a narrative context that repre-sents the socioeconomic home of so many people: the frayed and insecure conditions of lower-middle-class life, of make-work, underemployment, and retail labor in the bleak territories of suburban Los Angeles. As is also true in *Boys Don't Cry*, in *Me and You* insecurity conditions longing, which makes its gentle posing of the question of how to be the insight of getting by, not of confidence or pensive leisure.

My response to this insight is not to romanticize deprivation but to pay attention, rather than using these texts or any other to restate what is already understood by those inside and outside deprived conditions: that deprivation in the context of great wealth is unjust. This is undeniable but banal: in and of itself, it neither reveals nor changes anything. I don't anticipate change from a film or story collection, exactly, but receive *Me and You and Everyone We Know* (2005) and *No One Belongs Here More Than You* (2007) as early counsel toward new ways of thinking about relations among culture, feeling, and social possibility, about cultural forms as affective resources in the project of queer class solidarity (Berlant 2008).

Tellingly, among the near-lost souls in *Me and You and Everyone We Know* (2005), better found by the end of the film, is Christine Jesperson, a young video artist (played by July herself) with a day job chauffeuring elderly people. Thus one of the film's messages is that art makes a way to cut through misery and alienation: not so surprising from a filmmaker long working in the hallowed trenches of the underfunded avant-garde. But July's trench work includes creative communal endeavors, like her Big Miss Moviola Video Chainletter, a pre-MySpace postal distribution system for outsider video, particularly work by girls and old women, many of whom July never met (Bryan-Wilson 2004). Likewise, the use of Christine's art making in *Me and You* to ask "how to be?" is neither solipsistic nor rarefied but, rather, social and quiet, unmarked by liberal melodramas (such as crime-as-the-economy-of-last-resort in any number of gangster youth vehicles set in Los Angeles, or self-destruction-as-girls'-destiny in *Thirteen* [2003], also a contemporary suburban L.A. story). The film's message to critics such as myself is to watch and learn, which spoke to the reparative shift in my thinking under way when I first saw *Me and You*.

Reparative openness marks chapter 4 as well, perhaps better described as a reopening of the recognition question debated in Left social theory, a reopening pursued through the queering of class identification among readers of American writer Dorothy Allison.

I chose Allison readers because I knew, as a reader myself, that in their responses to Allison's work, including her first novel, *Bastard Out of Carolina* (1993), her second, *Cavedweller* (1998), her memoir, *Two or Three Things I Know for Sure* (1994b), and her several collections of stories, essays, and poetry, class questions and insights would surface unprovoked by research queries. They would arise in conversation and in the public, mixed-class settings in which Allison regularly speaks and performs as an openly feminist, lesbian author and as a sexual radical from a traumatized, working-class past in the South Carolina Piedmont. From 2001 to 2003, I took my project on the road, traveling to California, Massachusetts, and Pennsylvania for Allison's talks, readings, and public conversations with other writers and interviewing Allison readers whom I located through her public events. I would introduce myself and my project in the autograph line after a reading, where people would talk with me while they waited for the chance to speak with Allison herself.

Although I wasn't surprised that many readers would volunteer to be interviewed at a later time, I was struck that no one found my interest in "queer class identification" to be the least confusing. They didn't interpret the phrase uniformly, but they received it transparently, as relevant to their own reading, whether or not they would describe themselves as queer or as marked by their class location and history. As readers and viewers, we commonly use emotional, ethical, and poetic means to find an unself-conscious connection to characters and scenarios that bear little empirical resemblance to the worlds we know; how else would historical or fantasy genres work? But readers' responses to Allison through the lenses of family trauma, queer identification, and class escape were especially sensitive to class difference, expressing a quasi-conscious working out of ways to think about class location and survival in the United States. In chapter 4, then, several values of studying class in terms of recognition arise: one finds a conversation and a will to speak that so many critics miss, blinded as we can be by the near-mythical assertion that there is no popular language of class in the United States. One sees the ways class moves through social and cognitive space, through time and narration, as a dominant category at some moments and a more oblique one at others, but at all times in relations that are neither scattershot nor fixed, but patterned and creative. Class, again, is queered by recognition in this form, revealing the political potential of culture made public.

Queer class projects are everywhere, taking shape through discourse and social relations, sometimes challenging and rarely overturning familiar forms of distinction and hierarchy. One of those projects comes from the anticommercial politics of cultural production, those the analysis in chapter 3 would predict: if commercial culture recombines the most limited versions of queer-class possibility, look elsewhere for transformative expression. Broadly, I agree, except when anticommercial resistance produces a reactionary critique through historical standards of taste. Put more plainly, resistance to commerce easily morphs into cultural judgment, superiority, and contempt for popular pleasure, its producers, and its audiences. We reproduce that move at the expense of recognition and solidarity.

Such a move has its roots in periods and contexts quite apart from queer ones, most vociferously in the mass culture debates of the mid-twentieth century, authored by critics like Dwight MacDonald (e.g., 1957) and such theoretical arbiters as Theodor Adorno of the Frankfurt School of cultural theory and criticism. In a phrase, commercial production as a system is bad for civilization and democracy. I *still* agree at some level, except when the flattest interpretations of such a standard extend into contempt not only for systems but also for the people who occupy them. Thus my question, in the contemporary queer class case, is how to move away from imagining a cultural scene in terms that entrench and rank social distinctions and moralisms among commerce, anticommerce, and the supposed denizens of each camp. My interest is in freeing up other terms of critique and engagement and other subject positions not so bound by deadening judgment and opposition.

My response is chapter 5, "Queer Relay." This chapter continues social exploration through fieldwork to examine actually existing market conditions of queer cultural production at the crossroads of industrial and queer independent sectors—that figurative port of entry for much queer work that is later taken up in mainstream form and whose mainstream expressions flow back to queer cultures with each new half-generation of producers and audiences. The chapter narrates a field study designed to work against what I call the "commercial repressive hypothesis," the idea that the history of commerce in queer cultural production is a history of repression. My analysis comes from Foucault's (1986) writing on the sexual repressive hypothesis (SRH), the name Foucault gives to familiar accounts of the history of sexuality in the West: that it is a history of sexual repression with cumulative nods toward liberation, as liberationists have undone, first, the religious, then the carceral, and finally the medical ties that have bound us sexually in the Modern period. In the first volume of *The History of Sexuality* (1986), Foucault argues, contrary to the SRH, that modern Western sexuality is in fact a history of the proliferation of sexual discourses, including liberationist ones. A historian or philosopher is hard-pressed to find evidence of an overall pattern of repression or silencing, and more likely—much more likely—to find an expanding repertoire of ideas, languages, social rules, institutional practices, fantasies, and sexual identities in modernity, repertoires geared toward sexual control and management, not repression.

Foucault's displacement of repression in favor of proliferation as a model of Western sexual historiography does not deny histories of sexual injustice.

Instead, it frames repression and liberation as ideas within the same regulatory economy. In his analysis, jail time for public indecency, new diagnostic categories like gender-identity disorder, and the inclusion of same-sex couples as joint filers of income tax returns are not equivalent gestures merely *imagined* to be repressive (jail time) or liberatory (joint filing). Some may indeed heighten sexual autonomy or diminish repression for some of the people some of the time (or even many people much of the time). But all are part of a history of sexual regulation through the near-limitless production of discourses for naming and colonizing sex and gender, including those that liberationists may work for and welcome. This is why, for example, many activists were less than relieved by what others celebrated as the liberatory defeat of *Bowers v. Hardwick* (1986) by *Lawrence v. Texas* (2003).[8] Both are U.S. Supreme Court decisions, the first denying a right of privacy to same-sex practice, the second overturning the first but with a majority opinion whose language celebrated gay domesticity and sexual intimacy. The abolition of *Bowers v. Hardwick* is welcome, but the terms of *Lawrence v. Texas* are most promising for those prepared to keep their sex behind closed doors and who can count on private resources, like jobs, incomes, and property. Those same terms are mixed for those unwilling or unable to play by the rules of privacy—people committed to public sexual cultures, to having access to public resources regardless of sexual style and practice, and to elective privacy but not legislated secrecy in the name of "home," an effect that has condemned so many to entrapment, violence, and domestic control (Willse and Spade 2005).

My critique of the commercial repressive hypothesis (CRH) uses Foucault's insights in an attempt to partially escape the commerce-versus-liberation logic that entraps queer cultural politics, and thus to slow down the queer-class taste hierarchy that such a politics can deliver. *Relay* is a term designed to capture the movement of cultural producers and production practices across such zones of imagined and theorized opposition and, from there, recalibrate cultural political possibility beyond the claims and counterclaims of the queer mass-culture critique. My argument is not that those oppositions don't exist after all, but that their compulsive rearticulation within and beyond queer contexts is not self-evident but a form of theorizing at once formal and practical (see Williams 1961, Gibson-Graham 2006) and that a theoretical shake-up out of the impasse of such queer cultural politics is due. But, rooted in July's soft aesthetic and Sedgwick's weak theory (formed less to colonize theoretical possibility than recognize and enable survival and change), relay aims small, at grounded contexts of queer cultural practice, in this instance illustrated by the making and festival release of writer-director

Liza Johnson's queer short film, *Desert Motel* (2005). What difference, I ask, would it make to read culture and cultural production for its relay effects and to imagine *class* relay in queer culture?

"Plausible Optimism," chapter 6, returns to criticism for an exposing comparison of two recent films in the queer canon—*Brokeback Mountain* (2005) and *By Hook or By Crook* (2001). Both can be read as queer class texts. Adapted from Annie Proulx's story of the same title, *Brokeback Mountain* was heralded as the watershed entry of queer material into a classic commercial genre, the Western or cowboy movie, with the vital result of revealing that genre's homoerotic roots and creating space for the public memorializing of prices paid, in the 1960s and since, by men finding same-sex love in the expansive but harsh world of the American West.

By Hook or By Crook is smaller, grainier, artier, cheaper, and consciously more alternative than *Brokeback Mountain*. Cowritten and codirected by its two leads, Silas Howard and Harry Dodge, *By Hook or By Crook* tells a contemporary story of butch friendship against the odds in the day-at-a-time world of poor, queer San Francisco. It is an exhilarating film, an opinion I share with adoring fans on and off line. Where *Brokeback Mountain* celebrates the entry of queerness into the grandeur of Hollywood romantic melodrama (its other genre), *By Hook or By Crook* is a work whose do-it-yourself aesthetic, brilliant performances, and characters off the radar of central casting hail viewers into a universe of subcultural aliveness and possibility.

My choice of these two films for *Love and Money*'s closing chapter may appear to throw into question my critique of the commercial repressive hypothesis, by reaffirming the liberatory character of subcultural production. In response, I would offer that the critique is not intended to suggest that there is no such value in queer independence, nor to wave away the differences between industrial and queer sectors. Instead, it enables us to read against the grain of that opposition in the spirit of more cultural political room to move. Relay thinking is intended to provoke questions of border crossing and boundary change in both dominant and nondominant spheres of cultural production, to better describe how queer cultural producers and citizens actually live and work, and thus to better imagine a cultural future at least partly unbound by political habit in the present. Relay questions can be asked, in other words, of *By Hook or By Crook* and *Brokeback Mountain*, both of which introduce changes to genre, the former borrowing from the canon of Hollywood independents like *Midnight Cowboy* (1969), the latter reflecting the changing status of a director like Ang Lee and a producer like James Schamus, who were finally able to green-light a historically unproducible script like *Brokeback Mountain*.

My reading of *Brokeback Mountain* and *By Hook or By Crook* does, finally, argue in favor of the politics and energies of communal art-making in this instance. But it argues more strongly in favor of the optimism of friendship in contrast to the romantic but ultimately suffocating losses and bad attachments in *Brokeback Mountain*. The critical question, then, is not whether all subcultural films promise release and all Hollywood coproductions promise death. It is whether queer critics and citizens might question collective fantasies about romance as love's best form, to reinvent a queer history of social organization through multiple expressions of love and solidarity, where romance is neither demeaned nor promoted but takes its place among other forms of attachment in a hopefully more sustaining array.

As queer *class* texts, moreover, both of which feature strapped or poor characters and one of which—*Brokeback Mountain*—features social bargains made in the name of economic survival and mobility, the comparison of *Brokeback Mountain* and *By Hook or By Crook* speaks to the terms and limits of creativity in deprived contexts. This is not to imagine the category of "class" as signifying working class while unmarking everything else, but to look to work that troubles the relation between optimism and resources. *Brokeback Mountain* is fairly traditional in that equation, projecting its lead characters' abjection in large part through a story of exploited cowboy labor. *By Hook or By Crook* treats it differently, neither ignoring deprivation nor exploiting its image for narrative foreclosure, whether as "poor means noble survival" or "poor means death." Instead, it opens up the relationship, respecting its characters and aerating its narrative through contingency and insecurity in everyday life. In combination with its style, and drawing on Lauren Berlant's work in *The Female Complaint* (2008) and the critical disposition first arising (in this volume) in response to *Me and You an Everyone We Know*, I use *By Hook or By Crook*'s images and story to steer myself toward optimism as plausible political affect. As Berlant writes, not all practices bearing upon political futures are themselves politics. Some are what she calls *juxtapolitical* (8), running parallel to politics or even as relief from the antagonism and loss that official political worlds impose, but still essential to political futures as a source of collective sensibility and feeling. I offer my comparison of *Brokeback Mountain* and *By Hook or By Crook* to arrive at optimism as a critical, collective, and juxtapolitical affect, rooted in friendship, not only in market-authored narratives of individual survival and transcendence.

Love and Money concludes with reflections on criticism as itself a form of cultural production and political intervention. This is not an unfamiliar claim; most queer scholarship shares some stake in imagining how the world might be, beyond our inventories and diagnoses of how it is. In my scholarly corner, however, studies in cultural production are still imagined to be "out there," as accounts of worlds in which critics and fieldworkers are guests, not locals. We may become locals, honorary ones anyway, when we commit the dubious gesture of going native, dubious despite it being our native status as queers that leads us to those contexts in the first place. But *as* queers, we are not so practiced at recognizing our native lives in class terms, a boundary *Love and Money* wants to break.

In a more fully throated cultural political voice, I also want a research practice designed less to keep me apart from the worlds I study than to let them unfold, first, in some of their own terms. If I do that, when my terms consciously intervene, I may have reasonable (not ideal) knowledge of how things happen elsewhere, enough that I am open to new modes of thinking and living, guided by others' cultural work rather than perpetually returning to my own authority. Such a return strikes me as less paranoid than flat (though it can be both), since the variations are so familiar, so easy to repeat. Imagining criticism as cultural production rather than as about it puts me in creative company among other critics and fieldworkers, and among artists, citizens, media, genres, languages, affects, and cultural political possibilities I do not already know. In queer class terms, that strikes me as a critical resource for discovery and solidarity, in a relay world never structured in queerness alone, nor structured apart from the density of class relation.

1

The Class Character of *Boys Don't Cry*

What might be the value of reading *Boys Don't Cry* (1999) as a social class narrative? More precisely, how might we interpret the film as a story of transgender becoming and punishment in a representational field whose class idioms are conspicuously coherent? I pose this question to explore popular discourses of transgender experience, the meanings of class belonging and difference in the commercial media, and the mediations of transgender embodiment and working-class life. The pattern I want to illustrate, which turns up again and again at the nexus of queerness and class, is the displacement of the trauma of one category onto the trauma of the other. In popular culture and its reception, queer and class suffering is an easy switch.

Such themes are amplified in *Boys Don't Cry* by the film's roots in the social reality of Brandon Teena's life in the months before his death, naturalizing or at least stabilizing the film's account of cultural locale and persona.[1] Here, though, I want to emphasize the "based on" rather than the true story, to signify the continuities between text and life from which *Boys Don't Cry* emerges as probably the best-known version of Brandon Teena's death.

Brandon Teena—the person—has been described and redescribed by various interlocutors as alternately a young transman, a genetic girl, a tomboy, a teenage woman, a butch lesbian who passed as male in the absence of an affirming lesbian community, and as a universal subject who courageously sought to become his "true self." These are not just variations, however, but claims, and each carries different political weight. For me, Brandon was a young, female-bodied person who identified and passed as a man, and whose physical style and attraction to heterosexual girls and women were expressions and confirmations of his gender identity.[2] Whether and how Brandon might have further materialized his masculinity through hormone treatments or surgery had he the resources—and had he lived—is not clear.

In familiar parlance, Brandon was transgendered, though to my knowledge that is not a term he used to describe himself. In threatening contexts, for example in the sheriff's recordings of investigative interviews following his rape,[3] Brandon described himself in more clinical terms as having a

Lana and Brandon at pool table (still), *The Brandon Teena Story* © 1998 Bless Bless Productions.

"sexual identity crisis." It is uncertain, however, exactly what that meant to him or whether he might have used other phrases on other occasions.

In *Boys Don't Cry*, the terms of Brandon's gender identification are mixed. Brandon regards himself as a boy, though sometimes even his self-descriptions shift for strategic reasons. Others see him as a boy, too—until they stop doing so, at which point he is at the mercy of their chaotic and hostile attributions. He finally becomes a transitional body made violently accountable to gender binarism, permitting no alternative embodiment or subjectivity, demanding instead that both one's body and claims about one's self conform to (born) male masculinity or (born) female femininity and to heterosexuality as their normative counterpart. Brandon as a character is not quite exposed and killed for being a dyke (though he is sometimes identified as one), but as a freak, a gender liar whose nerve in reporting his rape provokes the homicidal rage and fear of his attackers, men whose masculine excess and precarious homosocial bond Brandon had earlier sought to be included in.

Boys Don't Cry had unnerved me since its release. Like many viewers, I knew to expect Brandon's murder and the abjection, intimidation, and violence that preceded it. But while most of the violence comes from those fictional others in the social world of the film, gender malevolence also comes from the film's plot, particularly the romantic recuperation of Brandon as

Teena in a late (and short-lived) rendering of his and Lana's love affair as a lesbian relationship. This is particularly visible in the surprising, even perverse, love scene that follows Brandon's rape. "Were you a girly girl, like me?" Lana asks Brandon, as he props himself up on one elbow and she gently removes his shirt and the Ace bandage strapping down his breasts. "I don't know what to do," Lana continues. It is her first declaration of sexual inexperience (despite earlier love scenes), and thus becomes a self-conscious reference to the specifically lesbian sex Lana has never had but is about to, with Brandon as a girl. The scene affirms what Brandon's rapists had imposed (while reclaiming him later as their "little buddy")—that Brandon is female. While other moments of sex-gender uncertainty or even duplicity are contained by the plot (when, for example, in order to explain biographical inconsistencies and his illegally assumed identities, an incarcerated Brandon tells Lana he is a hermaphrodite), it is disturbing to watch Brandon be recovered by the script into a love that refuses the masculine gender he has struggled to become and for which, indeed, he is finally killed.

As Judith Halberstam suggested, however, the conventional romantic style of the scene may work for those audiences who would prefer to receive *Boys Don't Cry* in its universalizing, promotional terms—as a tragic love story between two people (Lana, and especially Brandon) who sought personal truth (Halberstam 2001), a gesture familiar and even necessary among commercial protagonists, whose transgender version had also appeared in Neil Jordan's *The Crying Game* (1992) and would be richly reborn on television in Frank Pierson's *Soldier's Girl* in 2003, and whose gay male version would hit the 2005 A-list with *Brokeback Mountain*.

To be fair, first-time feature director Kimberly Peirce and her colleagues had a complicated artistic task on their hands in bringing history and license to Brandon's volatile biography. But perhaps especially in fiction films based on true stories, license is the blessing and the curse that provokes ideological questions (and culturally telling answers) about events excluded and the terms and conditions of those left in. The most pointed exclusion in *Boys Don't Cry* is Phillip DeVine, the young African American man who had been dating Lisa Lambert (renamed Candace in the film), who was killed alongside Lisa and Brandon by John Lotter and Tom Nissen in Humboldt, Nebraska in 1993 (an exclusion Peirce referred to in a National Public Radio interview as a subplot she just had no room for). But also troubling for me, alongside the unsettling "lesbian" scene, is the extravagant coherence of the film's class-cultural overlay. In *Boys Don't Cry,* working-class life does not cause transphobic murder, but it does overdetermine it in ways that we need to understand more deeply.

My reading of *Boys Don't Cry* through the lens of class representation is not born of a search for so-called positive images, but I wince at the repetition of popular images of working-class pathology. Whatever may have been the circumstances of citizens in Falls City, Nebraska, in *Boys Don't Cry* everyone is trapped by limited options in a limited place, by duplicity, by histories of violence and a lack of autonomy, by single motherhood, by numbing and underpaid work ("You don't have to be sober to weigh spinach," Lana tells Brandon), by drinking too much and thinking too little, by rosy, unrealistic images of the future, by a destructive impulsiveness and, in John and Tom's case, a murderous rage born of its own history of psychic torture and incarceration. "Cutting," Tom explains (displaying the self-inflicted knife wounds on his calf), "snaps me back, lets me get a grip."

None of these conditions is intrinsically the stuff of working-class life, and each might be understood as a stereotype of some other social form, including youthful immaturity and self-destruction or a regional culture that imposes conformities and distrusts outsiders. But dramatized together, such conditions become the very scaffolding of working-class sensibility in *Boys Don't Cry,* a gothic, elemental portrait of a community whose citizens are rarely able to act on their own behalf and that finally ends in deadly events.[4]

My response to this image is not recuperation, a wish for a nobler portrait of thoughtful and hard-working people, among whom a few bad apples wreak havoc and commit murder. The conditions that define life in *Boys Don't Cry* exist and have provoked recognition for many viewers and critics. Those viewers might be more offended still by a "condescending glamorizing" of working-class subversiveness amid the deprivations and cruelties of poverty, or by working-class images burdened by an expectation of stoicism or grace.[5] But the gothic shorthand, like its flipside narrative of class transcendence, diminishes the human complexity of how and why people act as they do—good and bad—in conditions of privation, exclusion, and rage. In *Boys Don't Cry,* when Brandon shows a photograph of Lana to his cousin Lonnie and asks, "Isn't she pretty?" Lonnie responds, "Yeah, if you like trash." It is a moment when the film makes explicit what it has suggested from the first few frames—a bleak landscape populated by "white trash" (whose racialization may partly explain why there was no room for DeVine as subplot). As the story unfolds, events known from the historical record become outcomes predicted by class pathology for an audience of cultural consumers too primed for such a judgment and too attracted by its gritty and exotic brand of realism.

But that is not the whole story. Within this universe of feeling and reaction, structured by lack and tinted blue by country lyrics and a protective

Lana's mother inspects Brandon's face, *Boys Don't Cry* © 1999 Twentieth Century Fox Film Corporation.

and threatening nighttime light, characters fuse gender and class through their longings for love, acceptance, and a better life. For Candace and Lana, Brandon's charm and attentiveness outweigh his ineptitude in such hyper-masculine rituals as bar fights and bumper skiing. He is a different kind of man—radiant, beautiful, clear-skinned, and clean, the promise of masculinity and mobility beside Tom and John, who stand instead as scarred and mottled failures. They are condemned to prison and poverty, while Brandon and Lana aspire to adventure and romantic escape, however unlikely their plan of karaoke for pay. Brandon's gender-passing, moreover, is anchored in a self-promoting tall tale of class status, with a father in oil and a sister in Hollywood—an erasure of his hustling and criminal evasions made plausible by his angular, unhardened, boyishly feminine good looks. Even as Lana's mother (Jeanette Arnette) calls him over to inspect his face more closely (while Brandon and the audience hold their breath), the judgment is splendor, not duplicity, though that judgment will not save him when his passing is discovered and his shame and vulnerability are redoubled by gender and class exposure.

Received by others as a young man, Brandon's "pussy" masculinity embodies hope for romance and social mobility, and his careful observation of others' gender style becomes reflexively thoughtful, in contrast to John's brutal reactivity and Tom's copycat impotence. Exposed as a sex-gender trickster, those same qualities make Brandon fair game for the violent reenactment of normative gender difference and hierarchy.[6]

My interest in the articulations of class and gender in *Boys Don't Cry* and my anxiety about the film's supersaturated typifications of working-class fate speak to the reentry into cultural studies of class belonging and representation. As Sally Munt (2000) charted so clearly, cultural studies began with a leftist commitment to working-class inclusion and liberation, a commitment later challenged for its inattention to other axes of social difference and power. In the 1990s, class cultures in Left terms were pushed to the rearground even as class difference continued to operate and to make itself felt. As a cultural studies of class renews itself, it does so conscious not only of the historical reproduction of class position and the persistence of exploitation and struggle, but also of the complex trajectories of class location and identity that occur within the lives of persons and populations. "We tend now," wrote Cora Kaplan in 2000, "to think of class consciousness past and present more polymorphously and perversely: its desires, its object choices, and its antagonisms are neither so straightforward nor so singular as they once seemed" (13). Here Kaplan expresses a queered form of class analysis to which my comments on *Boys Don't Cry* respond, an analysis that not only connects class to (trans)gender and sexuality but also articulates the complexity and recursiveness of the category and its variants. Class cultures are produced not least by popular representations, and complexly so, in contexts where class life is sometimes central, other times not, structured and structuring in critical but incomplete ways.

Pressed to identify the primary representational and political terms of *Boys Don't Cry*, I would call the film a transgender story. Pressing further to the layered conditions of social life takes me to the film's class character. That kind of pressing on, reading queerness for class and class for queerness, exposes the availability and malleability of shaming and excess in pathologizing queer and class others. Shame and excess are essential to suturing and even interchanging the categories of queerness and class, a substitution often accomplished by means of violent exposure. The rumble of popular surprise and anxiety about Jaye's revealed penis in *The Crying Game* (1992), for example, can still be felt in *Boys Don't Cry*. As working-class club performer and transgender woman, Jaye suffers many of the same impositions as Brandon, but she survives, disoriented, brutalized, and stripped of feminine glory and power. Here, too, shame and excess are rapid infusers of cultural hierarchy, at work in commercial image and everyday expression and equally at work in the move out of shame into respectability and status. That's the trade: a superabundance of queer and class shame for the mean distribution of status and regard, some spared and others sacrificed over and over again.

2

Queer Visibility and Social Class

In his beautiful essay "Intellectual Desire," Allan Bérubé (1997) disentangles a lifetime of border living and territorial and symbolic migration. Growing up poor of French Canadian descent in the United States and surviving the shame and hostility rained down on his speech community, his family's Catholic religiosity, and their position and culture in the working class, Bérubé came out as homosexual and intellectual in conditions that predicted neither but courted both. A consciously bookish kid, he read, and envisioned "a different world, full of poetry, literature, great music, philosophy, and art" (52) through the *Encyclopedia Britannica* volumes purchased from the door-to-door salesman in his family's trailer park and the classical records his parents played on a hi-fi his father had constructed from a DIY kit.

Amid his father's job relocations, brief periods of middle-class surroundings, returns to the family farm, and permanent economic struggle following the unsuccessful strike of his father's labor union, Bérubé's family endured the historic uncertainties of striving, achievement, and loss—liminal states that mark so many personal and community narratives (even happy ones) of class and other forms of mobility in the United States. Lovingly, and nostalgically, Bérubé traces the reciprocities of class, sexuality, language, ethnicity, and region, writing first to an audience of queer conferencegoers in Montreal, a city he had never before visited in a province from which his family had hailed a generation before his parents. I attended that conference ("La Ville En Rose," November 1992) and, like so many others in the audience, was riveted by Bérubé's warm invitation to imagine queerness through the sociocultural kaleidoscope of class migration. In his talk, he made no appeal to a uniform definition of social class or even a stable if multiform one; instead he spoke of a writerly model of narration and identification that exposed class experience at the historical conjuncture of many things: money, labor, desire, opportunity, alliance, displacement, education, and the stabilities and instabilities of privilege.

Neither Bérubé's story nor his title, "Intellectual Desire," is a likely candidate for production at NBC or Showtime—outlets that typically require more glamour and less anxiety, more triumph and less uncertainty, and more humor and less loss to cultivate a favorable narrative environment for the sale of cars and cruises and to sustain the right audience of middle-class gay and straight consumers and subscribers. Bérubé's story is also openly attentive to questions of class desire and instability, a discourse many critics claim to be missing from U.S. popular culture and especially from the commercial media, bound as those media are by the transparency of middle-class norms like American dreaming and upward mobility.

Why, then, do I lead with Bérubé in a chapter on the class markers of queer worth in contemporary commercial media? Because his essay reminds us that the forms of distinction, pleasure, and injury that make up the cultures of class run unevenly through a range of social locations and symbolic contexts, among them everyday interaction, memoir, testimony, and popular narrative. In each context, the terms are recast by technical, aesthetic, and economic requirements, but resonances arise across forms. We can look, for example, from "Intellectual Desire" to *Will & Grace* or *Modern Family*, asking whether there is common ground in their discourses of class difference despite dramatic contrasts in form and genre. Discovering that there is reminds us that no example invents class and its entanglement with what it means to be queer, or gay, or lesbian, or trans, though each roots that relationship in distinctive ways. In literary memoir ("Intellectual Desire") and the camp sarcasm of commercial situation comedy (*Will & Grace, Modern Family*), class aspiration and arrival structure gay meaning, and sexual identification as gay underwrites both stigma and the promise of cultural taste and refinement. "Intellectual Desire," *Will & Grace,* and *Modern Family* are hardly the same texts, but, as queer class stories, they draw from the same deep well of class discourse and value.

We can take this further, looking for resonance between these examples and social exchange in everyday life. When we find them, we recognize that the stories, fantasies, and desires organized by class and sexual difference are part of our public formation, and that those media forms that critics and others refer to as if they exist unto themselves, with sealed boundaries and external influence (think of the phrase "the effect of media on society"), are more continuous with social life—with households, cultural scenes, love affairs, political campaigns, or public policies—than critics suggest. We are mistaken to ignore the organizational routines and practices of cultural production in asking why media texts appear as they do. But we are equally mistaken to forget that popular narratives become popular in part because the fantasies they distill and promote have a social and even psychic life that precedes—not only follows—commercial genres.

Class Projects

Queering class and interrogating the class character of queerness across genres is a critical form of what Sherry Ortner (2003) calls *the class project*, a phrase that challenges the static image of class categories (such as working class, middle class, bourgeois). "Class project" marks the practice of social class, not so much who we are or what we have in Liberal, Marxist, or popular terms, but the things we *do*—as workers, producers, citizens, dreamers, policymakers, elected officials, business leaders, and critics—in the ongoing formation of class difference. The class project returns us to Bérubé's recognition of class identification as historical, both within and outside an individual life, and to cultural representation (including Bérubé's) as itself a class practice. It also demands that we consider the indissolubly material and symbolic dimensions of class, as (1) a relative and potentially unstable economic position in a social system committed to economic hierarchy and exclusion, (2) a form of social power over others and vulnerability to discrimination, prejudice, stigmatization, and pain, and (3) recognizable in the cultural practices of everyday life that are closely calibrated to and by those forms of economic and institutional hierarchy—speech, taste, the ways in which we can and do attend to our bodies. In this chapter, I address the second and third of these three categories—images of social power and cultural practice—mindful of the forms of labor and labor value to which power and practice are linked.

In commercial media, class is queered by the slow drip of queer characters into an otherwise unchanged stream of class difference. But we can also imagine "class project" as queer in Kaplan's metaphoric terms (2000), where transparent categories of class difference are destabilized and reimagined, enough to challenge the familiar assertion of class absence in popular discourse. Queering class in this second sense can be what makes it visible. It is no secret that in U.S. commercial popular culture the class spectrum is compressed. Both the ruling class and routine (not criminal) poverty are strikingly absent, and wealth is way out of proportion to the world as we know it. The underrepresentation of lower-middle-class citizens and communities meets an overabundance of superrich celebrities and corporate up-and-comers, and even modest living is more luxurious and better-heeled on television than in strapped neighborhoods and working households. That doesn't mean, however, that amid this compression the engines of class distinction are still. They aren't. But they are steady, neither thunderous nor silent but a coarse drone that demands a more deconstructive analysis—a series of hypothesis and critical moves—than the familiar language of class types offers us.

In the cultural comparisons that follow, I argue that queer class distinction is visible through four gestures across a range of forms and genres: (1) good queers (protagonists, familiars) are moved from the class margins to the class middle, where practices of bodily control are maximized; (2) bad queerness and powerlessness are represented as class marginality and are signified by performative excess and failures of physical control; (3) wealth becomes the expression of fabulousness, in a limited version of the good life *legitimately achieved*; and (4) class is displaced onto family and familialism as the locus of normalcy and civic viability. In the class project of queer media visibility, in other words, comportment, family, and modes of acquisition are the class markers of queer worth, pulling characters and scenarios toward a normative middle, but not without deploying an array of other class meanings and values.

The interaction between queerness and class has an economic logic, embedding enough fragmented class recognition to appeal to a range of consumers and still flatter those at the crest of advertising trade value, and sweetening content with just a *soupçon* of queer edge to draw newer, hipper, younger audiences in the hyperdiversified landscape of popular forms. Within this logic, queerness has delivered cultural expansion, a new commercial horizon broadened beyond old typifications of queer marginality but well shy of heterosexual disarmament. In the case of television, it is a horizon fitted to the "postnetwork" era (Lotz 2004), a competitive context in which smaller, more-defined "niche" audiences acquire industrial value, cable outlets compete as targeted brands with each other and with traditional broadcast networks, and distinction relies on a combination of old formats (situation comedy, nighttime soap opera, family melodrama) and new themes and characters, queers among them. In this new environment, an audience of "socially liberal, urban-minded professionals" (Becker, quoted in Lotz, 38) comes with a high price tag for advertisers and is thus especially desirable for networks, outlets, cable operators, portals, and production companies. Many producers and executives, gay and straight, are themselves a part of that audience, brokering class fantasies, queer trade value, and industrial ratings as they shuttle back and forth between the specialized domain of cultural production and more diffuse forms of meaning-making in everyday life. The class project of queer visibility takes shape through their creative, technical, and managerial labor.

History

Queer media visibility since the 1990s also replays historical discourses of class and sexual hierarchy rooted in bourgeois projections of proletarian excess and failures of bodily control (see Stallybrass and White 1986; Gamson 1998; Kipnis 1999; Skeggs 2004). Working-class people, who are both the majority of the U.S. population and the demeaned periphery of its symbolic universe, are imagined as physically just *too* much: too messy, too ill, too angry, too needy, too out of control, too unrestrained and, critically, too sexual. Consider, for example, the hostile discourse of "welfare dependency," dragged out and puffed up by conservative politicians and critics (and by President Clinton in 1996) whenever "fiscal restraint" and "family values" are the political capital of the moment. "Welfare dependents" expect too much and contribute too little. Their illnesses are said to be born of indulgent living, not overwork, deprivation, or a systematic reduction in opportunities of all kinds; they are too sexual, born of surrender to temptation, not human need or desire; they are the parents—usually the mothers—of too many children, born of accident, not choice. No matter that the same practices are less shamed and more generously received in affluent contexts than in strapped or poor ones.

And queer bodies? We are, in history and principle, a mess of inversion, temptation, abomination before God and government, anal fascination, unproductive desire, infantile drama, illness out of bounds, consumptive decadence. Even our stereotypical strengths mark us as excessive: too stylish, too expressive, too aggressive, politically uncivil, too shameless or shamed, too vulnerable to mental anguish born of bodily condemnation, too needful of recognition, too funny, and, often, just too angry. It's a lot of excess to manage on one's way back to the fold.

But that's what the promise of mobility exacts. In class and sexual forms, the movement from the outer limits to the hypocritical edges of the charmed circle (Rubin 1984/1993) demands management and bodily self-regulation. In lived circumstances, we witness, for example, the personal desexualization volunteered by the aspiring gay professional and his lover described by James Woods in *The Corporate Closet* (1993). In a professional universe that historically asserted a heterosexist double standard for the acknowledgment of one's sexual orientation, the obligatory dinner invitation to the boss has been known to be accompanied by the banishment of the gay lover (who has spent the day cooking, cleaning, and readying the home for the right impression) to the garage for the evening. Professional life and sexuality don't belong together, explain the gay professional and his lover (both self-laceratingly compliant, if not unrealistic), notwithstanding the boss's wife joining the invisibly catered festivities.

While such an impulse appears to surface from the primordial queer past, it lived on in the celebrated endorsements of *Lawrence v. Texas* and the

Massachusetts marriage decision,[1] the good-faith testimony of Bette Midler or the biting satire of Bill Maher (both of whom weighed in, in 2004, against a constitutional amendment banning gay marriage). All seek a same-sex extension of the sanctity of privacy and marriage as the proper platform for relations between two people and in turn between them and the state. Similar investments in marriage as federal management solution are extended to poor people needing assistance (the "welfare dependents" alluded to earlier), for example, in federal rewards for marriage as a launching pad off the welfare rolls. The poor population is disproportionately black, Latino, Asian, and Native, though its greatest constituency—by far—is white. In a persistent recoding of class as race, poor and working-class people of color bear a redoubled burden of the presumption of bodily excess (too strong, too weak, too fat, too sexual, too ill, and so on), and poor and working-class white people are racialized and sequestered as "trash" (like the characters in *Boys Don't Cry*) in contrast to racially unmarked white people in the middle and upper classes (see McElya 2001). In popular culture and social policy, race is the key arbiter of class and sexual difference.

As is true with many cultural impositions, such management means less the elimination of offending possibilities than their careful distribution. This is especially the case in commercial entertainment forms, where success depends on an unstable chemistry of familiarity and risk, and where propriety *hopes* to meet sexual and other bodily fascinations, but in only the right places. Consider the case of gay sex. In such nonsubscription forms as broadcast television, even in the postnetwork era, gay is good and so is sex, but queer sex remains the object of labored consideration, caution, and, oftentimes, aversion among program directors. Poor sexless Will, recall, had to make do through most of *Will & Grace* with the erotic charge of sitcom camp and the occasional, misbegotten roll in the hay with Grace. And even subscription forms like cable television (with the important Showtime exceptions of *Queer as Folk* and *The L Word*), famed for their latitude and edge, claimed the frisson of gay sex while also guarding the presumed modesties and class aspirations of their straight audiences. Miranda on *Sex and the City* may have discovered herself to be attractive to her law firm's senior partner and his wife because they mistakenly assume that she and her new softball friend are a lesbian professional couple who might expand the boss's social circle in fashionable ways. But at her boss's home for the first and only time, Miranda-as-lesbian is cinched to the neck in desexualized attire, in contrast to her looser professionalism as her straight self. The couple is also meticulously androgynous in style and dress (hence the cinching), not trading on the historically working-class codes of butch/fem difference.

On the same series, Samantha's lesbian sexual experiments were unrepentant and drenched in female ejaculate, but they were also just that, experiments, and the series' one expressively gay character, Sanford, almost never had sex until the closing season. Samantha's exploits were reconciled by the general sexual character of the program, by her established pansexual appetites, and by gloss: sex works best (on subscriber TV) among stylish, attractive, upscale players.

I loved Samantha. She was sexy, briefly queer, and exposed conventional pieties with witty intolerance. She straddled the class project of queer visibility, conforming to its demands for bodily control and consumer extravagance while resisting knee-jerk family attachment, save among her family of friends and her rare capitulation to babysitting. Recognizing her coy—and conspicuously white—position on the borders of class propriety, and recognizing the continuity of fantasy on television and off, my affection and others' makes sense. We loved Samantha because she was at once inside and outside the hierarchies we live by as natives and aspirants to the good life. She was not, however, the narrative or ideological anchor of *Sex and the City*, a position that went instead to the resolutely straight Carrie Bradshaw and the bashful—thus more versatile—branding of Sarah Jessica Parker.

Bearing in mind historical discourses, cultural impositions, and the frisson of queerness and class in postnetwork media, the comparisons that follow explore body, family, and modes of acquisition in the class project of queer visibility. They also ask how race and gender specify queer class relationships, and return, finally, to the place of class fantasy in everyday life.

Family Ties

To begin, consider some anticanonic examples of televisual representation in the (old) new queer visibility: not *Queer as Folk, Ellen, Will & Grace*, or *The L Word*, but that other staple, the one-off secondary character in shows elsewhere unmarked by sexual difference. In 2003, an episode of *My Wife and Kids*, a family situation comedy on ABC featuring a predominantly African American cast, had the wife chasing her husband out of the house in a fit of domestic exasperation. The series was a vehicle for its male star, Damon Wayans, fondly known for his early sketch comedy on *In Living Color*, whose most outrageous bit was "Men on Art," a community access television spot (and Siskel and Ebert parody) in which two flaming queens opined about recent film releases with the singsongy and now-iconic slogan "Hated it!" There was affection and nervousness for the audiences of that sketch, including black, gay audiences who loved the nuances but feared the reproduction

Wayans (back to camera) poses as Steve's boyfriend in *My Wife and Kids*, "Jay the Artist,"
Season 3, Episode 11 © 2002 Touchstone Television.

of stereotype among nongay viewers (Hemphill 1995). But the character
stuck, and Wayans resurrects it with every intertextual opportunity.

In this episode of *My Wife and Kids*, titled "Jay the Artist," turfed from his
own home, Wayans's character Michael Kyle goes to meet a male friend Steve
(Steve Harvey) at a local bar and finds his friend running a line with Monica
(Chene Lawson), a lady on her own. To interrupt his friend's smooth operation, Wayans kicks into his "Men on Art" character, chastising his friend for
running out on him and trying to hook up with the woman in the bar. So
much falsetto, scene making, finger pointing, hip canting, lip protruding,
hoochie posturing, and bitching about cheating and broken promises mark
the joke, whose female character retreats in horror, though whether she is
disgusted by gayness, effeminacy, or duplicity we can't quite tell.

When the woman is gone, the men resume their deep voices and com-
radely backslapping, the first acknowledging that Michael had indeed scored
in this bit of masculine grift, whose real losers are black women and male
effeminacy. It was an old joke, set in place long before *In Living Color* (and
practiced by such Wayans mentors as Eddie Murphy in the first installment
of *Beverly Hills Cop* [1994]). Here, though, it is recycled and updated to meet

contemporary standards of queer media visibility: run the joke about a bad queer but disavow the hostility it expresses, preserve the normal family at the series' center by situating the joke outside the household, and make the gay type an out-of-control gold digger. In exaggerated homegirl style, she protests the loss of future vacations in Aguila. She acts out, fails to know when not to make a scene, and is unproductively dependent on another's discreet desire and economic largesse. Performative excess marks the character's transgression of racial, sexual, gender, and class propriety amid the urbane elegances, hushed tones, and solo piano music of the bar and the subdued ruthlessness of the scene's sexual-moral economy.

An inversion of the joke in fonder form comes from a 2003 episode of *George Lopez*. Like *My Wife and Kids* and many other family sitcoms (such as *Roseanne, Home Improvement, The Bernie Mac Show, The Hughleys*), *George Lopez* was a series based loosely on the biography and stand-up comedy of its star. In this episode, titled "Guess Who's Coming to Dinner," Lopez and his costars are joined by Cheech Marin as a former employee in the factory where Lopez's mother Benny (Belita Moreno) still works and Lopez himself has become a manager. A running theme in the series is Lopez not knowing for sure who his father is, since Benny (in a friendly Chicana rewrite of the sexually-active character Blanche and the irascible Ma from *The Golden Girls*) was quite the girl about town in her youth, and she makes no apologies in retrospect. A misunderstanding arises that moves George and his sidekick to visit the home of Marin's character, Lalo Montenegro, George believing that in Lalo he may finally have found his dad. George's mother knows it isn't the case: however inebriated she might have been one night forty years ago with her male coworker, they didn't have sex. Lalo knows it, too, but longs for the possibility of finding a family late in life and, at least briefly, latches onto an identity as George's father. George, longing for paternal connection, latches back.

The twist, of course, is that when George and his buddy arrive at Lalo's home, they discover that Lalo is openly gay and lives with his boyfriend of many years. Here the class formula for queer visibility begins to add up: unlike Wayans's homegirl caricature, Lalo is mild-mannered, friendly, earnest in his desire for family to the point of an entirely forgivable projection of a nonevent some forty years earlier. His boyfriend, played by John Michael Higgins, is more broadly mannered in his characterization of gayness (reminiscent of his earlier performance as the owner of a winning Shih Tzu in Christopher Guest's *Best in Show* [2000]). But he, too, is hospitable and understanding, offering his guests bruschetta and, in his devotion to Lalo and his own interest in family bonding, willing to consider unofficially

George Lopez at Lalo Montenegro's house, *George Lopez*, "Guess Who's Coming to Dinner," Season 2, Episode 13 © 2002 Warner Bros. Television.

adopting a forty-year-old son. Together, the two men live in an attractive, well-kept home, considerably more stylish than George's and his family's, marking gayness (and an ethnically mixed relationship between a Chicano and a white man) as the route to mobility, and further marking class mobility and taste as the measure of gay legitimacy.

Overall, the episode was irresistible in its kindness and its characters' resolve to relate "like family" even after the hope of blood kinship is dashed. It expressed the series' ethnically marked generosity toward modest departures from conventional propriety—like Benny's sexual troublemaking—in the name of humor. But its queer class logic is not so unlike that of the more hostile scene from *My Wife and Kids*. Good queers are modest, kind, hardworking—qualities that underwrite their ascendance from lower-middle-class respectability (Felski 2000). They also long for family even where they can't have it and are thus readily integrated into existing family formations rather than estranged. They are, finally, upwardly mobile and thus enjoy the stylish pleasures of midlife legitimately achieved.

Indeed, ethnic mobility and class arrival mark both narrative contexts. Wayans's gold digger (the bad queer) is sequestered from and thus identified in contrast to the deluxe image of suburban affluence of the Kyle household, whereas Marin's father figure (the good queer) is integrated into a more forgiving, less affluent, but still upwardly mobile extended family. Marin's character has controlled his desire, worked hard, established a life partnership, and maintained his family yearning. Consistent with the genre conventions of situation comedy, love and recognition are his rewards. This outcome stands in contrast, say, to the loss and uncertainty in Bérubé's memoir, marked though it also is by some of the same feelings of queer class longing expressed in *George Lopez*.

The comparison of *My Wife and Kids* and *George Lopez* reveals a queer-class economy whose gifts and deprivations are echoed elsewhere. Civil union and other homosexual commitment announcements, which started appearing in the Sunday edition of the *New York Times* in 2002, for example, also reproduce an equation in which a putative meritocracy meets quasi-marital attachment. Time was, wedding announcements were a staple ingredient of the society page. Their brides, grooms, and families drew from an aristocratic stratum whose denizens often already knew each other, though other readers were welcome to look on. But times have changed (Brooks 1997). In the updated nuptial pool, a couple's family pedigree is less conspicuous or necessary than the partners' education and professional occupation, which may either match or exceed their parents' schooling and employment. This is true for queer and straight announcements alike. I'm most charmed when the union occurs between partners from economically modest backgrounds (one partner's father retired from retail sales, say, their mother from service as a pubic librarian, and they are themselves theater scenics trained at Cooper Union and now working on Broadway). These, too, are white-collar scenarios, but their inclusion among all the unions fit to print feels like more of an accomplishment than those partners who've traveled the short distance from suburban Connecticut to Wellesley to Harvard to law-firm partnership by the age of thirty-two and whose fathers were law faculty at Yale.

Both scenarios, however, the less and the more elite, speak to and through the discourse of steady accomplishment, however foreordained the elite version. There are no featured partners, for example, whose fathers disappeared when they were toddlers and who are now marrying up after a lifetime of social assistance, high school withdrawal, and odd jobs (though it does happen). Instead, projections of careful upbringing and education combine with steady employment and interesting love stories, about wacky first dates and the transformation of early rejection into settled attachments.

The straight version of this has existed for some time, but the more recent, if contested, editorial arrival of same-sex versions into the fold in 2002 widened the stage for queer legitimacy through class ascendance marked by bodily control (love, not sex; marriage, not dating) and legitimate achievement (precocious lawyers and Broadway scenics). The payoff is good citizenship and happiness by national standards, in contrast to narratives of war and economic decline elsewhere in the paper. The unacknowledged cost is the compression of possibility and the misrecognition of other cultural equations and the people who live them, probably including the very people featured in the announcements.

There are no limits to what weddings reveal about American class life (see Ingraham 1999; Freeman 2001). Executives at Bravo knew this when, in 2002, they staged their *Gay Weddings* series, crosscutting among different same-sex couples soon to be betrothed. Some scenes revealed a loathsome bossiness between class-stratified partners, a high-end taste top routinely snubbing his blue-collar boyfriend's picks in the choice-riddled universe of wedding planning. Others portrayed a claustrophobic match between sex, class, taste, and aspiration, to my eye unburdened by personal effervescence or insight. Still another witnessed a kindness between two partners, one African American and one Latina, who felt they'd finally found a soft landing together after years of awkward and unsuccessful gestures in separate attempts to meet heterosexual partners and standards. I watched them, Sonja and Lupe, and I liked them. They were good to each other—forgiving, tenderhearted, and a little shy. Sonja's teenage son by an earlier marriage liked Lupe and, as often happens, recognized his mother's sexual relationship with her before Sonja was prepared to talk to him about it. Their upcoming wedding, both partners in silken, swishy, full-length gowns, would be a ritual attesting to the "truth of the self," in their own terms. They had discovered their lesbianism together, and the deepest and most public recognition of that discovery would come at their wedding.

What's not to love in such a portrait? For me, this is truthfully a difficult question to answer. "True self" narratives can be personally fruitful or, equally, a scourge softly spoken to justify all manner of indifference to others. As for the future, watching their episode I wished Sonja and Lupe well, but would never know how they fared; the wedding, not the marriage, was the show's premise. But even this loveliest example, ethnically marked, like the *George Lopez* episode and full of good faith, is equally inflated with inexorability, with the language of marriage as destiny and maturity. In all senses of the term, especially the class one, marriage consolidates.

Consolidation is echoed elsewhere in the program, as another couple acknowledged their intentions to a waitress serving them in a sidewalk café. "I didn't know men could marry in California," says the waitress. Technically, they can't, the couple explains, but they go on to describe the social if not legally sanctioned form of the commitment they intend to make. "Cool," the waitress responds, as she leaves the men to chat with gay friends about those straight people for whom the prospect of same-sex marriage just doesn't compute. As in the *Times* announcements, there are three kinds of people in the world: straights who support gay marriage, straights who don't, and queers who want to marry but can't and so do the next best thing.[2] The wedding-driven class form of the romantic couple (serious, sexually monogamous, mature, and consumer-based for all the right, life-building reasons) is the salable basis for a cable reality show about relationships, more so, say, than a program about all the creative, incomplete, contingent, and sometimes painful ways that queers and others hook up without the formative gesture of shopping. Add to this the innovation appeal of sexual sameness and we have *Bravo's Gay Weddings*, not *Bravo Presents Relationship Experiments We've All Tried Against the Grain of Confusion, Self-Doubt, and Social Demand*.

But entertainment genres do not tend to interrupt the very fantasies they are designed to reproduce. Rather than imagining sitcoms and wedding announcements as failures of empirical realism, we can receive them as expressing in queer class terms the limits of the fantasies now dominant. Each genre, moreover, brings a slightly different resource to the representation. Situation comedies offer a dense reduction of social desire in twenty-two minutes of typecasting and driven dialogue. *New York Times* wedding announcements and *Bravo's Gay Weddings* offer the heightened pleasure of a quasi-documentary form. Both the announcements and the gay weddings are products of intense social, economic, and editorial management, but in featuring nonactors they invite us to deepen our attachments to the romantic possibilities represented. As members of the audience, we know that even nonactors' stories are carefully selected and crafted, but their claim to originate outside the technical regimes of media work (in the "real world") adds a blast of expectation for fans and skeptics: Cheech Marin, we know, stopped being Lalo Montenegro once the *George Lopez* episode was in the can, but the same-sex couple in the *Sunday Times*, enjoying the wisdom of midlife romance and the pleasures of a tastefully appointed commitment ceremony, could one day be us or someone we know. Some of us may reject that prospect outright (though lots of antimarriage queers read the *New York Times* wedding page with a mix of zeal and guilty pleasure, flicking to the section and asking "What's up with the homosexuals this week?"). Or, we may find ourselves ambivalent for personal and political reasons. Such reactions, however, don't disqualify true-story images of marriage as a staple in the class project of queer visibility. What happens, though, when the marriage or relationship goes wrong?

Queer Therapeutics

January 2004 saw the debut of the long-awaited and much-promoted Showtime series *The L Word*. "Same sex, different city" was the network's clever billboard caption, designed to draw audiences who would soon lose HBO's *Sex and the City* as it entered its final season. It was a brilliant bit of network scheduling: follow *Sex and the City* and *Curb Your Enthusiasm* in HBO's Sunday-night lineup with *The L Word* on Showtime and see what materializes. Produced by long-standing queer independent Ilene Chaiken and directed by such young lesbian auteurs as Rose Troche (whose 1994 release *Go Fish* I consider a watershed moment in lesbian cinema [Henderson 1999]), *The L Word* promised what other queer portrayals lacked: lots of lesbians, a lesbian community, and explicit lesbian sex. On those promises it delivered, though some critics and viewers complained early on about the in-name-only character of the lesbians depicted and the limits of a community rooted in latte. In fairness, no television "first" can be all things to all people, least of all while adhering to popular standards of glamour and melodrama. But stylization and formula on *The L Word*'s first season complicated a fair response, as characters moved through a universe largely devoid of personal history or political horizon but brimming with well-dressed, soft-core lesbian and heterosexual sex—the calling cards of a risky venture that would need subscriber-viewers of many sexual dispositions to survive into a second and ultimately a sixth season. Characters' sexual styles, moreover, were troubling. Leads had four reduced choices: they could be consciously nonmonogamous and cold, maritally committed and destined for parenthood, confused and romantically frustrated, or closeted. Better, perhaps, to have four than one.

Consider *The L Word*'s version of that new emblem of televised, middle-class queer visibility. Not shopping—though the series was steeped in high-end good living—but couples' therapy. The therapy scenes offered expository efficiency: relationship dynamics were laid out and explained, and in principle the dialogue could reveal a character's vulnerability. But they also accomplished the class project of queer visibility. In the debut episode, the lead couple, Bette (Jennifer Beals) and Tina (Laurel Holloman), are deciding whether to pursue parenthood through donor insemination, and together they see a psychotherapist to consider their future as parents. Bette, a high-powered arts administrator, arrives late to the therapy session, crossing the office threshold while speaking into her ear-mic cellular telephone. Immediately

Tina and therapist await Bette.

Bette arrives, talking on her cell phone, *L Word*, Pilot © 2003 Showtime Networks.

we question the symmetry of their commitment, since Tina arrived early and has already given up her corporate career in anticipation of starting a family.

The therapist, a white man (Daryl Shuttleworth), notes that the two have been together for seven years and wonders whether the impulse toward child-bearing might have something to do with a loss of sexual attraction; call it compensatory intimacy. Bette and Tina resist this interpretation, reframe their desire as readiness, and, a little later in the episode, dismiss the therapist's cautionary questions with liberated indifference: "What does he know? We don't need his permission." Thus the characters bust out of one form of well-managed, middle-class maturity—therapy—and into another—pregnancy and family planning. From the therapist's office to the fertility specialist, body management and fee-for-service expertise converge and shift, from talk about commitment and intimacy to ovular record-keeping and biotechnology.

Late in the first season, however, the series introduced a couple of dramatic wrinkles into Bette and Tina's story. Tina, who is white, had acknowledged her ambivalence about the possibility of an African American sperm donor, and Bette, who is biracial, was hurt and disappointed, though the program never complicated Tina's response or framed it politically. It was a lifestyle choice, however misguided or insulting. In the end, when their intended (white) donor's sperm turns out to be inactive, they recruit an African American artist to serve as donor, a friendly, strapping guy who connotes nothing if not stereotypical black virility and who, we are frequently reassured, with the tenor of pedigree, is an *artist* whom Bette knows through her work, not just some black Average Joe or, worse, some young hood.[3]

A couple of episodes later, when the fertility procedure works and Bette and Tina announce Tina's pregnancy to Bette's African American father (played by Ossie Davis), Bette responds to his hostility at the prospect of a "grandchild" who bears no blood relation with the reassertion of the artist status of the African American donor. Her father is unassuaged; indeed he is incensed by the idea that by virtue of skin color he has anything in common with this man. He reminds Bette that she is Ivy League–educated, and that her lesbianism confounds what she should be doing instead: extending her father's wisdom and mode of living.

Later still, Tina miscarries toward the end of her first trimester, and religious-right foes of Bette's art organization exploit news of the miscarriage as evidence of God's will against homosexuality. Finally, a moment, however awkward, of political drama. Amid the series' hyperprofessionalism, hypercommercialism, hyperconsumerism, familialism, and fashion-model standards of gloss, we do learn that queer family-making is neither so easy nor so welcome, certainly no guarantee of broad social legitimacy. Bette's opponent from the religious right (played by lesbian favorite Helen Shaver, who earned heartthrob status as Vivian Bell in director Donna Dietch's 1985 feature *Desert Hearts*), has her own parental hypocrisy to conceal; her teenage daughter ran away from home and became a porn actress. Still, Bette's humiliation rests on the presumption that what is private and painful oughtn't be involuntarily exposed and, moreover, that enough members of the public who witness this disclosure during a fictional television program will secretly agree with the right-wing activist about queer procreation, even as they distance themselves from fundamentalist histrionics and mean-spiritedness. This episode of *The L Word* expressed the political vulnerability of even the most socially conforming if aesthetically liberal lesbian, who cannot depend on protection or support from her counter-typically elite, African American father. It was a moment in the series' first season where queerness was scripted to complicate the routine forms of class entitlement signaled, among other places, in the therapy scene.

In its gothic version of a shaky, entrepreneurial middle-class family, Season 3 of *Six Feet Under* (2003) also used the dramatic device of gay-couples therapy, presenting the scene as a visual triangle among three gay men: the white therapist (Arye Gross); Keith Charles (Matthew St. Patrick), the African American partner in the troubled duo who, late in Season 2, lost his career as a cop for outbursts of anger on the job; and David (Michael C. Hall), the oldest son in a white family of funeral directors whose founding patriarch died in the series debut. David's family bears all the marks of the barely domesticated haunted house from which they hail and in which is located the funeral parlor, chapel, and exhumation lab. Family members are arty, quirky, suffering, economically unstable, volatile, and alternately kind and hostile toward one another. In most respects, save for his gayness, David is the most conventional of the group— not quite venturesome, the least openly self-destructive, the most rational and accountable in matters of family business.

The dramatic characterization of Keith's family plays on some of the anxiety but, as a secondary-character unit, little of the fleshing out of David's. They are a tense, ex-military clan with an oppressive and angry father and a screwed-up sister whose child is dependent on family guardians, alternately Keith or his parents. Keith thus comes by his anger honestly, as the only son of a harsh and authoritarian father, but also stereotypically, as the only regular black character in the series. While David and Keith end up in therapy together, Keith is the more conspicuously out of control at that point, a dramatization that draws on two extradiegetic frames: the pressures that attach to being African American and male in the United States, and Hollywood's opportunistic brand of anti-positive-images "courage," which figures that since we've had Cliff Huxtable,[4] we can go back to loading black characters with rage and incompetence, with only the minor risk of being accused of stereotyping. David, by contrast, is fearful of Keith's anger. He tells the therapist that he feels like he's living in a minefield, that he can do nothing right, that he is routinely subject to criticism. This Keith dismisses as a whole lot of whining, at which point the therapist (in an arch scene) reminds him that now is the time to listen, and that his turn will come.

David and Keith, separated by therapist Frank Muehler.

Keith's turn. "You Never Know," Season 3, Episode 2, *Six Feet Under* © 2003 Home Box Office.

Thus basic, if still difficult, rules of reciprocity and recognition in domestic relationships are laid out in the scene, which also articulates the conflict between David and Keith in racial and class terms. Keith is a hothead from a military background—historically a key context for African American upward mobility—who needs to learn "anger management," that form of self-governance whose pedagogy is now routinely worked into court procedures and settlements in cases exacerbated by male aggression. David, in contrast, is a civil but repressed and conflict-averse white guy from a middle-class family whose fortunes have been on edge since early in the series, as competing firms seek to buy out (or disable) family-operated funeral services in and around Los Angeles. Keith's professional specialty is sanctioned strong-arming, a position he loses, late in Season 2, through his own failures of control, landing him in the humiliating and downwardly-mobile occupation of underpaid guard for a security firm that serves overendowed households. David, again in contrast, is a particular if morbid kind of body scientist, a funeral technician whose skill, exactitude, and social calm in the face of others' grief befit his race and class identification on the series. The difference is crystallized in the private (not court-ordered or agency-based) therapy scene, enough so that it is hard to remember that the class and racial types could be inverted, Keith becoming the second-generation funeral director and David the hothead ex-cop. But that is not the narrative or representational tradition the scene is trading on.

On *Six Feet Under*, then, the visibility of Keith and David's queer relationship intensified in the promising project of therapy; maybe that's where they could get enough control and mutual recognition to sustain a viable, quasi-nuclear, domestic scene rather than life in the clubs, on the street, or even in a more collective household. Later in the episode, for example, we see them practicing lessons learned in therapy about recognition and tempering their anger—tentatively, self-consciously, but in good faith—as they cook together at home. But that visibility also depends, I have argued, on a very familiar race-class reduction that might have been otherwise structured or recombined, perhaps featuring a volatile (white) middle-class type and a reticent (black) upwardly-mobile one.

Unlike its counterpart scene in *The L Word*, however, psychotherapy on *Six Feet Under* does preserve the sexual privilege of gay men in contrast to lesbians. "How's your sex life?" the therapist asks both David and Keith. "Great" says Keith, with an offhanded ease that registers in contrast to an otherwise tense scene. "Oh, yeah," says David, overlapping Keith's line, "that works." The trouble they're having is not expressed as sexual conflict; indeed, attraction and sexual involvement may save them. At the end of *The L Word*'s debut season, in contrast, the therapist's early inquiry about sexual malaise and troubled intimacy has resurfaced. We know Bette and Tina's life together is on the rocks because their sexual relationship has cooled and Bette—under the strain of political opposition and personal attack from the religious right—begins an affair with an installation carpenter at the gallery where the controversial exhibit is being mounted. This is quite a different symbolic economy for representing the relationship between class and queer sex, and gender defines the contrast. In Keith and David's case, at least for the time being, sex is unburdened as the measure of maturity, stability, or class arrival; the relationship can be sour, but the sex good, and sex with others outside the relationship does not constitute a betrayal. In Bette and Tina's case, sex is love, and sexual monogamy, like marriage on Bravo's *Gay Weddings*, consolidates their resources as a couple. An affair is not simply a matter of desire or the release of social and professional pressure; it is a more comprehensive crisis through which the world-is-their-oyster character of Bette and Tina's relationship begins to crumble. It is also a conventional cliff-hanger to resurface in the following season.[5]

Sexual Healing

If middle-class propriety is a condition of good queerness, how does the representational field of popular culture make room for worthy, sexual queers from nonprofessional and working-class circumstances? The answer is "infrequently." Still, bodily control and legitimate modes of acquiring things figure in working-class queer portrayals, and the comparison I make here—between *If These Walls Could Talk II* (2000) and the commercial independent feature *Set It Off* (1996)—returns to the interaction of race and class in marking queer worth.

If These Walls Could Talk II was the second of two HBO films to follow the life of a house over multiple decades and multiple dwellers. In the first film, the narrative theme was abortion; in the second, lesbianism. In the middle vignette in *II*, directed by Martha Coolidge, Chloë Sevigny as "Amy" and Michelle Williams as "Linda" pair up in the early 1970s as a working-class motorcycle butch and a college lesbian feminist. Giving in to the attraction her roommates deride as patriarchal, Linda arrives at Amy's home one evening to return a shirt borrowed during the college group's slumming in a local butch/fem bar. In her modest, clean, and well-organized apartment, Amy seduces Linda with a degree of butch top expertise and tenderness rarely performed in commercial or even independent portrayals.

Despite her nervousness about the sexual plunge she is about to take, Linda has no regrets, and thus the scene becomes a familiar but heartening rendition of butch/fem seduction across class lines, where blue-collar, butch sexuality is expert, not merely aggressive, and commanding, not cowed by middle-class entitlement or derision, though Amy is shy and otherwise self-conscious. Her sexiness makes Linda and the audience happy about a liberating discovery, not shamed by a supposedly antifeminist reproduction of gender difference. They have skilled butch/fem sex. Within the scene (which

Amy and Linda's sex scene in Amy's apartment, bed made, illuminated lamp on modest work table, *If These Walls Could Talk II* © 2000 Home Box Office.

includes their ballsy delight in response to a shocked neighbor who witnesses their goodbye kiss), there is no irresolution, no regret, no apprehension, and no price to pay. But in its very stealth and stylization, its shy seduction, and an economy of sexual gesture in which Sevigny wastes no moves, there returns the image of physical management, even in the service of desire. The sex is controlled, at once sexy and proper, amid class and gender variance between the two women.

The segment stands in marked contrast to another butch/fem love scene released a little earlier in *Set It Off* (1996), an independent bank-heist feature directed by F. Gary Gray. The film is vaguely reminiscent of Kathryn Bigelow's *Point Break* but stars a band of four young, African American women (instead of five young, white, male surfers) frustrated by underemployment, systemic dismissal, police brutality, and living in the sweltering projects of South Central Los Angeles. One of the four, Cleo (played by Queen Latifah), is a butch lesbian who likes to customize her car with all the latest chrome and hydraulics. She lives in her garage, which is where we find her mid-plot, seducing her voluptuous, short-haired, peroxide blond girlfriend, Ursula, for whom she has bought some luxurious black under-things with part of her take from the recent heist. It's a nice scene (notwithstanding Ursula's curious lack of lines or vocalization),[6] until the other three partners in crime (Viveca A. Fox as Frankie, Kimberly Elise as T.T., and Jada Pinkett as Stony,

Ursula dances for Cleo on the hood of Cleo's car as Stony, T.T., and Frankie enter garage, *Set It Off* © 1996 New Line Productions.

the brains behind the operation) arrive at the garage and respond with contempt to Cleo and her girlfriend.

It isn't clear, however, that they're upset by the sex so much as Cleo's profligacy and her lack of foresight. Cleo has spent a lot of money on her girlfriend and the car, but meanwhile the foursome needs more money and they need to plan, not hang out having sex on the car in the middle of the garage, where any attentive police officer might notice the influx of cash. Stony chastises Cleo, who responds with violent defense and, despite their having been friends for life, a gun briefly to Stony's head. With steely composure at the end of a gun barrel, Stony tells Cleo that she is "real high, and acting real stupid, and better get that thing the fuck out of my face." Agitated, Cleo complies.

Toward the end of the film, Cleo is among the first to die in a grossly overpopulated confrontation with police; indeed she sacrifices herself in the hopes of sparing the others (though only Stony survives) by driving her car pell-mell into a police blockade. It's a heroic sacrifice but, like Cleo's actions in the garage, it is also impulsive. In contrast to Amy's butch sexual prowess in *If These Walls Could Talk* (2000), Cleo's sexuality is part of a pattern of self-destruction: sexy, yes, but out of control, the only lesbian character among the four friends, and the one who doesn't plan, spends too much, and gives in to temptation. In her character, the excesses of black poverty and lesbianism converge, in contrast to Amy's white modesty and self-taught skill as a mechanic, or to Stony's intelligence, femininity, light skin, and good looks, all of which qualify her for an upwardly mobile love affair with an African American banker (played by Blair Underwood) and, ultimately, for a lonely survival in Mexico endowed with stolen cash. Amy's legitimacy is rooted in settled living and sexual control, whereas suicidal loyalty is Cleo's redemption, a high price to pay as the class formula for queer visibility reasserts itself against the black butch. As is often the case through illness and violence, Cleo becomes a good queer when she dies.

Renewal? Modern Families, Broadway Teens

In late August 2010, the 62nd Primetime Emmy Awards brimmed with queer talent. Among the nominees for best supporting actor in a comedy series, for example, were Eric Stonestreet, for his role as Cam, partner to Mitchell on *Modern Family*, Neil Patrick Harris for his role as bromancer Barney Stinson on *How I Met Your Mother*, and Chris Colfer for his role as gay teen Kurt Hummel on *Glee*. All actors (and two of their characters) are openly gay. Colfer didn't win—the Emmy went to Stonestreet—but Colfer's costar, Jane Lynch, won for her supporting role as twisted cheerleading coach Sue Sylvester, an over-the-top bully with one thin vein of gold for her mentally disabled sister. Lynch is an openly lesbian Hollywood stalwart, a working actor with a long list of advertising credits, a long partnership with director and actor Christopher Guest (in such Guest films as *Best in Show* and *A Mighty Wind*), her creative new role in *Glee*, star turns in such comedy features as *Talladega Nights*, *The 40-Year-Old Virgin*, and *Role Models*, a recent supporting role opposite perennial Oscar nominee Meryl Streep in *Julie and Julia*, and still more recent stints hosting *Saturday Night Live* (2010) and the 2011 Emmy Awards broadcast. She is also recognized for having fought jointly with her spouse, clinical psychologist Laura Embry (the couple was married in Massachusetts in the summer of 2010) for the right to share custody of Embry's daughter, whom Embry had adopted with her ex-girlfriend. Shared custody rights were granted.

Such legal complexities in queer family living are rarely the stuff of broadcast television, even where a season of queer liberalization delivers a majority of openly gay nominees to an Emmy category and, indeed, the award for best comedy series to *Modern Family*. *Modern Family* is a new-form sitcom featuring three households in an extended family, each presenting a structural variant on family living. The anchor family is headed by Claire and Phil Dunphy (Julie Bowen and Ty Burrell), long-married first spouses with two teenage daughters and a preteen son (Sarah Hyland, Ariel Winter, and Nolan Gould). Then come Cam and Mitchell (Eric Stonestreet and Jesse Tyler Ferguson) and their adopted Vietnamese infant daughter, Lily (played by twins Ella Hiller and Jaden Hiller). Mitchell is Claire's brother, and their father, Jay Pritchett (Ed O'Neill), married shapely, funny, warm-hearted, and hotheaded Colombian beauty Gloria Delgado (Sofia Vergara), some twenty years Jay's junior, who came into his life with her old soul of a preteen son Manny Delgado (Rico Rodriguez).

Modern Family is adorable with almost everyone's vulnerabilities and excesses, save perhaps those of the sensible Jay, though he, too, can be called on the cozy carpet (usually by Gloria) for his sternness or for the limits of his emotional expressivity, especially toward his adult son and daughter. The writing is swift and emotionally exposing, the comedy as physical as it is dialogic, the direct address to the camera (by lead couples or individuals) a clever, reflexive element that lets characters reveal things otherwise concealed or fibbed about in the main action, and the camp sensibility rich, pointed, and blended with sweetness. But as a show with a primary gay household, *Modern Family* begs the class question of queer worth and the intersecting question of ethnic typification. In its renewal of the sitcom genre through interethnic, May–September, and same-sex family variants, it floats on fantasy levels of privilege and designer living across all three households. Indeed taste, and the income to sustain it, are equalized, creating a level class playing field where sarcasm and sting are softened by the knowledge that everyone's life is on track—by the standards of resources and options—even where their family feeling, at least briefly, might not be.

The strategy of class leveling has its effect on the series' ethnic typification as well. The three primary characters who are not European-American—Gloria, Manny, and Lily—come by their class participation through a certain largesse on the part of white characters, whether their cooing and attentive gay dads, in Lily's case, or their established businessman husband and stepfather, in Gloria's and Manny's. Lily is, so far, a silent near-toddler, who sits contentedly in a highchair or perches on the forearm of one of her doting dads; hopefully, with time, she will vocalize, rather than suffering the fate of the strangely mute five- (or so) year-old Lily York Goldenblatt, adopted Chinese daughter of Charlotte York and Harry Goldenblatt in *Sex and the City* (the movie, 2008). At the moment, both adopted Asian girls are plot points and human accessories for white leads.

Gloria is anything but mute. Indeed her richly Spanish accent and her idiomatic errors as a second-language speaker of English are frequently made into a punchline or an extended bit of comedy. She says "doggy-dog world," to signify a warm world full of puppies rather than a harsh world of human dogfights (dog-eat-dog world), and orders a boxful of miniature statues of Baby Jesus, mishearing Jay's declared love of baby cheeses. There is passing recognition that Gloria speaks two languages, where everyone else speaks only one. But the counterweight to language teasing comes less in a critique

TOP: High-end house tableau #1: Claire, Phil, and the kids. MIDDLE: High-end house tableau #2: Lily, Mitchell, and Cameron. BOTTOM: High-end house tableau #3: Jay, Manny, and Gloria, *Modern Family* title sequence, Season 1 © 2009 Twentieth Century Fox Film Corporation.

of monolingualism than in Gloria's over-the-top sex appeal. Actor Sofia Vergara is gorgeous and, in publicity interviews, sensibly unself-conscious about her beauty and her 34DD bust size. "I'm grateful I have them," she told a *Self Magazine* interviewer for the October 2010 issue, "and I've always felt sexy." Fair enough, though I can't help thinking of the celebration of Vergara's front side as a renewed celebration of Jennifer Lopez's backside, Colombian and Nuyorican variants of Latina body spectacle. Healthy body image notwithstanding, *Modern Family* reserves the connection among feeling, intuition, superstition, and physical prowess for Gloria as both ethnic and gender stereotype. She is not *quite* Damon Wayans's gold digger from the episode of *My Wife and Kids* discussed earlier, and some critics have suggested that Gloria picks up where Chicana sister Hilda Suarez (Ana Ortiz) in *Ugly Betty* leaves off,[7] as a warmhearted and multidimensional stereotype set in a universe of campiness, cartoonlike excess, and immigrant family love. Gloria is a lead whose warmth and over-the-top registers she, herself, recognizes and values, a cross between Wayans' gold digger and *George Lopez*'s solidarity but with only Manny's ethnic company to keep. Everybody, meanwhile, envies her husband Jay, even as some of us in the audience are left to think "the mysteries of heterosexuality" whenever an average-looking late-middle-aged guy hooks up with a younger and seriously more beautiful woman. But, Jay comes with money and Gloria doesn't appear to, and the ethnic differences between them signal her upward mobility, much like Lalo Montenegro's with his white boyfriend. Gloria shares (and spends) Jay's money legitimately as his spouse, and she is enfranchised in the household. The things that make her lovable, however, are inseparable from the things that renew every Latin bombshell image Hollywood has ever exploited.

Thus the leveling of class among the three households tempers the gender and ethnic stereotyping otherwise given free rein in the series, as it tempers the lovable feyness and insecurity of the two gay leads, Mitchell and Cam. Both are hyperattentive parents, driven by conventional ambition to get their daughter into only the finest preschool but also by gay determination to be better fathers than straight men ever could be. "Leave it to the gays to produce the only underachieving Asian child," says Mitchell in exasperation when Cam is slow to be enthusiastic about Lily's admission to the Harvard of local nurseries. The punchline combines class ambition with ethnic typing and fear of gay failure in the overdrawn domain of sitcom parenthood. But its class register is articulated through parenthood, not the language of class per se.

As income, wealth, and taste, class privilege roots everything on *Modern Family*—the ethnic and gay humor, the plotlines, the characters, settings, and resolutions. Privilege consolidates the series' social foundation, as episodic circumstances fly humorously apart at the seams through ethnic, gender, and queer tokenism, an old word and an old strategy.

Like talent on *Glee*, in other words, class on *Modern Family* equalizes away class questions. Neither *Glee* nor *Modern Family* is *Roseanne*, whose class and queer registers (through Martin Mull's character, or Sandra Bernhard's) could be co-present without one being reduced to the other. *Roseanne* was not perfect, but the series voiced family life with the greatest semblance of honesty about class effects. In the current broadcast season, *The Middle* on ABC comes closest, as Hampton Stevens (2010) notes in *The Atlantic.com* in a commentary comparing *The Middle* and *Modern Family*. "Everyone on *Modern Family*," says Stevens, "seems quite comfortable, even if Mitchell did just quit his job. In contrast, absolutely nothing about *The Middle* is upscale. The Hecks struggle to make ends meet, with both parents working. They drink beer, not wine. Their home décor is unironically shabby. Their clothes, especially Sue's, are comically dated." I agree with Stevens: plots on *The Middle* take shape in a universe that bears emotional and empirical semblance to the cultural and economic class lives of those watching. But *Roseanne*'s class deconstruction and class politics, or *Friday Night Lights*', are missing, and there is nary a queer character in sight. (There is hope, though, for *The Middle*'s sweetly odd young son Brick Heck, played by Atticus Schaffer.)

Conclusion: The Class Project of Queer Visibility

The terms of my criticism are not designed to dismiss innovations in queer programming as simple reproductions of class or race dominance. Rather, they explore with greater attention the ways in which class has appeared, structuring queer difference and being restructured by queer specificity. This is not a survey of queer class types but a mode of analysis that interrogates patterns of comportment, familialism, and the legitimate acquisition of the good life in the commercial ratification of queerness. My examples are wrought largely from the media mainstream in the early stages of the new queer visibility plus more recent comparisons, and other sectors and periods make visible other patterns. Bérubé, for example, names and explores what *The L Word* only deploys. What is visible, however, is the availability of class difference for producing queerness (a different conclusion than "all media queers are rich and white"; they aren't), but also the density and constraint of class representation. In a series of discursive turns at once humorous, powerful, and incomplete, class variance is exposed, but even variance appears in order to pull queerness toward a normative middle. Queerness, in contrast, no longer exerts—or does not yet exert—enough countervailing force to pull class difference back from the flow of dominance to the field of critique.

These conditions speak to a particular historical moment, dating from the early 1990s but with a deeper postwar lineage (Gross 2001). The evolution of cable television and the development of niche audiences in such other media as theatrical film have met changing sociopolitical conditions in the lives of some, but not all, gay and lesbian people. On the one hand, this made for nongay interest in gay characters, like Michael on *My Wife and Kids* and Lalo on *George Lopez*, and, on the other, for queer-identified audiences willing to pay for programs of their own, like *The L Word*. Producers and marketers created this niche rather than discovering it, and did so as commercial arbiters long have: by exploiting historical deprivations of images and recognition and catering to deprived audiences at a moment when the industrial risk is worth it. Showtime, home to both *The L Word* and *Queer as Folk* (based on the British series of the same title), branded itself as the cable outlet for courageous (because sexually explicit) queer programming, a brand promoted in contradistinction to conventional network anxiety about so much as a gay kiss. It is a queer brand now suspended, however, as sexual intensity is packaged elsewhere, in vampire narratives and ancient Rome, both arguably program opportunities reopened by half a generation of Showtime's queer sex.

In one-off characters like Lalo Montenegro, we had an image of assimilation, the presence of gay characters on straight terms, and in *The L Word* the contrasting presence of lesbians on hopefully lesbian terms, an image less of assimilation than cultural difference and community integrity. But, while we should not dismiss the kick of recognition that made even the most skeptical lesbian viewers subscribe to Showtime for *The L Word*'s run, in both contexts the class markers of queer worth bring stories and characters into line with dominant discourses for dominant and nondominant audiences alike.

Those markers, finally, organize not only the concentrated narratives of popular culture, but the diffuse and contradictory partial narratives of everyday living. The most visible fantasies commercial culture offers are not a world apart, but a part of our world, elements of a continuous cultural stream in which ideologies of class and queer worth rooted in managed bodies, family attachments, and legitimately acquired things are as likely to surface off television as on. My political goal, then, is not to claim that adequate representation in commercial culture will promote adequate representation in social life, or that as critics we ought to expect that popular media will deconstruct popular fantasy. Instead, I suggest the continuity of affective investments inside the media and out, in a universe where people *really do* enjoy, endure, and equally suffer the terms of existing class projects, including the class project of queer visibility.

That is a draining conclusion, however, if it means that queer class life has nowhere to go and nothing to do except to live with the limits dominance imposes, learning class rules from the cultural ether, and infusing that air with resignation in turn. What, alternately, might solidarity look and feel like? If it is true that cultural forms and everyday life are more connected than the fear of media influence communicates, it is also true that attachments to other kinds of narratives and characters matter. But what other kinds? *Love and Money* offers some alternatives, including finding in film a gentleness of tone that does not signal the usual class proprieties; finding in literature the chance for queer class recognition and among readers the collective will to understand queer and class experience more deeply; finding among producers a world of relay living in which queerness expands the terms of culture-making and challenges the *queer* entrenchment of cultural hierarchy in the name of never, ever, crossing over; and, through optimism and queer friendship, finding a queer class future of love and solidarity.

3

Every Queer Thing We Know

How to live? Be soft, get by, go slow, open up, find others, try to be kind,
funny if you have it in you. Get things done, think justly, create, learn your
corner as best you can. There is nothing queer in this list as we know the
term, but the gentle vertigo it releases—an unclinical venturesomeness in
meeting parts of the world we don't already understand—brings courage
closer, buoys newness. I remember coming out as queer—neither buoyant
nor soft, a little courageous maybe as I stepped off the future as I had known
it. I remember the summer night at a friend's birthday party, held at a Philadelphia dance club in 1987. I stood beside a six-foot loudspeaker near the
dance floor, where straight couples were dancing and where my sobs of recognition—that this world was no longer for me—would neither be heard nor
seen. That grief and that release were not queer things either, but they were
experiences common among queers and thus part of what I came to understand as queer time and space, a move toward the material world that makes
us queer from the outside in.

Miranda July's first feature film, *Me and You and Everyone We Know*
(2005), is full of such sensibility, the queer-making vertigo and release,
enough for me to want to claim it—beyond July's personal identification as
bisexual—for a gentle canon of queer expression. A canon is gentle when
its inventory is supple, its poetry delicate, its constitutive insights revealing
enough to help us live minute to minute. These are not the usual terms of
canon formation; they step aside its charge of hierarchy and exclusion. But a
gentle canon (corduroy, maybe, not steel) might recognize the virtues of softness and be slow to judge, while still enabling us to celebrate expression and
its artists. Slowness, softness, decompression, repair—these are the graces of
Me and You that I want to fold into observation as diffusely (not distinctively) queer. In the film, they carry a tender world of people socially and
economically at risk.

Me and You and Everyone We Know is poignant, quirky, and not exactly
happy. Everyone in it aches, everyone wants contact. Video artist Christine
Jesperson (Miranda July) plays both characters in the romantic dialogues she
records, writing "ME" on the toe of one shoe and "YOU" on the other in a

Pam's nightshirt in mirror, *Me and You and Everyone We Know* © 2005 IFC and Film Four.

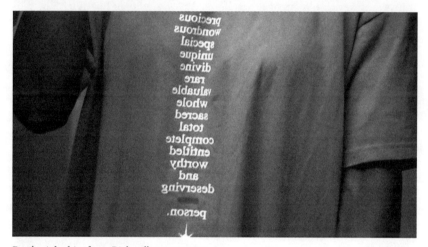

Pam's nightshirt from Richard's perspective

glossy pair of pink slippers sold to her by Richard Swersey (John Hawkes), a divorced dad and the new object of Christine's affection. In her digital view-finder, her "ME" and "YOU" feet approach, stop short, turn, withdraw, and finally they barely touch. Richard himself is unmoored by separation from his wife and the vicissitudes of custodial fatherhood. He needs his young sons, it appears, even more than they need him. "Do I seem okay?" he asks them. Six-year-old Robby (Brandon Ratcliff) is quizzical; fifteen-year-old Peter (Miles Thompson) responds, "Yeah, fine," a little panicky, conscious of the role reversal and the thin line between fact and reassurance. The boys' mother, Pam (JoNell Kennedy), is neither callous nor secure. Richard pleads with her to recognize their good times; she does, but wants more. She brushes her teeth wearing a nightshirt adorned with a column of affirmations printed backward, a column only she can read, in the mirror: wondrous, whole, deserving. When they were married, Richard felt left out by that nightshirt.

The boys make punctuation pictures on their computer (a Bengal tiger composed of colons and spaces), and after dark they exchange sexual chat online with Untitled, in idioms infused with knowingness and childhood speculation. Robby instructs Peter, chatting as Night Warrior, to say that he wants to poop into Untitled's butthole and Untitled can poop back into his. The same poop. Forever.

For her day job, Christine drives an Eldercab, chauffeuring people who "feel too old to drive." Her passenger, Michael (Hector Elias), spent fifty years traveling with a wife, now dead, whom he barely liked, and has since met Ellen (Ellen Geer), soon to die, in his assisted living complex. "Maybe it just took seventy years of life to be ready for a woman like Ellen," he tells Christine. Ten-year-old Sylvie (Carlie Westerman) spends her allowance on small appliances and linens, building her trousseau ("French for hope chest") for her future husband and daughter and pasting advertising pictures into a homemade pink catalogue of current and dreamed-of purchases. For all her bossy command over neighborhood children, whom she corrals in the park and orders to lie down and peep like birds in exchange for a Cheez-It, she has disconnection and longing for a world of love and comfort in common

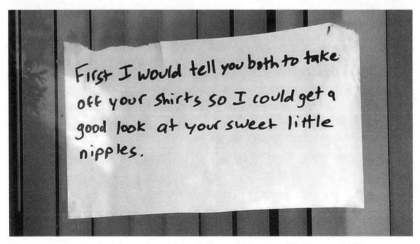

The message on Andrew's window, *Me and You and Everyone We Know* © 2005 IFC and Film Four.

with the adults around her. Teenage friends and local mean girls Heather (Natasha Slayton) and Rebecca (Najarra Townsend) taunt their chubby neighbor Andrew (Brad William Henke), who is also Richard's coworker in the shoe department, with challenges about what he might do with a couple of "lesbian sisters"—them—if he believed they were eighteen (they aren't). He responds first with sensible disengagement, then with big Magic Marker notes pasted to the window of the apartment complex: "First, I would tell you both to take off your shirts so I could get a good look at your sweet little nipples."

Robby touches Herrington's hair (#1).

Robby touches Herrington's hair (#2), *Me and You and Everyone We Know* © 2005 IFC and Film Four.

When the girls summon their curiosity and boldness and approach his apartment, Andrew nose-dives to the floor under the window, flattening and hopefully concealing himself against the wall. In his solitude and soft body, he is vulnerable to the girls' lean, experimental aggression.

Nancy Herrington (Tracy Wright), a depressed and unsentimental gallery curator, tells Christine to mail in the videotape she is holding in front of her. "It'll get lost" if she takes it by hand. Herrington is also Untitled. Moved by her correspondence with Robby (who cuts and pastes alluring phrases he barely understands), she asks to meet him in the park. Discovering he is a child, she receives his stroke of her hair—a July motif from earlier video work—tenderly kisses his mouth, and leaves.

This would seem like a sad tableau, but such a conclusion is tempered by moxie and curiosity. At the end of her mailed-in videotape, the part she believes Herrington will never see, Christine tells the curator that if she got that far and understands, she should call the number Christine holds up and say "macaroni," no questions asked. Late in *Me and You and Everyone We Know*, Christine receives a call, hoping it is Richard. "Eldercab," she says. "Macaroni," responds the female voice, and recognition tiptoes in.

Christine finds Richard later. Together, in a tree in the yard outside Richard's apartment complex, they hang a framed picture of a bird. Beholding the bird, Christine stands behind Richard, wraps her arms around his middle, closes her eyes, and lays her head on his back. If you are lucky, you know the feeling, tearful and almost nauseating in its wonder, of two wishful, halting bodies pressed together for the first time.

The social world of *Me and You and Everyone One We Know* is close to the bone; people are working and just getting by. Most are white, Pam is black, the boys are biracial. Most live in the nondescript Eden Roc complex in the uncelebrated suburbs of Los Angeles and survive through routine. The bleakness is reminiscent to me of my family's household after my parents' divorce, our activities constrained by genteel poverty and overwork, a child's life perforce unsupervised and a little gritty for that. Not enough space, not enough light, unmade beds, cereal for dinner. But *Me and You* is less bleak than quiet, an artful work of noise reduction that brings gesture into high relief. We can see and feel people reaching out, trying to be good.

Knowing her trousseau, we can imagine Sylvie's semiconscious calculations as she wonders how to receive Peter's gift of a plush toy beaver with a pink star in its paws. "For your daughter," he tells her. He has been thinking about her, child to child, and Sylvie now knows this. In aerial close-up, they lie side by side on Sylvie's pink patterned bedroom rug, being and gazing as children hopefully get to do. Peter asks Sylvie what she would say to

Christine and Richard embrace as Richard hangs picture.

Bird photograph in tree, *Me and You and Everyone We Know* © 2005 IFC and Film Four.

her daughter. "Hi, baby girl," Sylvie speaks into the air, "you are a precious treasure."

There are many such moments of exposure and generosity in the film: Herrington kisses Robby, avowing her affection and separating herself, as an attracted adult probably ought to do; Ellen loans a photograph of her daughter for Christine's art project; Richard acknowledges, in response to Sylvie's mother (Colette Kilroy), who has blithely claimed that "kids are so adaptable," that "kids have absolutely no control over their lives." *Me and You and Everyone We Know* is not a primer for queering children, but it shows us the delicacies and risks children undertake all the time, and thus an openness to their, and our, formation. Dependent on adults who are loving, broken, and sometimes know no better than they do, *Me and You*'s children fend and find for themselves.

It is in this fending and finding that new selves are made, new solutions tried, new possibilities wrought from novel arrangements of too few resources. This is not to recommend deprivation—in a cold world, it will happen anyway—but to see rather than judge (scold, lock up, treat, banish, categorize) the everyday social calculations of vulnerable people, children and adults among them. I don't mind envisioning queerness in such terms, as a kind of solution to an uncertain question—How to be?—rather than as a force of nature, God, or pride. It can be such a force, but it needn't. In its openness, *Me and You* restores the presence and contingency of being, and in its quirkiness of queer being. It is less defensive than reparative. Its redemptions are small, sustainable.

It is telling to read responses to *Me and You and Everyone We Know*. Critics and bloggers struggle to capture its tenor, making sociable the descriptive inadequacy the film arouses and in turn making that response a structured feeling more than a problem. "I really don't know how to describe the changing moods of the film, from humor to despair, without negatives: it's so off-kilter that its gloom and fatalism are never morbid or even sentimental, so . . . deadpan that its fundamental sweetness often passes by barely perceived," writes blogger Steven Shaviro on his Pinocchio Theory site (2005). "It hits too closely to the secret heart of most of us to invite duplication," says MaryAnn Johanson, "Flick Filosopher" on her blog (2005). "Deeply idiosyncratic yet strangely comforting," writes Eli Horowitz (2005) in *The Believer*. Even *New York Times* critic A. O. Scott (2005) scarcely resolves his skepticism in declaring that the film's "wide-eyed, quizzical approach . . . this guilelessness—which will either charm you or drive you up the wall—is more a calculated effect than the simple expression of a whimsical sensibility." Later, Scott calls July's flirtation "both brazen and coy."

"Her provocations may strike some people as overly cute," Scott (2005) continues, "and her self-consciousness as a tiresome form of solipsism. But *Me and You and Everyone We Know* is brave enough to risk this rejection, and generous enough not to deserve it. I like it very much, and I hope you will, too." Scott reverses his opening coolness, surrendering to the film's sweetness and complexity. It hardly matters whether characters' gestures are authentic or put on; as responses to sadness, they are simply possible. Says another reviewer at pollystaffle.com, "there's not a cruel moment in this film."

Not a cruel moment. I am neither naive nor guiltless enough to expect not a cruel moment in queerness, but in its sensible strangeness and its observation as light as lavender vapor, *Me and You and Everyone We Know* revives in me a curiosity, a wish, for a less self-righteous queer world. Amid the contemporary aggressions of Tea Partiers and generals, Judge Judy or Dr. Phil, self-righteousness is not a distinctly queer problem. But queerness has, historically, welcomed what others have shamed, inverted what others have damned or dismissed, deconstructed and reconstructed social possibility against the grain of misanthropy and accumulation. In a world high on greed and authority, how might queerness make things easier, not harder, and not only for queers? This is not an appeal to get along or abandon the multiple forms of social power that queer action has wrought. It is an aesthetic or dispositional appeal, a collective relaunch of the question "How to be?" This is a question in which July and her collaborators have kept the faith.

As cultural polymath, July followed *Me and You and Everyone We Know* with a collection of stories published in the summer of 2007, whose title—*No One Belongs Here More Than You*—extends the plainspoken solidarities of the film and whose pieces extend the film's reparative sense of observation and curiosity. They are empathic, unsentimental, sometimes "creepy" (to quote David Byrne from the jacket), and slow to judge. They invite their readers to go slow, too—a tonal beckoning more than a pedagogy, reached through spare expression and through characters who, themselves, have layered opinions about their experiences. In "Majesty," for example, a young woman dreams night after night of a sexual romance with Prince William, then makes a list of ways to meet him:

> Go to his school to give a lecture on earthquake safety.
> Go to the bars near his school and wait for him.

"They were not," she continues, "mutually exclusive":

> they were both reasonable ways to get to know someone. People meet in bars every day, and they often have sex with people they meet in bars. My sister does this all the time, or she did when she was in college. Afterward she would call and tell me every detail of her night, not because we are close— we are not. It is because there is something wrong with her. I would almost call what she does sexual abuse, but she's my younger sister, so there must be another word for it. She's over the top. That's all I can say about her. If the top is here, where I am, she's over it, hovering over me, naked. (23)

Alongside the William plot is the story of a neighbor's dog that has been killed by a car. The girl stands on the street with a young boy, also a witness to the event. The dog's bereft owner upbraids the girl for not finding the dog first:

I looked at the boy; he was the opposite of a prince. He had nothing. When my sister was in college, she used to sometimes take these boys home. She would call me the next morning.

I could see it in his pants, it was like half hard, so I could already tell it was big.

Please stop now.

The story continues, ignoring the request. Despite any marker, we realize that "I could see it" is the younger sister speaking, narrating her sex from the night before to her older sister, who finds herself aroused:

. . . Anyways, I was rubbing and rubbing and I was super wet and he's all pushing it in my face and I'm going crazy for it and then, you're not going to believe this, he jizzes all over my face. Before I even get it in. Can you believe that?

. . . And then my sister paused to listen to the sound of my breath over the phone. She could hear that I was done, I had come. So she said good-bye and I said goodbye and we hung up. It is this way between us; it has always been this way. She has always taken care of me like this. If I could quietly kill her without anyone knowing, I would. (29–30)

It is startling to encounter so soft a homicidal wish, sister to sister. The wish is legible, though, alongside the arousal, the older sister's self-contempt, the discernment of abuse and something wrong in the younger sister's bulldozing against the older's plea to stop, even as her arousal heightens.

As sexual practice, the sisters' phone calls take their place alongside Andrew's notes on the exterior walls of Eden Roc, Robby's single stroke of Herrington's hair, and Christine and Richard's back-to-front embrace. Such gestures converge in the unalarmed delicacy of their observation and in their oddity, not as good or corrupt, consensual, or coercive. July's tone, in other words, is not calibrated to the familiar divide between sexual pleasure and danger. Like *Me and You and Everyone We Know,* the stories recognize sexual suffering, aggression, and need as part of the same universe as arousal and delight. They open a door in what elsewhere seems like a solid and defensive wall, a sexual political cave from which there is no escape. In the stories, by contrast, we step right here, into a little *voilà!*—somewhere lighter, where people whose lives are open to attack know something about their circumstances and are not merely the objects of others' judgments or their own oblivion.

"My art," July has said in an interview, "is like my car, the way I get to the next place" (Bryan-Wilson 2004). In its enchantments, its recognitions, its invitations to see, July's work directs a graceful queer beam on the beaten turf of rage and pronouncement. On its own, such a beam cannot illuminate a queer future, but it can summon responsiveness, a preserving and consoling receptivity and recognition that are hard to find and harder to hold onto in these mean times.

4

Recognition: Queers, Class, and Dorothy Allison

Twenty years ago, shortly before Penn State University voted to include sexual orientation in its nondiscrimination policy, I crossed campus as a young faculty member, dressed in a suit and tie, wearing my hair short, dyed and spiky as befitted the moment, my mouth deeply tinted with red lipstick. A young white man walked past in the opposite direction, turned over his shoulder and scowled *"gender* bender . . . " Despite a crowded path and in classic Althusserian fashion, I recognized myself to be the one hailed by his contempt. I snorted back: "That'd be *Doctor* Gender Bender to you, pal."

I don't know whether the guy heard me, but in the early years after this encounter I would relay the story at school and students always laughed, cheering on my trumping of this young man's public contempt. But what about that "Doctor"? On the surface, it was the assertion of a status I could claim, but he presumably couldn't, in a setting built on the status distinctions of age and credentials. But it was also calculated to mess with a homophobic denunciation through a then-incoherent pairing of desired credentials and reviled sexual subjectivity, attaching faculty standing to the defensive pride of queerness. In that time and place, it was a gesture of recoding; it would be another three years before Penn State would include sexual orientation in its antidiscrimination policy, and meanwhile the tone on campus was set by famously homophobic women's basketball coach Rene Portland and an inert University leadership. (From 1988 to 1990, I was the only publicly lesbian member of a faculty of 2,500.)

I recount this occasion to think about the category of recognition in cultural politics, a category that marks my anecdote in several ways. First is the young man's hostile recognition of my gender (or sexual) perversion, perverse, that is, by his and others' standards. There is also my recognition of those terms, in understanding myself to be the one he was addressing. But then there is my recuperative version, rearticulating queerness as fierce, not vulnerable. Finally, there is the largely *un*-recoded bid for recognition in class terms, un-recoded because there was nothing new about dismissing the opinions or judgments of others (however hostile the judgment or righteous the dismissal) through an assertion of class authority. Mess with me, I told this young man, and I'll play the class card. When I do, you'll lose.

By most theoretical standards, I have conflated status and class here, to let the status difference between student and teacher and my hostile one-upmanship stand as homology for relative class power, on a campus where more faculty than students, in 1990, came from professional backgrounds. But rather than reading the conflation as sloppy, I offer it to illustrate the confusions and displacements routinely noted about discourses of class in the United States, displacements onto race, gender, language, money, and professional authority (e.g., Ortner 1991). Such displacements challenge the old claim that there is no language of class in the United States. Indeed, they *are* an American language of class, a category multiplied by the layers of class process and hierarchy present in any social encounter.

Class Recognition?

One conclusion from my story is that recognition takes many forms, though some categories of social difference, like sexuality, have been more amenable to a positive politics of recognition, while others, like class, have been less so. This is a point Beverly Skeggs (2000; 2004) makes more fully. Skeggs argues that for subjects suffused with the force and weight of *mis*recognition long imposed by bourgeois domination on the bodies, labor, and identities of working people, the goal is less recognition (or rearticulation, for example, from pervert to high-status queer) than unmarking the classed body. The route to such unmarking is economic redistribution—an equitable division of wealth and value produced by all kinds of labor, rather than the concentration of value up the class ladder. While identity politics recognize personhood and entitlement, in Skeggs's analysis class politics demand redistribution, not recognition. For some authors, moreover, cultivating recognition comes at the expense of redistribution.

Working on class and culture, I have been influenced by this line of thinking but slow to accept its opposition between recognition and redistribution and the uncoupling of class from recognition's language and value. The politics and strategies of redistribution are essential (among them, progressive social welfare and tax policy, living wages, cooperative ownership, health and education as public goods, and dismantling the war economy). But recognition and social class are not incompatible, given the routine displacement of class onto so-called cultural differences (racial, ethnic, national, and sexual) and given popular and scholarly attachment to status hierarchies marked by education, income, and taste. If recognition politics don't count, moreover, why are they so energetically practiced by people who claim a commitment to social change? There are skeptical answers: for example, those which presume the narrow self-interest of non-class-articulated (but deeply classed) subjectivities, like the stereotype of single-issue, bourgeois gay men more concerned with vodka advertisements, Beltway gossip, and well-catered weddings than with nationalizing health care—more interested, in other words, in joining the club than dismantling it. I want to resist such an explanation to consider a reconstructive approach to recognition in a cultural context where class hierarchy and sexual difference meet.

In a series of essays written between 1996 and 2000, political theorist Nancy Fraser sought to link recognition and redistribution.[1] Fraser was interested in connecting but not collapsing the two categories to identify the distinctive workings of maldistribution and misrecognition as forms of social injustice, and thus to find remedies that address both kinds of harm rather than limiting one only to heighten the other. In acknowledging what she calls the "bivalent" condition of virtually all social groups—for whom injustice takes form as maldistribution *and* misrecognition—Fraser (1996) is an undefensive Left theorist. She does not blame a historical shift in progressive priorities on the colonizing excesses of "identity politics," though she de-essentializes identity categories, refusing them as labels for absolute cultural difference and asking, instead, what difference such differences make in social participation.

I share Fraser's view of the political and social significance of identity, but I depart from what is perhaps the most frequent conclusion of that view— that cultural or identity differences have distributive significance after all (e.g., Butler 1997)—toward a less frequent but no less important one: that class difference and hierarchy provoke deep and important questions about recognition. The practice of class recognition, I argue, matters in the formation of selves and solidarity in ways that an analytic emphasis on redistribution alone cannot capture. Skeggs disagrees. "People," she says, "who cannot authorize themselves through their individual experience of pain, because they do not see everyday suffering as exceptional, are unable to participate" (2004, 59). It is a simple and critical point, but it leaves in place the presumed invisibility of class suffering. Under what conditions does suffering as class effect get expressed? How, moreover, do lives multiply marked by class, gender, race, and sexuality (among other forms of social difference and hierarchy) combine recognition practices and effects?

Another brake on the presumed value of recognition comes from Althusserian theories of ideology, where the practice of recognition is evidence of the workings of dominance (Hall 1982). Recognition refers to an experiential "aha!" that receives as simple, empirical truth what is in fact a process of sig-nification, or meaning-making, in relations of dominance and subordina-tion. For example, to recognize a statement as true, or a gesture or person as familiar or legitimate, is in fact to participate in the system of signification and authority that lies behind "truth," "familiarity," and "authority." To judge a statement as "making no sense" is, by contrast, to reject its very terms and frame the rejected item as a failed or suspect attempt by dominant (if unar-ticulated) standards. Such a theory would contend, for example, that in dom-inant ideology and everyday life, queers (especially at Penn State in 1990) were everywhere recognized as perverts, failed heterosexuals rather than the counter-cultural resistors of bourgeois sexual propriety. Similarly, working-class people become excessive bodies marked by multiple failures of control, rather than subjugated bodies produced by the formation of bourgeois sub-jectivity itself.

If domination is all that recognition sets in motion, then I, too, want to reject it. But is it? Why, given how people understand the term and how they or we experience its violence, does it endure as something we want from the world? Is this just selective self-interest? Is social class banished from even a reconstructive recognition politics? Is the very desire for recognition a second-order ideological effect fast in need of progressive indictment or is something more relational going on? This question is especially vital in a universe where people participate in multiple class processes simultane-ously and over time (as wage workers by day, say, and self-employed work-ers or students by night), and thus where no single class process can reliably be taken as the root of identification (Gibson-Graham, Resnick, and Wolff 2000). It is equally vital where mobilities up and down the class ladders of income and wealth do not readily correspond with changes in class affect. Class location and feeling, in other words, are commonly mixed, especially for those from working-class backgrounds who move into professional adulthoods and who describe themselves (as this chapter will later consider) as "class escapees."

Class, Queerness, and Dorothy Allison

I come to the study of class in queerness as a longtime reader of the work of Dorothy Allison, a southern, white, radical, queer, rural, working-class, feminist writer and performance artist relocated to Northern California. For close to thirty years, Allison's writing has inspired a mixed and open con-versation about social class that exposes the layered, recursive language and experience of class difference, hierarchy, and mobility in the contemporary

United States. Her books and essays have circulated as revered texts among lesbian and other queer readers and, since the publication of her best-known novel, *Bastard Out of Carolina* (1992), in the literary mainstream. Noticing the movement and reception of Allison's work among multiple readerships— queer, class-conscious, and neither—told me that I could turn to that conversation to explore class recognition in cultural practice, and could *queer* that recognition as I moved among Allison's audiences. I could ask what is queer or not about class, and about when class and queerness surface together, or recede, for readers who use both ideas.

Some of Allison's work is semiautobiographical, about her life as the child of poor white people in the South Carolina Piedmont. Her stories do not ennoble or conceal the abjection, violence, alcoholism, and suspicion present in her family and region, nor the depth of love and solidarity sometimes enacted there, or other times betrayed in the most painful and determining ways.[2] Nor does Allison gloss over the social conditions and everyday tyrannies that make her family's ways of living comprehensible to herself and to readers: exclusion from property, education, and decent employment, the withholding of social regard, and the equally repressive codes of masculine dominance and female dependence near the bottom of so many social hierarchies (Berlant 2007). Finally, Allison has written about the experience of liberation and abjection in the feminist, queer, and sexual radical communities in which she came of age as activist and author. There the conditions of alignment were sometimes receptive, other times hostile to working-class life and to Allison's personal legacies of poverty and mobility, the first treated to middle-class charity and authority, the second presumed to express an uncritical investment in the American dream.[3]

This chapter draws from Allison's writing and published responses to it, from her lectures and conversations with audiences, and from individual and group interviews with readers contacted through her public events, to track class and queer discourses in cultural reception and how those discourses are mediated by gender, race, and trauma. I wanted to know whether and how people recognize themselves and one another in class and queer terms, and whether and how they attach queerness to class in their engagement with cultural materials.

I did not undertake this study, however, as a vehicle for re-theorizing recognition. My writing responds to the consistency with which Allison and others in the course of our conversations articulated the value of recognition and the pain of misrecognition. I want to consider such expressions before dismissing the cultural politics of recognition as so much ideological distraction. In the process, I explore the cultural injuries of class domination (Ortner 1991),[4] the place of affect in class solidarity and difference, and the kinds of relief and even new understanding (*re-cognition*) some public occasions entail. Finally, I consider the sociality of popular and middlebrow pleasure in the formation of contingent communities, those relations in time and place whose feeling endure beyond the moment. Lauren Berlant (2007) has observed that the feelings and attachments we cultivate over time are not necessarily promising just because they're feelings. They can misdirect us and make us stuck.[5] But they can also bring survival that much closer.

Lived Recognition

An early occasion in my Allison travels took place one evening at the City Arts and Lectures Series in San Francisco. Held at the Herbst Theatre, a grand old venue near City Hall once threatened with demolition but revived by the series, City Arts and Lectures is in its fourth decade. The series invites about fifty guests annually, among them authors, artists, journalists, scientists, and other cultural figures, for live-to-tape interviews with a usually well-known and collegial interlocutor. Edited versions of the interviews are later broadcast on public radio, and tickets to the live event cost $15 to $20 in 2001 (less for students and seniors), which means that not everyone who wants to can attend. It isn't the case, however, that only affluent people show up or that ticket pricing homogenizes the City Arts and Lectures audience, though audience makeup changes depending on the guest. The group for Allison's date in 2001 was visibly more mixed than it was for earlier programs that season with authors Edmund White and Spaulding Gray.

This was Allison's fourth City Arts and Lectures occasion, for which she was interviewed by Michael Patrick MacDonald, a community antiviolence activist from Boston and the author of the award-winning *All Souls: A Family Story from Southie* (1999), a story of growing up Irish American and poor in the South Boston projects.[6] Allison wanted MacDonald, she told me, because he'd ask her difficult questions about social class rather than make polite conversation about being an author. With an audience of students, aspiring writers, friends, sponsors, philanthropists, social workers, former inmates, professionals from working-class backgrounds, lesbians, and "just readers," to name a few self-descriptions, the occasion offered a mix of impulses and interests among those who described themselves as fans of Dorothy Allison.[7] Following MacDonald's introduction of Allison and about half an hour of conversation between the two, audience members were invited to address questions to either author. Below, I quote selected comments from the introduction and the question period to think about the objects and meanings of queer class recognition.

One

MPM: I met Dorothy for the first time about a year ago, after I'd written my book [*All Souls*], and, we were speaking together on stage at the Children's Defense Fund. And I got up to do a reading, and it was a piece of my book that . . . had a lot of violence, and drugs, and death and suicide, and I sat down after doing my reading next to Dorothy and she turned to me and said "I think we're related." [*Laughter*] What she was talking about . . . she showed me pictures of my family members in my book, and showed how similar their faces were. And there were a lot of things about those faces . . . a lot of things that I saw in their faces that were very familiar to me when I went out and bought *Two or Three Things I Know for Sure*. And some of those things were of course a lot of the hardship and pain and struggle and pride . . . And the more I read from that book in particular and then went back and read *Trash*, the more related I felt, I think, to you and to your story.

Shortly after these comments, MacDonald described giving a copy of Allison's story collection *Trash* to a young man in Southie on the verge of suicide, and the solace the book had brought him despite his community's habitual disdain for homosexuality and his own embarrassment in carrying around a book labeled "lesbian literature." MacDonald quoted a line that had been especially meaningful to the young man, about deciding to live. "Thank you," he then said to Allison, "for writing."

"What I want to know," Allison responded, "is he datin' boys yet?" MacDonald looked shy and the audience laughed. "We'll have to see!"

Two

From the Q-and-A period, the audience member a white, middle-aged, carefully coiffed woman, elegantly styled in casual designer clothing:

Q: When did you start to write, when did you, did you have mentors?
DA: Did I have mentors . . .
Q: And how did you have the courage to persist in your young life?
DA: My *young* life . . . I had a television . . .
Q: Any writer . . . ?
DA: And I do actually think that the television can be your mentor in the absence of anything else. . . . No, honey no! When you grow up in a family in which, um, your mother's a waitress, your father's a truck

driver and nobody in your family has ever graduated from high school, you don't have a mentor . . .

And later in the same exchange:

DA: A funny thing happens, I've been thinking about it a lot, 'cause I've been thinking about genius, lately. Who gets rescued, and who doesn't. I always talk about being a working-class escapee, because I do not work in a textile mill, and I do not work waitress no more. So I'm a working-class escapee, and some of us get rescued. And I got rescued at an early age. I got my glasses from the Lions Club, the Mormon missionary elders were really a powerful force in my family. They had books! . . . But that rescue thing that happens to working-class kids, you get picked. The next thing you know they're giving you books, they're giving you encouragement. That happened to me very young. That's not exactly what I would think of as a mentor, because I was afraid of those people. Because they had power. My life was in some sense dependent on them and I knew it. And also because I was pretty clear that they had enormous contempt for my mother and my brothers and sisters. It was like *I* was okay but the rest of my family was dirt. That's the thing that happens that's very problematic . . . to this day. And then you start trying to please them, and then you just become a little slut for their admiration. So you start writing stories that they will like . . . the good poor stories. You start telling good poor stories to people who have all . . . most of them have really good intentions, and they don't know that they are, that on some level they're treating you with a kind of condescension, that's awkward and painful. And meanwhile they're giving you books! They help you figure out how to go to college, and they tell you that you're wonderful. Nobody else in your life but your mother is telling you that you're wonderful. It's a great thing. That's a kind of mentoring that I got. But it was very backhanded and dangerous. Still trying to sort some of that out. I don't know if it was because my mother was such a great waitress that I can be charming. Or if it's because at an early age I had to hustle people with money to help me get out of where I was.

There are many ways of reading these first two excerpts: as the public discourse of celebrity writers, Allison more senior, MacDonald more deferent, each appreciative of the other; or as the q-and-a-speak of cultural programming, a familiar audience question ("did you have a mentor?") that invites a writer of deprived and troubled beginnings to account for her apparent transcendence—the regional, cultural, and economic distance she has traveled between past and present. A description of genre, however, does not acknowledge the energetic bids for recognition occurring in the interactions, first, between MacDonald and Allison, and second, between Allison and the woman from the audience. Allison recognizes, literally *sees,* her own family in pictures of MacDonald's, and he reciprocates. Both emerge as survivors, one of only a handful of honored subject positions for poor and working-class people, but no less vexed for that and honored most reliably in the exceptional conditions of upward mobility that both Allison and MacDonald inhabit. But, in addition to the writerly class solidarity built into their pairing—which MacDonald's introduction acknowledges—Allison deftly refuses its terms, naming the queerness of her life and work and wondering about the sexual interests of the young man who read *Trash.* Has he started dating boys yet?

For Allison's queer fans, whose lives are not captured by class alone, it is a moment of recognition. The moment registers against the expectations of a different cohort of readers who came to Allison's work through *Bastard Out of Carolina* unaware of her writing and publishing in the feminist and gay press for some fifteen years before *Bastard,* of her sexual radicalism as S/M practitioner, and of her explicitly sexual, self-referential writing as a fem lesbian (an early hook for me). The conditions of prestige literary recognition have long required a judgment of universal voice—read "just like us in the critical elite." But Allison resists, her swift gesture toward MacDonald rewriting even his revisionist terms for the evening's conversation. With fluster and affection he goes along, and so do we. Class and sex difference lose their conventionally bounded meanings as each is recast in terms of the other. MacDonald describes the boy's class desperation in presumptively heterosexual terms (he's "embarrassed" by lesbian literature, not, say, fearful of identification), whereas Allison imagines his class survival in queer ones.

Queer-class interdependence would surface routinely in readers' responses to Allison's work. More than a year later, I attended a reading by Allison held as a fund-raiser for Boston GLASS, a multiracial community center devoted to the emotional, intellectual, and physical well-being of queer young people. Most GLASS participants come from working-class and poor households. At the fund-raiser that night, participants were dressed to celebrate in faux snakeskin skirts (for boys), thrift-shop suit jackets (for butches), and pink hair, feathers, and army boots (for young fems). It was impossible not to recognize their queerness alongside their working-class and ethnic identities as African-, European-, Latino/a-, and Asian American.

In the women's room before the show, one black girl asked her friend, a white girl, about Allison's performance. "What's she doing? Reading?" "Yeah," said the white girl, "from . . ." "From *Dirt*?" asked the first. "No, *Trash*!" The girls fell out laughing. All the kids in the hall that night had received a copy of the new edition of *Trash*, included in their ticket price. "I'm a bit of a Dorothy Allison freak," said a young white woman in high fem style, waiting in the autograph line with a grocery bag of Allison titles. A young butch in line behind me described Allison as "so raw." "Once you pick it up," she said, "you have to keep going." For all those queer kids—safe and at risk, celebrating and needful—social attribution without queerness would be misrecognition, and indeed Boston GLASS was founded to organize resources without the threat of misrecognition and the antiqueer hostility so often directed at young people.

And what about the mentoring question at the Herbst? Judging by speech style and appearance, the audience member was a part of San Francisco's cultural elite. Was she making her own bid for connection with Allison, embedding in her query a familiar guess about the route to Allison's success? Allison responds thoughtfully but interrupts the bid, at least in its own terms—"No, honey, no! Poor people don't have mentors." Her response is part overstatement, part put-down, part challenge to the idea of mentorship as a solution to class entrapment, an idea that has long brought some people to the service of others, but whose benevolence better consoles the benevolent than frees its subjects. I didn't speak with the blond woman and do not know her story, but in that moment I watched her press her torso, hard, into the back of her seat, a familiar enough gesture that reminded me of my own reflexive impulse to escape the feeling of public exposure and vulnerability. Is there recognition in such apparent discomfort, in the revelation that hopeful ideas about opportunity are historically rooted in privilege? And who in the audience might have been consoled by the recognition in Allison's critique? Others who later described themselves as "working-class escapees" and who, like Allison, were wrestling with the guilt, relief, contempt, and contradiction of having been "picked," by teachers, clergy, and sometimes "dumb luck," from their class cultures and families of origin.

Three

"Escape" had long been the term Burt Garrison used to describe his own uneven upward mobility. A young, white college student whom I later interviewed with his girlfriend Audrey, Garrison recalled the sense of "strings attached" to his middle school math teacher's recruitment of him into the academic track. He attributed this gesture to the teacher's kindness and her judgment of him as adept at math, but also to her reception of him as polite and well mannered—a boy refined by a visibly feminine quality that separated him from working-class toughness and the low expectations to which teachers routinely held his peers.[8] In our interview, Garrison recalled his childhood realization that if he acted a certain way—polite, appreciative— he could expect protection and modest promotion from some teachers, a realization that had produced as much anxiety as reassurance against the grain of his family, whose other members would not or could not present themselves in the same way. Such a scenario promised a painful exchange: trading connection with one's family and the scene of one's upbringing for an isolated and uncertain ascendance to and through the ranks of middle-class distinction, an ascendance that, Garrison felt, could be withdrawn at any time.[9] This is a harsh bargain, with no guarantee of encouragement from the first location, no guarantee of admission to the next, and no language of class identification, in a long transition that might never produce the luxury of unself-consciousness even as it became less anxious over time. The new condition of middle-class particularity into which Garrison and others are invited is therefore better described as the press of enforced secrecy about one's class origins than the distinctive or celebrated character of the person.

At the Herbst, Garrison asked Allison about class disclosure, a question privately recognized by other "escapees" as especially courageous in so public a context.

> BG: Hi. I'm someone who was, uh, rescued from the poverty class, and I'm a young writer myself, and, uh, and was wondering how you exorcise the demons at the same time, not letting the structure, of like society . . . without feeding into the prejudices that society already has about your people, and your family?
>
> MPM: Mmm, that was hard.
>
> DA: Yeah.
>
> MPM: That was, um, really hard for me to want to tell the truth about my neighborhood, but not to give people the also humorous depiction of "white trash," liberals *and* conservatives, often, since "white trash" is fodder for both views.
>
> DA: For me the tricky part is, um, it would be nice if this separated out, if the contempt of society was separate from some of this contempt you feel for yourself. Where I get in trouble is that I think it's very deeply related. If I'm gonna tell what I think is a true story . . . it's a complete lie, of course, I make these people up. Maybe I stole 'em, but still, I

make 'em up. But I'm gonna try to tell a true story. So I'm gonna have to tell the truth as I know it. And the truth as I know it is, you know [*pitch and inflection rise*] we're not paragons of virtue! I can't tell a *Bobsey Twins* story, and not hate myself for it. But in the writing, one of the things I've learned, is that I've discovered all the places where my contempt for myself, for my family, and for people I love, completely dovetails the social contempt that the upper classes have for the lower. And I have to sort it out. I keep telling myself all this . . . let's be real . . . namby pamby Christian bullshit, you know, "if I bring enough love to the table it'll be okay." Well no it won't. There'll be some fool that will use stuff I've written against us. But if I lie? Well, then your young person who wants to kill himself wouldn't find anything that's strong in what I'm writing 'cause he'd see I'm lying. I believe that telling the truth is the only way to win in that thing, but we don't win completely. 'Cause there are people who will hold us in contempt for the very things we know are virtues—our stubbornness, our determination, our ability to endure and survive, and some of our hatefulness. You got to take that as a given. Some of this is not going to come out easy or clean. Tell a mean enough story with enough love, you got a chance to survive it. Tell a cleaned-up story? It'll come back on you.

This exchange expresses both the risk of poverty-class identification (framing and expressing one's life in these terms) and the multiple valences of recognition circulating that evening, some of them the upside of that risk. The risk itself barely needs explanation, since for even the most guarded audience members, it is difficult *not* to conjure the abundance of punitive frames and stereotypes for denouncing the lives, struggles, defeats, and excesses of poor and working-class people. Allison acknowledges that hostile others will use those frames, fixing in place the links between social and self-contempt. Some will use them no matter how carefully a writer portrays the oppressions, degradations, or self-destructions of people living in poverty, and no matter that such things are more easily forgiven in middle-class or elite contexts. There, problems, like strengths, are imagined to belong to the person, not the class.[10]

Allison could not reassure Garrison, could not tell him how to write both truthfully and safely, but she could acknowledge the risk. There is recognition in that gesture, both the artistic recognition that makes "young-writer-from-the-poverty-classes" a viable and honorable chain of signifiers (since Allison was once that, too) and psychic recognition in the very act of *witnessing* the risk publicly acknowledged. The occasion is literary and polite, but it is not programmed harmony. It enabled delicate truths in mixed company, delicate especially for those, like Garrison, who live them most immediately.

A skeptical response might conclude that all writing is risky, a claim that includes Allison and Garrison but does not recognize the class component in their work. But, as those who cautiously congratulated Garrison for his question understood, the exchange was remarkable, the social surfacing of a well-known but usually hidden transcript (Scott 1990). It arose in a public context where poverty-class escapees don't have to pay the usual price of exposure—indifference, refusal, punitive references to bootstrap mobility. Instead, they can be open to the reflective recognition of Allison, MacDonald, and Garrison's exchange. That exchange is generous and direct, witty but not driven by the irony and distance often characteristic of literary chat, a class form present on other occasions at City Arts and Lectures.

Another response might receive Garrison's question less as courageous than a conventional gesture at a public event, a play of the "class card" that establishes insider status with Allison and elicits guilt or compliance from class outsiders. Public cultural performances produce genres and characters and enact partial scripts, some of which—like class—are echoed in other contexts. But to read the exchange in these terms alone substitutes ritual meaning for psychic recognition, an either/or displacement to which, I would argue, working-class people are routinely treated.[11] Overwhelmingly, working-class escapees do not "play the class card," especially in professional class settings, which reveals the particularity of any such disclosure when it is made. Garrison was struck, for example, by the nervousness with which other "escapees" had approached him off-stage, people whom he tenderly and ruefully described as he had described himself, as "white trash in disguise":

BG: Yeah, I got a lot of greetings that day . . . from several people who kind of came out as "white trash" in disguise, actually . . . at least four people. One guy . . . he was totally like, you know, just the perfect—I don't know how to describe it but he was just total San Francisco . . .

AB: [Garrison's girlfriend, who had also attended the Herbst]Clean cut, city look . . .

BG: . . . city look, had it down . . . but then he, I think he said he grew up in what, Alabama or something like that?

AB: . . . some "redneck country" . . .

BG: Yeah, he said "I grew up total redneck, my family is total white trash," and he was asking me, kind of like saying that he went through a period of running away from his family, and now as an adult he has been able to go back to his family, and visit them, and how therapeutic and healing that has been for everybody. And a few other people, too, asked me about the . . . One man came out to me and he said something about do the demons ever go away, and I said "I don't know yet, I'm still too young" [*laughter*]. And he said, well, I am nearly fifty and they haven't [*laughter*].

AB: Good luck!

BG: I mean, he was trying to be encouraging, but he himself seemed kind of at a loss of what to say. And his friend came out of the bathroom, and they left, but yeah, it was like he wanted to be encouraging, but he was at a loss, what to say. But a couple of other people just kind of gave me nods, asked me if I was the one who asked the question (. . .) And I felt so weird, so many different questions were asked, but I had . . . I don't know, a few people came and asked me if I was the one who asked *the* question [*laughter*] and just kind of gave me some nod of approval or some kind of gesture. I don't know, I just felt there was a lot of people who, you know, either had distant relatives or had themselves grown up poorer than they know their social status now was . . . kind of like "white trash" in hiding.

Amid solidarity, "escapees" in the audience had still shielded their class locations and their acknowledgment of Garrison with cautious glances and comments, gestures that may have expressed shame, self-consciousness, or uncertainty in the absence of a common language of class or a common practice of class identification. "Class isn't absent," Garrison later told me, "just secret."

Four

Garrison's distinction between absence and secrecy reminded me of an earlier occasion in 1999 with a colleague who was openly lesbian but guarded, I learned, about class. I joined my colleague (who had recently moved to the city) at a poetry and story reading by Allison and other writers. The reading was part of a Queer Arts Festival at the Harvey Milk School for Civil Rights, a San Francisco grass-roots organization housed in a former public school. My friend and I arrived a little late and took seats at the back of the room. It was difficult to know who was in the audience, based on appearances, but overall we looked to be in our thirties and forties (some younger, some older), ethnically mixed but predominantly European-American, and loosely bohemian. The architecture of the room was informal, constructed of functional and since dilapidated public school materials, and the occasion was solitary, full of shared sensibility and purpose rather than competitive projections of status.

Although Allison was then on tour for the paperback issue of her second novel, *Cavedweller* (1999), she read something more explicitly queer, an essay called "A Lesbian Appetite" from *Trash*, a piece I knew and loved but had never heard read aloud. The story draws on the convergence of sex and food and the ways both express *habitus* and desire. Writes Allison early in the essay, "I remember women by what we ate together, what they dug out of the freezer after we'd made love for hours. I've only had one lover who didn't want to eat at all. We didn't last long. The sex was good, but I couldn't think what to do with her when the sex was finished. We drank spring water together and fought a lot" (151–52). Throughout the essay, sex is sustenance and food the object of desire, and both mark personal and political history through region, class, and political alliance. Allison literally longs for the salt and fat—the biscuits, beans, and pork—of her working-class, southern upbringing, finding in them pleasure, satisfaction, and solace in visceral contrast to the terror of pretending to enjoy oysters at an upscale reception (a scene from her memoir *Two or Three Things I Know for Sure* [1994]), or the drudgery and promotion of brown rice and boiled carrots at a feminist encampment, carrots that Dorothy, more often than her middle-class *compagneras*, was asked to prepare. The audience at Harvey Milk conveyed our pleasures and self-mockeries in response to "The Lesbian Appetite" with titters as some of us recognized ourselves among the feminist food police, and sighs as Allison spoke the language of sexual pleasure.

After standing in the autograph line listening to a range of English-language accents that conveyed a cultural range beyond my first impression, my friend and I left to get something to eat. We ate in a diner and talked about the reading. I discovered new things about my friend, secrets, to echo Garrison, about her class upbringing unknown to me despite our long-standing disclosure of that other identification—lesbianism—that had carried its own risks in so sexually modest a field as Communication. Her schooling at a prestigious private university (admission to which she considered an uneven mix of ability, effort, and elite compensation) was preceded by a rural and working-class southwestern upbringing, some of whose idioms resembled Allison's. She had recently left academic life (which I did know) for a research position elsewhere, a shift that brought more money but the disappointments of someone trained—as I had been—to want an academic job and its intellectual and cultural autonomies. She told me that her decision to leave came from years of frustration trying to find a permanent teaching post somewhere hospitable to queers, the elusiveness of which seemed a function of both a changing and proletarianizing academic marketplace and her own sense of being shut out for not *quite* possessing the cultural ease or pretense academic life so often requires, an ease semisecretly presumed to be birthright more than acquisition.

We ordered our food, and my friend talked about her anxiety during the reading as Allison had spoken, with delectation, of the pleasures of salt and fat. Both are essential in fine, Mediterranean olives, say, but those were not the salt-fat forms Allison referred to. In her childhood, my friend wanted biscuits and barbecue and got them, but still she was punished as a big-bodied girl for eating at all. She was nervous during the reading, she told me, because she felt laid bare by Allison's memory of taste and worried that the audience might react scornfully, shaming her again as a fat woman. Her economic opportunities had been secured, if not by the academic job she wanted, but that did not set aside the psychic reach of her class identity or her vulnerability to bodily shame.

Allison's story hadn't created my friend as a class subject, but the reading and our conversation had summonsed her story in class terms that had gone unspoken on previous occasions, despite the amplified language of other identities, like lesbianism, in academic contexts. Other lesbian colleagues made similar observations: the identity disallowed by their families of origin—lesbianism—could be acknowledged at school, while the common identity at home—poverty, working-class, or "lower-middle-class" status[12]—was deeply guarded on campus by some of the most assertive and well-recognized queer scholars then writing.

Class Avowal, Sexual Solidarity

Recognition is not limited to affirmation, as I hope my examples suggest. Recognition is a gesture, a relationship whose meanings are keyed to the social capital and cultural power present in interactions among people, things, institutions, and discourses. Consider the anxiety of misrecognition expressed in a conversation with two Philadelphian women, a couple, Barbara, European-American and Jewish from an upper-middle-class suburban family, and Joy, African American (and not Jewish), from a family whose mix of educational capital, specialized military training and employment, partial enfranchisement, and chronic financial pressure left her uncertain about how to describe herself in class terms. Barbara and Joy were both in their mid-fifties at the time and had fallen in love some twenty years earlier. I met them at a lecture of Allison's at the University of Pennsylvania a few months before our conversation. As we talked, Barbara, a registered nurse, recalled with some annoyance having been harshly misidentified as wealthy by her blue-collar coworkers in a regional hospital. Joy joined the conversation with insights about how certain practices are read by others through the lens of social class.

Five

J: Yeah, yeah. I mean . . . there are people who think that, that my manners are [*pause*] upper class, very, very proper, that's sort of . . .

B: I got that too . . .

J: Yeah, and it's all because of my parents, just how they are.

B: I always got "you must come from a lot, you must have a lot of money." No, you can have decent manners without having a lot of money, honestly. It's just a matter of what you choose to do or say.

J: It's like manners go with money.

B: It's really what they thought . . . A lot of the . . . people at work were like "oh we ha . . ."—it's a very blue-collar place . . .

J: Blue collar . . . ?

B: It is . . . No?

LH: Manayunk, you mean up, up the Schuylkill . . .

B: Yeah, I worked at the home-care department there, and I worked in the hospital for awhile, and many of the other nurses were like "well you don't really need to do this, you have a lot of money." Well, why do you think so? And . . . "well, it's obvious, you just do."

J: Yeah, and . . . I get the same kind of an . . . well, I don't want to call it an accusation, but that's almost what it feels like! Because of how I speak, and, and the fact I have manners, drilled into me by my parents.

B: Do you notice that? Yourself?

LH: Well, I got manners drilled into me, and I didn't come from a family with a lot of money, although . . .

B: See! You don't have to have money to have manners . . .

(. . .)

B: Even just an interest in reading.

J: That is something that somehow is perceived as, as not something . . . that either black people do, or people of a certain . . . economic class do. At least that's how I'm reading, that's how I perceive others' perceptions of me.

B: Well they say that, that poor kids that read get a lot of trouble from their schoolmates and stuff like that, they get, there's a real problem with that, that some kids deliberately fail or deliberately get bad grades just to survive elementary school and junior high.

J: Yeah . . .

LH: So this comes as an accusation?

J: I sometimes feel like it is.

LH: Who is speaking that? Do you know? I don't mean specific individuals, but where . . .

B: These nurses? Were very jealous. I'm not sure what they were jealous of, but they perceived me . . .

J: You drove a foreign car . . .

B: Yeah, a car that was so old, it was probably older than some of them . . .

J: But still it was a foreign car, it was exotic. [To LH] She used to drive a Saab.

B: An old Saab, a leaded gas Saab. [*Laughter*]

J: When you worked in Manayunk . . .

B: I had an unleaded gas one, but it was still . . .

J: Was that Red Jamiece or were you still doing Blue Jamiece?

B: That was Blue Jamiece . . . then Red Jamiece . . .

J: She had several Saabs in a row. [*Laughter*]

B: But they . . . it was like "you're not like us . . ."

J: . . . well, sure . . .

B: "We're Catholic" [Barbara is Jewish], you know, "we have to really work hard." And the other thing is that . . .

J: Language . . .

B: I really did figure this out—part of it is language—but I also figured out that, if you work hard but you don't appear to be working hard, that does not go over well in some circles.

LH: You get your job done?

B: Yeah, but you don't complain about it, and you act like you enjoy it. And . . . I mean I, I don't know, maybe it's an affectation but I sort of grew up, somewhere I got the idea that, you know, it, it was important to look like things were easy for you.

J: Never let 'em see you sweat.

B: Yeah . . . They didn't like, appreciate that.

J: What do you think they were making of that?

B: "You're a different class." You know, "we're a blue collar," whatever . . . "We cheat." It's true . . .

J: And yet, I have cousins who live in Manayunk . . .

B: They're unusual.

J: Yes they are unusual.

B: But they live in Manayunk . . . None of them were these nurses.

J: This is also true!

Barbara and Joy's exchange crystallizes the ways class difference and its judgments are (mis)recognized, assigned, rerouted, and reassigned among individuals, practices, and other forms of social identification. I was not witness to Barbara's interactions with coworkers in Manayunk, but instead to her recollections several years later. She remembers being singled out as Jewish, and feeling religious difference and suspicion expressed as her coworkers' hostility toward the class position stereotypically attributed to Jewishness— "you don't have to work." She also recounts a competition among systems of class attribution based on what Pierre Bourdieu (1984) called *habitus*—the familiar social gestures, practices, styles, and tastes that identify a class or class fraction. For her (and for Joy), manners and reading do not necessarily mean money, but for others they've encountered, manners and reading *do* mean money. This becomes particularly vexed for Joy, who feels herself perceived as a person of some contradiction: educated, well mannered, well read, and well spoken by dominant standards, in racialized contexts where black people, by white and sometimes black others, are presumed to be none of these things.

Cultural systems of class attribution are sometimes reliable but always partial. Careful manners and a particular expressive stance toward work ("never let 'em see you sweat") may signify hereditary affluence or high levels of cultural capital, but they may also signify, say, working-class modesty or self-conscious entrance into the culture of professionalism (Bledstein 1976). Thus Barbara's memory of misrecognition and hostility from her coworkers expresses less the absolute class position or value of habits than an internal tension between class compliance and class resistance *within* the ranks of skilled hospital workers.[13] It isn't a case of conflict between high-status management and low-status employees, but a bid for dominance in which, according to Barbara, insiders marked outsiders in terms of their perceived motives for working: either "fulfillment"—a virtue long attached to professional employment—or paying the bills.

Barbara's recollection is a reminder, as Sherry Ortner (1991) points out, that classes are relationally constituted: "[W]hile we normally think of class relations as taking place *between* classes, in fact each class contains the other(s) within itself, though in distorted and ambivalent forms. This is particularly visible in the working class, where the class structure of the society is introjected into the culture of the working-class itself, appearing as a problematic choice of 'life-styles' . . . a choice between a life style modeled essentially on middle-class values and practices and one modeled on more distinctively working- or lower-class values and practices" (172). The working person who embodies professional dispositions can expect chastisement from other workers in the same milieu, rather than solidarity for doing the same kind of work. This does not set aside, however, what may also have been real differences between Barbara's class history and those of other nurses in the Manayunk hospital, or the displacements of class hostility onto religious exclusion in a robustly Catholic workplace culture.

Barbara also has a stake, in this recollection, in what I would call class disavowal. Her coworkers were wrong about her, she says, her series of old Saabs notwithstanding. Here the cultural hierarchy that makes an old Saab preferable to an old Ford (though a Ford might have been cheaper to operate) is muted by another position in that same hierarchy, where a new Saab is preferable to an old one. (For her coworkers, Barbara has a Saab, not a Ford; for Barbara, she has an old car, not a new one.) It is muted, that is, until Joy recognizes the meaning of an exotic old European car in a hospital parking lot in Northeast Philadelphia, with gentle challenges to Barbara and conspiratorial glances to me.

Joy's sensibility in this exchange is fond, acknowledging that she and Barbara have had this conversation and disagreement before. Their difference of opinion is mediated by time and affection and by other sources of mutual identification, including a sexual sensibility rooted in shared experiences of domestic abuse in their very different families of origin. As founding members of a local circle of lesbian women who practice sadomasochistic sex, both Joy and Barbara imagine their desire in relation to experiences of childhood sexual and physical abuse. Though they were more allusive than specific in conversation with me, they also linked their affection for Allison's work to her sexual radicalism against the grain of antipornography feminism in the 1980s and 1990s, and to her writing about her own masochistic desire as a woman who had survived childhood sexual abuse. In a long part of our conversation about leaving lives, places, and people we once knew and whether and how one could ever return (a conversation sparked by Allison's acknowledgment that she had never returned to live in the South), Barbara and Joy concluded that you can't go back to an earlier life and expect to find the sensations or comforts that had once been there, but you can avow and use your past, even your traumatic past, in the present. This, said Barbara, was also what attracted her to Allison's work—her attention to circumstance and process in making a life and writing a character. That same combination—of avowing the past and attention to "process"—was, she added, an important part of her interest in S/M:

B: . . . Seeing how people change or arrive at decisions, arrive at life
        choices, like Dede [in *Cavedweller*] fools herself, she doesn't want
        to get married, doesn't know it . . . She [Allison] teases it all out, and
        brings it in . . . very *delicately* . . .

J: Very seductive . . .

B: Yeah, she's very seductive.

LH: She is that, isn't she? Did you notice that about her talk, was that a
        vibe?

B: Oh yeah . . .

(. . .)

LH: I can't help but think that Dorothy knows this so consciously, that it's a
        power she can wield.

B: Oh yeah . . .

J: . . . I certainly hope so! . . .

B: Oh yeah!

J: I hope so!

LH: You hope so! You enjoy it?!

J: Yeah.

B: She must, she's crafted it. Nobody just gets there, I don't think.

LH: So publicly . . . it's *shame*less!

B: Yeah, she really enjoys it.

J: That's the fun of it.

B: And that's probably part of the "poor white trash," you don't have to,
        like, you know, be WASP and quiet . . .

J: . . . You can *be* shameless . . .

B: . . . you wouldn't want to show off or anything, you know.

LH: Well, it has a flip side, because she talks about growing up with intense
        shame. I've just been listening to that tape again. Being shamed for
        being from a mean family, an unschooled family . . .

B: And she used it, she used the whole thing . . .

LH: . . . Yeah, an inversion? . . .

B: Yeah, it's a very clever way of dealing with things. Makes much more
        sense than going to a psychiatrist three times a week for so many years.

LH: Well, maybe she's done that too.

B: But I mean . . . and . . . somehow learning to . . . grow. I don't know . . .
        It's like so many people think you should just get over things, and
        instead of getting over it, she's used it.

J: Maybe she's gotten over it too.

B: Well, okay. Instead of renouncing it, she's gotten over it . . .

J: Okay.

B: . . . Instead of renouncing it, she's gotten over . . . she's used it. Instead of saying "well I'm not like that anymore," she's kept her identity and managed to use it to her advantage.

LH: She writes about having renounced it at one time, and then having to confront the fact that the legacy doesn't go away, and what would it mean to hold onto your family, your crazy family even, your abusive family, in some contexts.

B: Yeah. And that's part of S/M. Because people, you know, you're not supposed to be this way. And that's part . . .

LH: Taking pleasure in those things?

B: Yeah, you're not supposed to do that. The whole world knows that, right, like this is really sick behavior, you know?

J: Depends who you talk to.

Like Allison, Barbara and Joy have lived life keenly aware of the resistance they can expect from others, including women in their lesbian and feminist community who see their S/M practice as pathological rather than restorative, intimate, or otherwise pleasurable. They are also among a minority of readers who know Allison's writing as a sexual radical, since her public conversations were, by then, less marked by sexual disclosure than her writing and perhaps her life had once been. As we spoke, it became clear that Barbara and Joy's commitment to each other was founded partly on sexual recognition and creativity in a sexually hostile universe. Such recognition did not level the racialized class difference or the difference of class perception between them, but they described it as the shared ground on which such differences had become negotiable over time.

Six

As I joined this conversation and later listened on tape, I thought about a relationship of my own, which had ended several years earlier. I had come to the affair with a mixed-class background. Long stretches in my life could be roughly described by the contradictory category of "genteel poverty," but I did grow up more or less confident that I could get an education and live well.[14] Still, some memories of class exclusion and shame were uncomfortable enough that I resisted conceding to my working-class and upwardly-mobile girlfriend—who described herself as an "escapee" from class deprivation and family trauma—that my expectations and entitlements were born and raised in the middle class and represented a historical relationship to the present that she could never claim. Our time

together was a long instance of class difference experienced and repro-
duced through human relationships, to paraphrase E. P. Thompson, an
instance that exposed both the embattled instability of class position and
the long history of social-class conflict.[15] We did, after all, fall in love and
in that state talked openly and revealingly about class difference. But we
also ended things in a haze of distrust marked by profound differences
in status and *habitus*, despite similar ages and vocations—myself a junior
faculty member and my lover an advanced graduate student—and despite
great fidelity of sex and style.

I was reminded of our routine slippage from intimate pleasure to hurtful
misrecognition by a passage in Allison's essay "A Question of Class" in *Skin:
Talking About Sex, Class, and Literature* (1994a):

> While I raged, my girlfriend held me and comforted me and tried to get me
> to explain what was hurting me so bad, but I could not. She had told me
> so often about her awkward relationship with her own family, the father
> who ran his own business and still sent her checks every other month. She
> knew almost nothing about my family, only the jokes and careful stories I
> had given her. I felt so alone and at risk lying in her arms that I could not
> have explained anything at all. I thought about those girls in the deten-
> tion center and the stories they told in brutal shorthand about their sisters,
> brothers, cousins, and lovers. I thought about their one-note references to
> those they had lost, never mentioning the loss of their own hopes, their
> own futures, the bent and painful shape of their lives when they would
> finally get free. Cried-out and dry-eyed, I lay watching my sleeping girl-
> friend and thinking about what I had not been able to say to her. After a
> few hours I got up and made some notes for a poem I wanted to write, a
> bare, painful litany of loss shaped as a conversation between two women,
> one who cannot understand the other, and one who cannot tell all she
> knows. (33)

When I read this passage for the first time, the love affair over, but memo-
rable, I recognized myself in the character of Allison's affectionate and deeply
uncomprehending girlfriend. It was a slightly sickening invitation to stand
in the footprint of class histories like Allison's and see myself in high relief,
on terrain I had carefully avoided. My lover and I had been queers together,
but not the same kind of queers. That became clear in retrospect, but had
been obscured by the pressure of everyday life (as newly- and not-yet-profes-
sional) and by antagonistic class attachments, hers historically working class,
upwardly mobile but insecure, mine historically middle class, eager to be

recognized for class consciousness, and entitled in its expectation of solidarity. We never got to Barbara and Joy's gentleness with each other.

Reading and Recognition

My encounter with "A Question of Class" is an example of the cultural work of recognition that literature and other expressive forms do. Our responses to characters and scenes link felt reaction to the material details of their represented lives.[16] Here identification may surface in unlikely places, between, say, a privileged reader who has known abjection and an abjectly poor character who has never known privilege of any kind. There is a danger in the translation of such a readerly experience to the world beyond the book, a danger signified by a reader's thought about a character "I am like you." What is squelched in such a claim? The difference between poverty and privilege. What is enabled? Attachment? What, then, is required to produce an unsquelching attachment? Readers of Dorothy Allison sometimes do this, cautious, in fact, about not wanting to claim heroic forms of survival for themselves while recognizing versions of human experience in her characters. Their very caution suggests a disposition toward class consciousness, one heightened by their sense of accountability to Allison's class. An example comes from Joanna Frank, whom I met following Allison's talk at the University of Pennsylvania and who was once a working-class Southerner, "but not really," and was then a graduate student and lecturer in English literature at Temple University. Joanna had brought several undergraduate students to Allison's talk and found herself a little awkwardly moved to tears by Allison's comments, recognizing in parts of Allison's story her mother's effort to make a professional life out of few opportunities and her own labor in continuing the trajectory her mother had begun.

Seven

JF: I kind of feel like part of my response to her, my response to her fiction and my response to her talk, comes out of what I was saying before about there being things that resonate with me, but also the fact that I'm not quite Southern, and I'm not quite . . . working class or lower socioeconomic class in the way that she describes. So, in a way, the things that she talks about and the struggles that she talks about unlock or crack open all these questions and issues for me, but, I can imagine there are people for whom the story is much more similar. And there are parallels there that I don't know about. So I kind of feel

like . . . I don't want to come across as inauthentic, or claiming to have
this Southern . . . you know . . . struggle, class struggle that's not as real
for me as it was for her, or other people. And yet, that's exactly something that I was responding to in her talk, the feeling of in-between-
ness, the feeling that you went away [from the South] and then who
are you? What are you?

Joanna draws a movable line between Allison's characters and her own
Southern background, where relative poverty signaled "modesty" rather
than "trash."[17] With pinpoint caution, she narrates closeness to and separation from Allison's characters, broaching but not quite claiming a place in
their universe despite the depth of feeling summonsed by Allison's reading. Joanna's story isn't queer, but it expresses a social demand for crossing some lines while backing away from others. Sometimes the demand is
about learned exclusion and self-preservation in a segregated world of rich
and poor. Other times it signals accountability—don't pretend to be who you
aren't. In a careful state of quasi-recognition, Joanna's seeks to meet the second standard without reproducing the class hostility of the first.

Eight

San Franciscan Lee Belton expressed a more driven relation to Allison's characters and to the students she taught in a San Francisco elementary school.
I met Lee after Allison's City Arts and Lectures interview; she enthusiasti-
cally introduced herself to me in the autograph line and volunteered to talk
with me later. Like Joanna's story, Lee's is not expressly queer, though Lee
described her life in San Francisco as closely connected to queer culture and
to the queers who had introduced her to Allison's work.

By her own telling, Lee's story is a mix of urban class privilege and family
violence, a history that draws her to Allison's writing and provokes a kind
of expressive contortionism in describing her identification with Allison's
characters. The daughter of a self-made man, Lee, then twenty-four, grew
up in New York City and spent her prep-school years witnessing her parents'
wrenching and near-murderous divorce. For years, her father had unleashed
both the most impulsive and most calculated violence upon her mother, to
the blind eye of local police in New York and in their elite summer resort
town. Lee spent a lot of time, she told me, stoned and acting out, loving and
hating her parents, hating herself, many times on the brink of self-destruction. She was "rescued" as a late teenager by her mother and a residential

treatment program into a young adulthood of active addiction recovery and profound family distrust.

In Allison's writing, especially her novel *Cavedweller* and her memoir *Two or Three Things I Know for Sure*, Lee found an image of redemption and the possibility of human recognition between her once-abusive and now-aging and infirm father. Her friends told her that she was crazy to want a relationship with a man who more than once had tried to kill her mother. But wishing for distance or indifference wasn't working. Lee knew, she told me, that her father had given her many fortunate things and she wanted to be able to take care of him in some way. Since her parents' divorce had been finalized, her mother was safe and deeply regretted the turmoil of Lee and her brother's upbringing. It was her mother's safety and accountability that made some kind of reconciliation with her father possible.

In *Two or Three Things I Know for Sure*, Lee was overwhelmed by Allison's bravery in remembering her stepfather's violence and mother's abandonment in the language of nonfiction, a reaction Lee received in contrast to her own family's secrets. In *Cavedweller*, she found Delia, a character who years earlier had abandoned her two daughters to escape an abusive husband, and who, as the novel begins, returns from a music career in Los Angeles to remake her life in her small Georgia town, third daughter in tow. Delia slowly redeems herself in her older daughters' eyes in the course of caring for Clint, her once-abusive and now dying ex-husband.

Lee adored *Cavedweller*. In it, she found a reflection of her own experience despite huge differences of class and culture between her life and the lives of Allison's characters, and against the grain of those critics who discounted the premise that Delia, a singer, would trade the raw glamour and intensity of L.A. rock and roll for a redemptive return to small-town Georgia. For Lee, the book made Delia's impulse for redemption and her reconnection to the scene of terror both comprehensible and sane, qualities that then became available for telling her own story. In the course of our conversation, however, Lee struggled to articulate her connection to Allison's characters, sensitive to the differences that class and race make:

LH: When you read Dorothy Allison, it sounds like your connections are so strong, and at the same time, there are so many differences.

LB: Right, like the class differences, the regional differences, the environmental differences, yeah, um, see when I read her I always feel connected to her characters, like her characters go pretty way beyond the regional and environmental setting or the context or even like, you know, that they are in this house that's really disgusting, especially when they move back into Clint's house. There is this really sick man in there, who has just been so horrible . . . Do I relate to that? I won't, like, try to fool myself into thinking that I can relate to what it might feel like to be a man. Well, I mean I definitely try to make things harder for myself, so I will understand in life . . . So, that's definitely been, yeah, I even tried to hide that I had money for a long time . . . Now I just think that's stupid. It was like, it's like the opposite of somebody who doesn't have money, any money, who tries to wear nice clothes, and then the rich person who has way too much money and way too much compassion and like too much thinking this is really not fair and like unjust that I come from all this, and then be embarrassed by that and hide.

Later in the same conversation, Lee acknowledged how difficult it had been to earn the trust of the parents of her working-class and poor African American and Chicano students in the San Francisco public school where she had taught. Indeed, sensitized by addiction treatment and community self-help programs, and tried as she had at the school, she never felt trusted or even trustworthy. After a couple of years, she left:

LB: I still feel like a lot of teachers feel like, you know, you can cross those cultural boundaries and have understanding for those kids and I . . . don't believe in that anymore, so . . .

LH: Did you believe that when you started?

LB: I entered the job believing that I could be somebody that could enter American homes and understand where that mother is coming from, and when she told me she's got five kids, and no money, and was on welfare, kids whose father had just left, and all that shit, and I always thought I could understand, you know, or even just the kids, I thought I might have understood. But I really think that culturally, I am a true believer, I really think it matters. I could change again . . . but I definitely think that cultural background and how you were socialized and raised in your situation, even the soc-lingo, you know. Socialization into a lingo of *ain't* and *don't*, you know that is . . . I don't think that separates me from them as a human being, we have similar experiences, but I know for a fact when, like, we had a black woman that I hired to the welfare to work program . . . she had no counseling background, you know, she had no training at all in how to relate to people, she didn't even believe in counseling, you know . . . and she had an effect with people. I mean, the children responded to her within a second, it took months to respond to me, you know, just because of their, it was just different, do you know what I mean? . . . But the thing that hurt me and why I loved it so much, was that . . . everybody is human, you know. And we are all so human, and maybe the mother who is on crack and is addicted and is in the house and beating her kids is not so different than me. Like we have those propensities in ourselves, too, you know?

As I read the transcript of this part of our conversation, I was overwhelmed by Lee's uncertainty and self-consciousness in trying to work out how much privileged compassion is too much or on what bases students, teachers, and parents might trust one another. At the outset, I was anxious about Lee's use of the language of addiction recovery in what seemed like a fantasy of cross-class and cross-race recognition, in a school setting of unequal power among teachers, students, and parents. But the very terms and feel of her struggle to articulate her place at the nexus of privilege and trauma ran deeper than that. Her appeal to a common humanity was honest, arising from the recognition that the boundaries of stratification and segregation are real, not there for the crossing by complex good intentions. Her remarks became uncomfortable testimony to a broader social desire for connection to others in a world of cultural and class apartheid. I am not responding to the historical details of Lee's story or anyone else's, since I have no way of estimating them apart from the telling. But I do not want to lose sight of Lee's longing, less as an expression of the fuzzy utopianism of privilege or youth than of defeat in a divided world, a disappointed class awareness that goes missing in claims about the absence of class discourse in the United States.

Recognition/Obligation?

For the readers I have quoted, Allison's work stands as an invitation or beacon, a brightness on the social horizon through which painful, sometimes shameful, experiences and feelings are pressed into recognition as art and through which anxieties sequestered as personal secrets are socialized as collective narratives, "turning sites of shame into dramas of inclusion" (Appadurai 2002, 40).[18] This is a gift for those thus served. But for skeptical observers and critics, that same gift can be a kind of manipulation in which the possibility of redemption is presented as the reader's reward for attachment to a deeply drawn link between author and story. Allison tells gritty stories whose characters survive social indifference and brutality and intimate attempts to destroy them. As a survivor herself, and as a public performer, she stands for her stories and they for her. The classical American narrative of heroic transcendence becomes a generic expression of working-class life, to which others (including admiring others from more secure positions) owe queer and class recognition and solidarity.

In my itinerant experience as a member of Allison's audience, dissenting readers have not shown up, voiced contrary opinions, waited in line for Allison's autograph, or volunteered for interviews with me.[19] Such absences are a reminder that the occasions are, for the most part, gatherings of fans and recruits, people who have already found or believe they will find in Allison's work something revealing and meaningful, something worth reading. The skeptic might respond that this returns us to the Althusserian meaning of recognition as ideological affirmation and reproduction, with Allison as star Subject interpellating readers as reverent class subjects themselves, subject, that is, to the truth as Allison tells it. Allison's public personification of class subjectivity might be seen to remake working-class status into a discrete, identitarian category in possession of its own idioms, its own traumas, its own heroes, and its own conditions of membership, unalloyed to other positions or groupings. In such a critique, class recognition is sequestered as *thing*, less a critical or transformative gesture than an object of celebrity trade value or prefabricated attachment in the domain of cultural production.

In my fitful navigation of the cultural politics of recognition and redistribution, I have heard this critique and the contradictions it identifies. Finally, though, it is unsatisfying because it invites negative foreclosure rather than curiosity, and because it reduces instead of capturing layers of signification and resonance in the public conversations about class that I have described. Those conversations were not called upon to analyze the conditions of capitalist production that efface class trauma in the first place.[20] The Allison readers quoted here, moreover, do not isolate class from other forms of difference, though they struggle for a language that signifies class experience, drawing into their narratives the reciprocal meanings and aggressions of race, gender, region, trauma, and especially queerness. It is true: the felt relief readers experience in queer and class recognition could turn into identitarian reduction. It is also true that many of those I have interviewed here see the contours of their class experience through "escape" from deprivation and suffering; they are at once of their working-class origins and not. Mobility, they acknowledge, has sharpened their story, partly through the discomfiting differences they recognize between their lives and those of others in their families. But there is nothing in the character of their recognition or relief that predicts social or personal stuckness or political reduction, any more than it assures liberation. The presumptive move from recognition to essentialism is an assertion of theory, not the necessary artifact of cultural participation. It depends on what happens afterward, on what people do with recognition, what it loosens up, what forms of common cause it illuminates and invites.

Conclusion: Distributing Recognition

My point, finally, is neither to affirm the distinction between recognition and redistribution, nor to determine which is more urgent in challenging the reproduction of inequality. Instead, I have asked how cultural materials, long identified as expressions and objects of attachment—of deeply-felt, sometimes unarticulated truths about one's character, origins, possibilities, and worth—are brought into active and public production of class identity and recognition. This process takes place in a social universe whose any given moment is marked by economic and cultural imperatives, neither of which prevails (except as theoretical metaphor) unstructured by the other. Looking at queerness and class together, indeed looking at social conjunctures of all kinds, reveals the distributive effects of culture, and the cultural effects of distribution.

Such cultural production is ontologically *new*—despite resemblances, whatever we make today isn't what was made yesterday—but it is also *reproduction*. But to emphasize reproduction too quickly subsumes the uneven value of recognition, the collective act of seeing oneself and others in queer and class terms that are embodied, relational, sometimes defensive. It may block acquiring even an imprecise language through which to produce and practice such recognition consciously and, in the process, reveal and reconstruct unconscious habits of misrecognition, habits that claim that working-class people aren't queer, nor queers working class; that mobility is a matter of mettle; that the world offers equal opportunity to hard workers; that poverty is noble and ignoble poor people have only themselves to blame; that marriage and its conventional moralities will solve welfare dependency; that upward mobility leaves the pain and fury behind; that Jews are rich.[21]

The project of class recognition in queerness also seeks to recognize the array, internal density, and social significance of mixed-class encounters, some fleeting (Allison's and her audiences' performances, say, or public transportation), others enduring, for better or worse (queer love affairs gone well or gone bad, most forms of employment in a service economy).[22] It seeks as well to articulate the array of dynamic class positioning (upward and downward mobility; class escape, entrapment, and security; genteel poverty;

patrician bohemianism; the anxiety of productivity across the class spec-trum)[23] in contrast to familiar, more static categories and their presumptive attributes. People might talk more about class in culture if available idioms weren't so categorical.

The project of recognition also asks whether one can calm class and queer shame by socializing it, not by denying or dispelling it or by displacing it with a shaky or assertive pride, but by imagining and politicizing a commu-nal form rooted in the vulnerabilities, privileges, and relations of economic, cultural, and sexual hierarchy. This has never been simple to do. To quote George Lipsitz (1997) about the state university students he has taught, "All most of them know about the working class is that they don't want to be a part of it" (12). Calming class shame is especially difficult—and here I return to Beverly Skeggs (2000)—where class ascendancy is made the route to enfranchisement for nondominant subjects, be they gay, female, persons of color, or all three. The politics of respectability, waged within a hegemonic narrative of class mobility and long fought over in the institutionalization of political movements for rights and recognition, cannot but entrench hos-tilities toward those still judged disrespectable.[24] Lipsitz's students may know more than they can explain.

Class recognition is not an immediate distributive remedy. But filtering class subjectivity and subjection out of the domain of recognition, including queer recognition, makes the harm and privilege of class hierarchy inarticu-late, leaving such filtering to become its own form of cultural injustice. My desire, then, is to find and speak the not-so-common senses of social class exposed by a range of cultural contexts, imagining these occasions of recog-nition—in their mixed, sociable, and unstable expression—as one form of class consciousness to be used in queer critique and solidarity. In cultural reception, Dorothy Allison's work offers a revealing place to start. In cultural production, on the other hand, the boundary conditions of queerness and class emerge in the practice and logic of crossover.

5

Queer Relay

Crossing Over

In April 2006, at the Anthology Film Archives in New York, I ran into distinguished writer, artist, and cultural producer Sarah Schulman during the
MIX-NY Queer Experimental Film and Video Festival. Schulman asked
what had brought me to MIX, and I told her that I'd come to see a program of
shorts that included writer-director Liza Johnson's film *Desert Motel* (2005).
As fieldworker and script supervisor, I had joined Johnson's crew on *Desert
Motel* to write about queer filmmaking at the interstices of industry and independent resources and aesthetics. "Ah," said Schulman, "crossover dreaming." It was an instructive response, one that left me feeling a little defensive
on Johnson's behalf and that quickly exposed my anxieties about a queerness
defiled by markets and commerce. It equally exposed the alternative fantasy
of a cultural milieu that answers only to queer sexual and political impulses.

Weeks later, Schulman's and my exchange had me thinking about formulations that resist that ideological split, a split that Schulman herself has had
to negotiate as novelist, archivist, and playwright.[1] In the queer case, crossover dreaming signifies a spatial and cultural polarity between a queer *here*
that is pure and sequestered and thus makes outsiders want in and some
denizens want out, and a nonqueer *there*, mixed, polluted, driven by capital
and cultural normativity, both morally compromised and the target of recognition and success—a dream, after all, not conscription.

Were I to recount my own history with the idea of crossover dreams, it
would probably begin with Leon Ichaso's film of the same title (1985, starring
Rubén Blades) about making it as a Latino salsa performer in the Anglo-
American mainstream of popular music. But the polarities themselves evoke
a centuries-long standoff between art and commerce, a standoff reinvested
with moral import when the differences are not purely aesthetic (when are
they ever purely aesthetic?) but mindfully political. This is certainly true
in the queer case, even more so as the conscious, marketable presence of
queer cultural forms displaces their coded or haunting one in the history of
commercial cultural production. Such an effect—of crossover tension and

anxiety—is heightened when what once was haunting becomes the hook, as in the feverish and repressed love between Jack Twist and Ennis del Mar in Ang Lee's film version of *Brokeback Mountain* (2005)—a hook aesthetically celebrated, liberally welcomed, and politically misrecognized. Along with many critics, *Brokeback Mountain*'s director and male leads (Lee, Heath Ledger, and Jake Gyllenhaal, respectively) claimed that the film spoke to anyone stricken by the loss and grief of deep but unnavigable love or the sadness of a closed and troubled soul. But *Brokeback Mountain* drew many to something more particular—to its image of sexual and emotional urgency and its raw and tender physicality between two men perilously in love in rural Wyoming in the 1960s, a distinctly queer effect available in the film but downplayed in mainstream publicity.

When the cultural costs of commercial representation include another round of anxious marketing at queer expense, renewed accolades to non-queer actors for brave gay performances (when queer actors can count on effacement, not reciprocity, for playing straight characters), and little opportunity to explore the queer foundations of American culture save when queers are shopping or dying, it is no wonder that "crossover dreaming" stirs up the defensiveness that Schulman's comment drew from me. But alongside the histories of exclusion and aggression that make queer political and cultural distrust sensible, in its own way queer anxiety about crossover sustains the opposition between queer and not queer, also at queer expense.

What would a different critique look like? One whose primary move is not to rush in with self-preserving refusal at the first or last sign of queer encounter with nonqueer market culture? In the interest of a different kind of self-preservation, can we resist what, borrowing from Michel Foucault (1986), I call the commercial repressive hypothesis, the idea that for queer culture, politics, and sexuality, the history of commerce is a history of repression? So often it is, but trading in dismissals of *Queer Eye for the Straight Guy* or anxiety about *Brokeback Mountain* as evidence of a critic's undefiled queerness and her hostility to market cultures moves too quickly inside the very symbolic economy it seeks to upend. You say mainstream? I say upstream.

What might be gained in a countermove that finds traction against the grain of queer/nonqueer opposition in the politics of cultural production? Can we make that move in a charged and politically aggressive time without joining the ranks of ambitious apologists settled into the spoils of reading the drum calls of queer life for cultural conservatives? Can we do so without ignoring the forces that hijack nondominant cultural forms onto the neoliberal tarmac of privatization and upward distribution?

History says yes. The history, that is, of cultural producers like John Waters, Pedro Zamora, Jean-Michel Basquiat, and the coming-and-going club circuit of drag kinging on both sides of the Atlantic, to name just a few examples whose knotty relations inside capital have long stood as a queer resource. Waters's over-the-top melodramas of fem nuttiness at the cross-roads of patriarchy, cult cinema, and the avant-garde (*Hairspray* [1988], *Serial Mom* [1994], *A Dirty Shame* [2004]); Zamora's measured disidentifi-cations on the world stage of MTV as a queer man of color with HIV; Bas-quiat's untempered attachment to and infusion of the pop-art world of Andy Warhol; and the figurative entry of subcultural kingyness into such apotheo-oses of commercial culture as *Austin Powers: International Man of Mystery* (1997) trouble the anxious version of crossover that signifies a move from good culture to bad capital.[2] Taken together, such examples channel the cri-tique not toward hanging on or selling out but instead toward relay, a differ-ent trajectory in imagining relations between subcultures and their domi-nant alternatives (Halberstam 2005, 110).[3] While the critique of capital offers the language of market determination and appropriation, the subcategory of relay within commercial cultural production multiplies and redirects deter-mination in favor of determin*isms* and other, more reciprocal forms of influ-ence.[4] It imagines a historical braid of changing production conditions and the hunger of commercial systems for subcultural energy and artistry.

Relay refers to an ongoing, uneven process of cultural passing off, catch-ing, and passing on, if not always among members of the same team. It is not assimilation, exactly, or hybridity or bricolage, although it shares with those ideas a mediating impulse and a lively aversion to hardened catego-ries in cultural analysis. Instead, I intend relay to mark—in ways those terms do not—cultural-economic difference and relation, a particular (if movable) politics of recognition, and the materiality of practice, the idea that practice matters in nondominant cultural production.

Such a formulation doesn't protect subcultures from theft or suffering, nor reliably reward queer producers like Waters, Zamora, Basquiat, Schulman, or the finest of drag kings. Nor does it level the signifying fields of cultural production on the buying and bullying fields of neoliberalism. But it does recognize a charge in a different direction than the one promised by cross-over nightmares, a charge in which subcultures become the fantasy target of recognition and success and where dominant culture itself is necessarily *in play*, not at the mercy of subcultural forms but lifeless without them.

Relay, in other words, suspends or pauses cultural anxiety and the pre-sumption of market degradation. It returns queer cultural power while depleting the speaker's benefit in queer refusal, the moral and libidinal energy that comes from opposing dominance through separation and the condensation of that charge as political capital.[5] What is lost in oppositional resolve may be gained in recognizing and redistributing critical cultural resources, including new subjectivities as producers and audience members find room to move in a cultural middle range where choices are not so constrained by the dominance of capital versus no-budget subversion. For class critique, this means an alternative to the queer taste aversion and cultural hierarchy that mark so much crossover anxiety.

Relay also harnesses a cultural political question to an empirical one in studies of contemporary cultural production, a gesture at the heart of my interest in *Desert Motel*. How do queer filmmakers produce their films and what difference does it make? My account of *Desert Motel* and the world of its production and festival release is small and grounded enough to follow the process intimately—its arcs and deviations, its deliveries of people and stories to different cultural locales, the reflections and reconciliations of its producers and other practitioners, its gathering and disbursement of creative and financial resources, and its aesthetic and ideological reconfigurations among genres, forms, and cultural professions. These are the layers familiar to ethnographic work and the boundary crossings characteristic of field research in changing times and places, rooted less in the site than in the project and its migrations. Imagined this way, ethnography's intimacy—its face-to-face character, the engagement it demands and enables—opens onto the broad field of cultural practice and change, making visible the sediments of old habits amid productions and transformations in the present. Such a high-contact exploration of structure, practice, meaning, and the reciprocities among them makes case studies like *Desert Motel* less particularistic than deeply articulated, less novel than conjunctural, less transparent than analytic in their subjectivity and commitment to local speakers. *Desert Motel* can't stand for queer filmmaking *tout court*. But by presuming the significance of practice in an uneven universe of cultural production (rather than practical indifference and commercial determination), those questions— how *do* queer filmmakers produce their films, and what difference does their practice make?—expose the inadequacy and cultural hierarchy of the commercial repressive hypothesis across a range of media, genres, and formats in queer cultural production.[6]

The Queerness of *Desert Motel*

A twelve-minute narrative short, shot in color on sync-sound Super 16 and blown up to 35 mm for festival distribution, *Desert Motel* is the story of Leslie

(Candice Hussain) and her girlfriend, Kate (Kara Lipson), a butch-fem couple who travel one holiday weekend in 1996 from San Francisco to Desert Hot Springs in Southern California and there encounter an acquaintance visiting with his transgender support group. All members of the racially mixed group are undergoing female-to-male transition, and Connor (Max Madrigal), the acquaintance, takes this chance encounter to explain his new gender expression to his uncertain friends. Leslie, the butch member of the couple, is troubled by the news and finds her own embodied masculinity exposed and vulnerable. Acting out, she strips down and challenges Connor to do the same and to join her in the motel pool—an inversion of the usual traumatic stripping in transgender narrative, where the trans character's clothes are forcibly removed to reveal the "lie" of gender transitivity and the "truth" of embodiment. The inversion is driven by Leslie's anxiety and enabled by her visible whiteness, in a racially mixed swimming-pool scene marked by historical memories of segregation and gender surveillance. It is hard to imagine a scene in which even a belligerent butch woman of color so readily exposes herself in a racially mixed pool setting.

Connor declines the provocation, but Leslie pulls him into the water, fully clothed, to the surprise and contempt of Connor's compatriots at the pool's edge and to Kate's dismay and frustration. Connor hoists himself out as Leslie taunts him and as she suffers her own physical exposure above and below the water line. Expertly lit nighttime underwater exteriors signify Leslie's ambivalent relationship to her own body and its distinctly female parts—her breasts, hands, hips, thighs, and crotch. *Desert Motel* closes after she surfaces and exits the pool.

Desert Motel is a consciously atmospheric film, communicating situations and characters through rich production values, languid environmental and architectural images, sparse physical performance and dialogue, and, except for Leslie's aggression, a tenor of queer indirection and dislocation in a desert context outside routine images of space and time. The film was broadly and well received on the festival circuit, including at such high-profile queer festivals as Outfest in Los Angeles (2005), the New Festival and MIX in New York (2005) (Johnson had served as a member of the MIX programming committee from 1999 to 2004), and Toronto's Inside/Out (2006), as well as in a variety of programs at such mainstream international festivals as Rotterdam (2005) and Berlin (2005).

What is queer about *Desert Motel*? In a cultural universe and an era where distributable "gay films" are likely to be feature-length and to affirm gay and lesbian communities through coming-out stories, happy endings, and same-sex kisses, the depth and range of queer feeling and representation are

Leslie and Kate (publicity still), *Desert Motel.*

Connor acknowledges his transition to Leslie and Kate, *Desert Motel* © Liza Johnson 2005; used with permission.

compressed. Such a distribution standard is not merely skeptical overdrive on my part. As Johnson noted in one of our conversations, two women in Berlin buying lesbian films for a German distributor had commented that they'd seen *Desert Motel* and thought it was good. But, they added, "We are instructed only to buy the fun and happy ones." I looked askance at this story, but Johnson was unsurprised. *Desert Motel*, like most queer shorts on the festival circuit, is not *Kissing Jessica Stein* (2001). It excavates the lesser-known inside of butch embodiment and the known but popularly unarticulated tension between butch lesbian and transgender masculinity. It is not a happy, fun film, exactly, but it is tender in its vision, harnessing empathy and irresolution to bad butch behavior and thus inviting its audience to inhabit the queer sensation of butch melodrama.

I adapt this phrase, "butch melodrama," from Matthew Tinkcom's (2002) work on the films of John Waters to signal a narrative about the entanglements and contradictions of masculinity (in contrast to Waters's femininity) in patriarchy, a narrative that speaks to both the material artifice and the unsettled affect of female gender variance. We encounter Leslie and Kate on their holiday weekend in one of the most iconic, gender-resonant locales in U.S. popular culture: the golf and Rat Pack scene of midcentury Palm Springs, remade in Desert Hot Springs as mid-1990s vintage culture, replete with local thrift shops selling white buck loafers and "funny old man shorts," molded Populuxe ashtrays, and wasp-waisted print dresses. For Leslie and Kate, what was once the stylized environment of Mr. and Mrs. Middle America has become a butch-fem ruin, overcooked and still raw, where gender trouble is at once deepened and buoyed by Connor and his support group of FTM friends.

By "butch melodrama," I do not mean "dyke drama," a lesbian insider's vernacular exasperation with romantic intrigue, betrayal, and boundary transgression (think "issues" on *The L Word*). Such an overtone is always available as both stereotype and subcultural knowledge, but the feel in *Desert Motel* is quieter, richer, more exposed, less dismissive than dyke drama as a catchall for lesbian neurosis. Tall, broad-shouldered, long-haired, and striking but unadorned, Leslie lives her queer irresolution in her body. Erotically, she is defensive, charged but not quite open; publicly, she is self-conscious and thus a little awkward. She reacts to Kate's advances in their motel room with hurt feelings, insisting that in sex their gender difference is not pretend. "But it is pretend," Kate responds, "make it more pretend." At each step, Kate draws Leslie out of wounded sensitivity. For Leslie, it isn't an easy time; for Kate, fem subjectivity and gesture in Desert Hot Springs are rooted in sociability and empathy; for both, gender intensity is echoed in the environmental intensity of the desert's bright light and rippling heat and in the film's slow, expressive rhythms. Each scene offers saturated attention to place and space (in the motel room, at the pool, at the thrift shop) and a gendered punchline, sometimes about butch-fem sex, transgender acknowledgment, or anxious butch embodiment, other times about excavating a gendered past through thrift consumption and restyling in a playful, self-conscious present.

At the pool with Connor and his friends, Kate is reassuring, but Leslie's aggression has a life of its own, unchanged by Kate's efforts to calm things down. A butch-fem reduction of affect and relationality—masculine antagonism, feminine understanding—is rendered and then complicated by Leslie's vulnerability, as she strips down and as Connor and his friends look on in skeptical surprise, shaking their heads into their hands. Has Leslie lost it? From an onlooker's perspective, she has. Her taunting and belligerence and her "what's the problem?" attitude once out of the pool reveal someone exposed by bad behavior she cannot acknowledge. Such a failure expresses both gendered and racial self-consciousness in the company of a racially mixed FTM group, and the arrogance of someone historically unbound by gender passing and racial hierarchy at a semipublic swimming pool.

But underwater, Leslie is panicking and she knows it. She alternately surfaces long enough to goad Connor (who isn't biting), then submerges to be alone with her mortification. Leaving the pool and returning to her motel room, where Kate awaits, quiet and bewildered, Leslie acknowledges the exuberant, transgender pool party under way in the background. As *Desert Motel* closes, Connor and his friends have moved on to a splashing reverie, Leslie's moment of self-recognition has returned to willful oblivion, and Kate's empathy has surrendered to frustration. Characters' responses are legible, if in different terms for different viewers, and Leslie's is delicately excruciating. In *Desert Motel*'s unresolved melodrama of butch and fem, Leslie and Kate are stuck but not done. They are in a state of gendered becoming, marked by their time—1996—and the heightened, if halting, accountability the period demanded of lesbians across the gender spectrum to transgender and transsexual identity and practice.

Anticipating the first festival screening of *Desert Motel* in the winter of 2005, Johnson wondered whether the film would be received as provoking

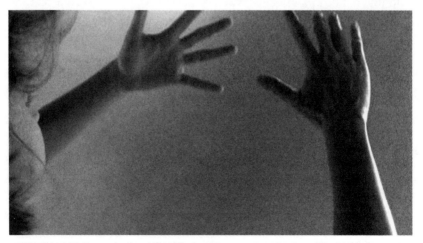

Underwater, Leslie anxiously studies her hands, *Desert Motel* © Liza Johnson 2005; used with permission.

the butch and trans resentment it explores. As audience responses took shape, Johnson reported, those possibilities settled:

> After I screened it in New York, no one really [responded] that way. In New York, I had longer discussions with people because I knew people here. After the screening, lots of people, mostly lesbians, came up and talked to me. Though one person—I'm not sure how he or she identifies, as a lesbian, I think—responded that this is similar to experiences they have all the time . . . of witnessing this kind of discomfort. . . . When you make a work, you have to stand behind it. . . . And you never really know what feelings things will set off for people. But I realized I wasn't making a film to make everyone feel comfortable. . . . I was trying to invert what is common in narrative films about trans people, which is that at some point they have to be stripped down so that you can see the supposed truth of their gender through their body. I wanted to make a film where that experience was put on the person experiencing panic.[7]

Echoing the gendered forms it depicts, *Desert Motel* had been released into a state of queer becoming.

Making Desert Motel

Like all independent shorts or features, especially those shot in sync-sound with high production values, *Desert Motel* was made by a network of friends and referrals. Johnson collaborated with Anne Etheridge, a college friend who had spent years as president of the board of Frameline, the San Francisco distributor and festival organization, before enrolling in the American Film Institute for training as a cinematographer. Etheridge, director of photography, brought on Domini Hofmann, a former actor and now an independent producer in Los Angeles whom Etheridge had met following her Mandy.com solicitation a year earlier for a line producer for Etheridge's AFI project. Hofmann recruited Kara Lipson, an up-and-comer between jobs in the Los Angeles television and film industries, to be casting director, and Lipson located Candice Hussain, who plays "Leslie," through an open call. In a novel (and, for Lipson, complicated) gesture, Johnson cast Lipson herself as "Kate," having witnessed the success of her pairing with Hussain in an audition reading.[8]

With the assistance of friends and networks in Los Angeles, Johnson cast Max Madrigal as "Connor" and several actors as the FTM support group through the Los Angeles FTM Alliance. Etheridge recruited Kate Hoffman, a photographer and decorative painter by trade, who had worked with Etheridge as a production designer on earlier projects. Bob Alotta, a longtime friend of Johnson's in New York, an experienced assistant director and, by day, a technology manager at the Columbia University film school, was AD and referred Johnson to Andrea Chignoli, a professional film editor from Chile then enrolled in Columbia's MFA program. Etheridge recruited the underwater cinematographers and camera and electrical crew members, and Hofmann recruited the sound recordist. The film was catered by friends of Johnson's from New York and script-supervised by me, as a critic, fieldworker, and friend and colleague of Johnson's who'd brushed up her script skills to join the project. Except for script supervision and catering, cast and crew were modestly paid, although virtually everyone acknowledged the aesthetic and professional value—apart from their day-rate—of working on *Desert Motel* with so "talented" and "promising" a writer-director-cinematographer duo as Johnson and Etheridge. As collaborators at similar stages in their filmmaking careers—with substantial production credits and festival exhibition but not, as yet, agents or commercial sales—principal crew members were part of a natural alliance in independent production.

Crew formation on *Desert Motel* is a familiar story; what makes it distinctive (in addition to its women bosses) is the production team's metamorphosis into a small, queer, five-day world in the California desert. About half the crew members were now or once queer identified, about half were not. The script, however, encouraged a queer sensibility on the set through its tale of butch-fem romance, anxious butch embodiment, and tender but resolved gender transition. The balance was further tipped by the location, the Beat Hotel in Desert Hot Springs, then a small, stylish place filled to shrine proportions with owner Steven Lowe's collection of artwork and writing by William S. Burroughs, and made available, as both set and crew accommodation, at very nominal cost. Fueled by good food and standard twelve-hour (not overworked) production days, queer sensibility and solidarity flourished on the set, making it possible to envision a world gently changed by the return of each of us to our own landscapes, some newly attuned to a tale of queer embodiment brought to life by a mixed and creative assembly of cultural workers.

The budget for *Desert Motel* came from a familiar range of sources: most from Johnson's savings; some in the form of a faculty grant (for the lighting truck) from Williams College, Johnson's employer as (then) assistant professor of art; and the usual loaves-and-fishes approach to marshaling equipment, materials, and personnel in independent filmmaking. A major camera house gave Etheridge a break on what would have otherwise been an out-of-service camera package; Lowe offered the location well below his off-season rates as a contribution to queer art-making; Hofmann hired crew members for modest pay on days they would otherwise have been unscheduled to work for commercial industry scale; those in the camera department looked forward to future projects with Etheridge and appreciated the chance to work with her on *Desert Motel* in the interest of cultivating a professional relationship; the caterers—whose workdays started two hours before and ended two hours after everyone else's—worked *gratis* as Johnson's friends, a critical resource on a project where limited pay is made up for with good food, reasonably comfortable accommodations, and decent treatment.

In preproduction, Johnson, Etheridge, and Hofmann pursued but did not receive a handful of resources available for specifically lesbian productions, such as production insurance from PowerUP, a lesbian nonprofit founded by the former writer-producer Stacy Codikow in Los Angeles, whose mission is to "promote the visibility and integration of gay women in entertainment, arts and all forms of media" (www.powerupfilms.org), offering its members production information, networking resources, and the chance to compete to have their short scripts produced. Etheridge and Johnson also tried, unsuccessfully, to secure a camera deal from Panavision as part of the firm's New Directors program. The rejection left collaborators wondering—inconclusively—whether the story itself had affected the decision.[9]

In other parts of the production process, most dramatically in finding and using the principal location, the film's queer theme was a confirmed resource, not a speculative liability. Queer cultural attributions were thus continually and unevenly in play as producers assembled resources, deciding as they went whether they'd be better off describing the film as queer or whether a fiction film of unspecified theme would be more attractive. This latter judgment was made, for example, about the proprietors of a local thrift shop, where the crew spent half a day shooting in exchange for a small fee and Hoffman's elegant new store sign, which was fabricated as part of the production design and then installed as a permanent fixture. Despite the overall ease of queer presence on *Desert Motel*, an old rule prevailed: when in doubt, hold back.

From this sketch of the everyday life of a queer short in the making, we get some sense of the environment queer relay creates and in which it occurs: a combination of informal queer and nonqueer networks, set in motion by a distinctive story in the now more or less viable context of queer narration and cultural recognition. It is a scene held together by professional norms (one finishes the jobs one starts); by sensitive treatment of cast and crew, enough so that the completion norm was not routinely tested; and by collective faith in the artistic and industry promise of the principal collaborators, who are cultural workers themselves on the edges of a production sector in which career peers exchange labor and opportunity. I would call it a quasi-industrial scene, structurally exploitive in the sense that cultural workers (crew as well as artistic principals) invest hard labor, untold hours, and personal savings in the present in the hope of a future payoff. In uneven ways, the payoff returns to the workers themselves, in the form of employment opportunities, new artistic collaborations, and potentially money (where, in the event of a sale, musicians and actors are paid first after expenses are recouped), marking the cooperative side of this and other independent projects on the margins of high commerce. In *Desert Motel*'s case, cooperation comes on the heels (or wings) of aboveground queer commitment, and cultural change is further apparent in the knowledge—at all stages—that queer work is inching toward par with other independent productions, no more a guarantee of that future in aesthetic or economic terms but, increasingly, no less. If the "new queer cinema" has disappeared, as B. Ruby Rich (who coined the phrase in the early 1990s) argues in an interview (Rose 2004), it may not be only the effect of squashing or economic dry-up in one production sector but also the softening of queer profile that relay induces.

"Feeling Costs Money"

Johnson's oeuvre preceding *Desert Motel* is partly narrative and largely experimental, and thus I was curious about her impulse to move toward sync-sound narrative on film, with its considerable labor and infrastructure demands. During our conversations about this move, Johnson said that "feeling costs money." This is a claim I would ask her to explain and that I would later repeat as a question in my conversations with other collaborators. Does feeling cost money?

For Johnson, the phrase signifies less the cost of filming feeling per se than the price tag on visual transparency in cinema, a transparency sought to invite lay viewers into characters' emotional states. A film about empathy for bad behavior in the context of butch anxiety, in other words, needs to give its audience something human to go on, such as enough embarrassment and vulnerability in witnessing Leslie's gestures toward Connor, to produce more recognition than contempt. Johnson wanted the audience to watch characters and their responses, not grainy film surfaces, artful jump cuts, objects evocatively but incomprehensibly standing in for people, or found footage—not, in other words, the creative hallmarks of no-budget production. She wanted actors, rehearsals, location scouting, expressive design, and continuity shooting. She wanted moderately complete crews, underwater cinematography, and high production value; she wanted to make decisions that occasionally favored style or performance over shooting schedule. Still, time would be tight and the room for error minimal with a shooting ratio of less than 10:1—low, by the standards of narrative sync and technical finesse.[10]

Johnson wanted, in other words, to make a movie with a queer story, but small moviemaking, not big; delicate, not aggrandized. In a conversation about future projects, including a moderately priced feature she was then writing, Johnson described her ambitions by quoting the critic Dana Stevens (aka Liz Penn), whose phrase "juice bomb" (Penn, 2005), coined to describe Agnes Jaoui's feature *Look at Me* (2004), captured the qualities of character and feeling Johnson sought to create:

> [Stevens] likes to call this kind of film a "juice bomb," which she describes as a kind of intimate, miniaturist film, not usually driven by crimes and plots, more driven by the everyday niceties of experience. In that respect, it is often characterized as a woman's film, although it may or may not have to do with women. A great deal of emotional force, or, in a way, story, comes from very small, miniature gestures. A raised eyebrow can constitute a major plot development. And I thought, "I want to make a juice bomb." A juice bomb probably has to cost . . . I mean, I am not talking *Waterworld* . . . but it just has to cost more than $100,000 [many times the cost of *Desert* Motel] because I think that if you can see the boom or see through the texture of the video, the raised eyebrow does not constitute a plot development.

This is the sense in which "feeling costs money": having the resources of time, personnel, equipment, and materials to amplify and control the texture of the image, sound, and performance. It is not an absolute aesthetic relation. As Etheridge pointed out, formal experiments can cost money, too. In my conversation with Etheridge, the films of Matthew Barney and the video triptychs of Isaac Julien came to mind, both examples produced in fine art, avant-garde contexts better capitalized than the scenes in which short, queer films are produced. Likewise, such no-budget examples as the wrenching and underlit childhood drag scene from *Tarnation* (2003; shot on Super 8 by Jonathan Caouette as an eight-year-old boy, although paired with an expressive and expensive music track in the feature film) or any number of open-hearted student video productions, including by students of Johnson, contest the claim that "feeling costs money." And money can be spent without feeling. *Waterworld* (1995) is a routinely mocked example. But, relative to the cost per minute of Johnson's earlier projects and their formats, the budget-affect ratio had grown on *Desert Motel*, with new aesthetic motives and skills evolving alongside existing ones.

"Feeling costs money" also expressed Johnson's and her collaborators' desire to communicate with audiences at a distance. In the popular universe of narrative fiction, where filmmakers and filmgoers are strangers to each other (unlike underground avant-garde scenes, where, as Johnson joked, filmmakers can name the people who will see their work), expressive transparency rooted in character, detail, and continuity is a resource. In the politics of art, however, such a resource is haunted by moral narratives of aesthetic distinction and commercial refusal: better to be rough, cheap, and moving than slick, pricey, and flat. The tension between these two standards—popular legibility and political adequacy (a tension at the heart of crossover anxiety)—makes short films a good risk, especially where the affective qualities in play are *other* than "happy, funny," which makes them hard to sell. Short films remain difficult to distribute, and as nontheatrical works their potential revenues are limited. But you can't distribute or even show a film you haven't made, and thus the production imperative—first, make the movie—rules both newcomers and writer-directors on the rise, symbolically balancing the benefit against the cost, especially with outsider work that "gives voice" to underrepresented characters and experiences. "I think the beauty of the economics of the short film," said Johnson in conversation, "is that I can make a short film that doesn't have good feelings in it, and if I never sell it, no one went broke over it. It all happened in ways that were economically possible for me. It didn't compromise me, it didn't compromise the crew, it didn't compromise the cast. It would be better for us all if we can sell it, but it is not the same kind of economic crisis as if I made a bad-feeling feature film and owed somebody half a million dollars."

Story and production value in *Desert Motel* would qualify the film for more queer and nonqueer festivals and be legible to more audiences. It would circulate more widely as a festival release, possibly enter negotiation for a cable sale, and have a life beyond those audiences for whom Johnson could personally screen the film. As outcome, if not by Johnson's intent or design, *Desert Motel* would thus become a mobile queer text whose production was rooted in skimming resources from multiple edges of the commercial industry. In Los Angeles, said Etheridge, such skimming was easier than in New York, given the scale and dominance of L.A.'s commercial filmmaking sector and New York's dying market for 16 mm. Camera houses and labs kept busy by studio production could afford to make short-term deals for up-and-comers, and a well-populated network of craftspeople alternately thrilled and bored by bread and butter employment would make themselves available—for a few days at a time—for something more artistically, socially, and professionally compelling.

Short films thus have a distinctive position in economies of filmmaking and film feeling and in the cultural politics of queer relay. Like poetry in Audre Lorde's famous maxim, they are not a luxury; cheaper to make, they enable experiments in queer bad feeling and vital queer cinema (Lorde 1984, 36–39). If their collaborators are lucky and the timing is good, they may also become calling cards for developing future projects.

Relay Worlds

We finished shooting *Desert Motel* in early June 2004. In July 2005, I traveled from western Massachusetts to Los Angeles for thirty-eight hours to attend a screening of the film at Outfest, the Los Angeles Gay and Lesbian Film Festival. I was out of research money, and it was an extravagant trip. What compelled me? Inclusion? Ethnographic attachment with the L.A. cast and crew? Curiosity about a Director's Guild screening?[11]

Catching up in Los Angeles with Lipson, Etheridge, Hoffman, Johnson, the film's makeup artist, Martha Cuan, and the actors Laurence Vincent Grey and Joey Aspen, I was struck by the mixture of film-related and other work they had each taken on since the previous summer; Cuan, for example, had been licensed as an esthetician, and Hoffman had been doing a lot of decorative painting and design. Etheridge had done more shooting in film and television; Hofmann was home for the weekend after preproduction consulting in Los Angeles on a series budget. Lipson had just finished a job as assistant casting director on a feature and had joined forces with its casting director to form a new partnership, a small office with studio clients. From our conversations, I gleaned a sense of careers in the making, of the perils of creative freelance employment in Los Angeles, and of where—outside queer life and queer cinema—the experience of *Desert Motel* would travel. The apparent coherence and continuity of our scene on the set would give way to a sense of lighthearted impermanence. In the bodies of its cast and crew, *Desert Motel* was migrating to worlds beyond the film and beyond filmmaking.

From Lipson's apartment, we walked over to Sunset Boulevard like a happy parade of four-year-olds. We landed in an otherworldly combination of architectural grandeur, Hollywood buzz, Donna Karan–clad press photographers, life-size character cutouts from *The L Word* and *Queer as Folk*, plush, insulated screening rooms and high-end projection technology, and the sweetest, motliest group of queer kids and festivalgoers imaginable, not the leads from queer serial television but the walk-ons from club and hospital scenes, not stylin' professionals (although they were there, too) but heartland tourists making a vacation trip to Outfest, not critics and academics but enthusiasts who would ask Lipson—discovering she had an on-camera role in *Desert Motel*—"Is it hot?" Not, in other words, weary festival cognoscenti who had seen it all, but some semblance of the mixed populations, motives, and responses that Rich hoped for in a comment on queer film festivals as ephemeral democratic utopias (White et al. 1999).

Earlier in the evening, Johnson had commented on Outfest having programmed *Desert Motel* as a "trans short." It shared the bill with a sports documentary from British Columbia called *100% Woman* (2004), about the MTF athlete Michelle Dumaresq, whose eligibility for competing as a woman was hotly contested by many nontrans athletes on her downhill mountain-bike racing circuit. "I understand what the programmers have in mind," said Johnson, "they're creating market groups. But I've seen this film work very well in a lesbian program, too." Being part of the trans program at Outfest (paired with *100% Woman*, and not, say, *Transamerica* [2005]) would mean a smaller audience for *Desert Motel*, something Johnson recognized as a seasoned festival curator. More to the point for Johnson, however, was that the film is Leslie's story, not Connor's.

For my part, despite the fact that the films bore scant resemblance in terms of format and style, I did see thematic continuity between *Desert Motel* and *100% Woman* in the personal and cultural anxiety both articulated about gender difference and embodiment. When I read the script early on, moreover, perhaps in a gesture of overidentification I received *Desert Motel* as also *Kate's* story—a film about fem subjectivity whose root affect is empathy for the wounded aggression of a gender-nonconforming lover. Just before we started shooting, I asked Johnson about this angle, about what narrative role Kate played in the film, and she responded that it wasn't Kate's story. I sensed that my reading it that way would make the film less empathic (Johnson's goal) than flatteringly self-descriptive for fem women, Johnson and myself among them.

Johnson did incorporate Kate's character in a later academic account of *Desert Motel*. In a 2005 unpublished self-evaluation she shared with me, she wrote that "the film produces a profound sense of discomfort, and allows for empathy with the men, with the badly-behaving protagonist, and with Kate, who is left in an awkward and feminine position, asked to understand and empathize with all the other characters' masculine needs and behaviors." I was struck to read this new gloss a year after our conversation in the tender hours before we started shooting, when a settled sense of the story is essential, although the story that had settled then was a little different than the one now offered.

As time passed, however, and as *Desert Motel* circulated, the story had accrued versions among collaborators, as a "universal tale" (Hofmann) whose gendered anxiety was legible to anyone who had experienced bodily self-doubt or exposure, as butch melodrama, as trans narrative, as fem expression, and as a multigendered story of empathy and recognition. We can thus see in *Desert Motel* some of the productive instabilities that are part of meaning formation within a mixed universe of queer cultural production. Speaking both to putatively internal (queer) and external (nonqueer) semantic and political variation, and thus softening the boundaries between inside and out, *Desert Motel* reveals the relay character of cultural form and value.

At Outfest, cast and crew were a supportive ensemble of queer and nonqueer, trans and nontrans, responding to each other in awkward good faith. Outfest itself was a protected milieu, a reincarnation of the small queer world from the production set, a world whose boundaries were both real and permeable, made and dissolved by social time and social space. So evanescent a scene does not challenge the most entrenched commercial meanings of crossover, where cultural workers obey and transcend the boundaries made and promoted by commerce itself. But it does remind us of the materiality of even temporary formations and the net cultural effect of their ongoing production and decay. Lives, communities, and populations are wrought from such cycles as much as from more visible structures and their impositions, including the commercial and quasi-commercial logics backstage at Outfest.

Relay, then, is a term coined less to displace structural critique than to rematerialize people and practices—most of us and most of what we do— and our routine navigation of cultural and institutional fault lines as we perform in, on, through, and across the received stages of everyday cultural life.

The Politics of Queer Relay

But such a project—making concrete the everyday life of cultural production—arouses its own critique. If we imagine our resistance to crossover and its excesses as protecting us from the cultural dangers of commerce, what, in contrast, can relay thinking do? To view multidimensional and multivalent scenes and practices in motion, to view, in other words, the world of queer relay as it already exists, doesn't demand that we do anything different, doesn't demand that we separate ourselves, be wary, expect the worst, and then stave it off with fierce refusal and avant-garde taste. A relay view might appear to be an invitation to settle, to leave or redeem things as they are. In a universe of artistic and political urgency, this is never enough.

But neither is this what I intend. Instead, I want to connect the scenes, practices, and practitioners of queer relay to a variable politics of representation, asking, rather than claiming, where such practices leave us in political terms. What is accomplished in the domain of representation? What images of a better world—indeed what better worlds—might surface through the loam and lens of relay? To get at these questions through *Desert Motel*, I spoke with principal collaborators about the film as cultural intervention and about politics and stakes in the filmmaking worlds they inhabit as writer-directors, producers, casting directors, actors, visual artists, and festival programmers.

Johnson, Etheridge, Lipson, and Hofmann are not representatives here of their respective roles (Johnson speaking for directors, Hofmann for producers). They are situated purveyors of discourses about art, media, and queerness, discourses that are familiar but whose juxtaposition speaks to the tension between crossover and relay and to the productivity of that tension in reimagining cultural production. In other words, I want to listen to what they say and track their different and similar claims about politics and film. The kinds of political claims about representation that I might present elsewhere as arguments or truths (for example, about the suspect status of "universal appeal" as a criterion of aesthetic accomplishment) here become other speakers' expressions in context, statements whose truth-value is neither in doubt nor transparent. Receiving their statements in this way (rather than foreclosing on their politics) enables me to witness the movement of their claims and counterclaims on the field of queer filmmaking and their attachment to social and professional imperatives. It thus briefly enables me to exit familiar oppositions, rather than reproduce them. Many of those oppositions have become staples in queer culture's commercial repressive hypothesis.

Immediately, *relay* points to a number of runners and positions and thus to the idea that political interest attaches to a speaker's position, such as that of writer-directors, like Johnson, who are emerging in rarified art-world and experimental contexts, but also in queer narrative ones for more popular audiences; casting directors, like Lipson, leaving television work as casting assistant and taking on both industrial projects as second in command and small, independent films like *Desert Motel* as a promising next step out of network employment and into film; independent producers, like Hofmann, who have bypassed incremental promotion up the ladder of paid industrial work in favor of working for less or for free in more advanced positions (and thus with greater production authority) as an alternate way to establish a track record; and cinematographers, like Etheridge, rooted in a technical-aesthetic practice that can be purveyed across production sectors, and equipped with art-world, popular, and (through her work with Frameline) distinctly queer repertoires and politics.[12]

As these four cultural workers migrate across production sectors, many of them could be described at least partly in the terms now assigned to the others. Strict comparisons by professional title, as relay suggests, do not hold up in a structured mapping of location, practice, and rhetoric. But the glosses help me navigate discursive unevenness born of location: where people are and what they are trying to do. As young women (in their late twenties to mid-thirties) on uncertain trajectories in volatile professional spheres, their work introduces considerable variance and, within individual conversations, sometimes an ambivalence or apparent contradiction that I am eager not to reduce. This has meant reading and comparing their stories and statements for insights about the conditions and practices of relay and leaving the contrasts open. Sometimes, for example, it is easy to read opposition (and easy for speakers to insist on the clear difference between their position and another's), but that is an ease the concept of relay seeks to temporarily suspend.

And, unexpectedly, I was struck by convergence among the queerest and most art-minded of the contributors and those more identified with the commercial industry. At moments, I could have asked speakers to challenge others' statements only to discover that no one disagrees. There are vernacular differences through which I can locate political variance of a subtle but revealing kind, differences tentatively attached, for example, to Michael Warner's (1999, 27–33) distinction between a stigmaphobe or stigmaphile ethos, the first eager to distance itself from the stigma of queerness (usually by refusing the shame of queer sex and its practitioners), the second assuming the stigma of queerness and counting for survival on the dignity of shame and exposure in common. But, as clarifying as Warner's distinction is in this context, and given the historical moment in which Johnson and others were speaking, even the stigmaphobe–phile distinction is too stark. In other words, speakers might not put things in the same terms, but they would not exactly disagree. My question therefore becomes: What do convergences and differences among claims about queer representation suggest about political stakes for queer producers and for queer cultures at large?

To begin, consider the convergences: Johnson, Hofmann, Etheridge, and Lipson all want relative professional autonomy and the chance to do "quality" work. Most imagine their futures in terms of feature films, historically an industry standard, given the costs and infrastructure demands of even the most economical productions and the limited paid venues for distributing anything else. Most would like to work with others who share their vision of life and filmmaking in some significant way. Most take pleasure in production scenes that are sexually and culturally mixed and hospitable. Everyone needs resources that already are in short supply (although no one has stopped working as a consequence); and everyone agrees that film has a place in changing the world for the better. How film might change things, how swiftly it might do so, and what the measures of such change might be are matters of variation, but no one is indifferent to the possibility of film and change. Johnson, Etheridge, Lipson, and Hofmann are neither guerrilla filmmakers nor the unrepentant capitalists of studio Hollywood. Rather, they are relay runners on a quirkier, edgier, and often beholden track.

From that perspective, the comparison in Table 1 can be read for its continuities, or at least for the pliancy of its distinctions, imagining not two opposed groups but contiguous cultural spaces whose borders are open and whose inhabitants are sometimes locals and other times guests, with both states in formation and transition. In the world of filmmaking, narrative and aesthetic repertoires—films themselves and the stories and styles they fix— are made and transformed through the situated decisions of cultural workers. In turn, this makes the space of their work an ethical space, a context that poses the question of cultural workers about what their, and our, cultural repertoires will be like, regardless of the degree of autonomy or dependence that workers experience in that space (Gibson-Graham 2006, xxvii-xxxiii). But filmmakers are also made by their filmmaking, and thus cultural production is also the space of subject formation. Conversations about producers' stakes therefore weave together insights about films, forms, selves, production contexts, and careers, and so must a scheme designed to represent those conversations, including the one in Table 1. The cultural space of relay in queer filmmaking, then, includes productions, careers, stories, and images, each category mediated by the other three.

In my conversations with Johnson, Etheridge, Hofmann, and Lipson, I was struck by the significance for them of the cultural conditions of film work and their attachment of those conditions to stories and style. As a persistently collaborative form, filmmaking brings people together, and that encounter becomes the ground of cultural possibility. For a non-queer-identified producer like Hofmann, that possibility is rooted in queer cinema being, "in fact," a queer variation on such "universal" themes as anxiety about gender performance and the emotional recognition that one is behaving badly and is out of control, like Leslie in *Desert Motel*. The evidence of *Desert Motel*'s accomplishment, for Hofmann, was not only that it was readily received in a broad range of international festivals, but that her spouse, a

Table 1: The Space of Relay in Queer Cultural Production

→→→→→ **Industry Orientation**	←←←←← **Queer Orientation**
Integration: making queer space from isolation	Queer worldmaking: remaking the world in queerness
Recognition: by the mainstream, educating the world	Recognition: from queer to queer, expressing the world
De-specification, "universalism" as aesthetic and cultural goals	Specification, representation as aesthetic and cultural goals
Responding to an objective social hierarchy that needs conquering (an irony, given emphasis on integration)	Worlds as intersecting, moving back and forth
Stigmaphobic	Stigmaphilic
Industrial career markers	Art/queer world career markers
• clout	• autonomy of expression
• feature production	• feature production
• big budgets	• budgets getting bigger
• individual development and success model: signature position in the field	• evolving film culture toward a better world
Aesthetic convergence	Aesthetic innovation
• all stories are the same, there are no new stories	• variation matters
	• beauty, form as communicative and contested
Audiences	Audiences
• Mainstream audience is the priority but don't ignore "specialized census" (Domini Hoffman)	• cultivate one's community
	• predictable and small
	• expanding the audience through film form
	• preserve world view
Crossover avowed	Crossover disavowed
Seeking economic clout and wealth	Seeking economic enablement
Queerness transforming from a bad financial risk to a risk worth taking	Queerness as given

thoughtful moviegoer and honest respondent but neither queer nor "a film guy," found that *Desert Motel* spoke to him: "He watched it and he loved it. He said it was a great story. And what I liked about that was that he saw it for what it was, a story about some people. It really doesn't have anything to do with their sexual orientation. It's not a gay film, well, not *not* a gay film. You know what I mean? He was just a guy who saw it and he loved it and he appreciated it for the story that it was ... one person's interior struggle to accept themself or to understand themself."

As our conversation continued, Hofmann made clear that among the virtues of a story legible to viewers outside a film's character group was that high-quality work like *Desert Motel* would get seen and would draw an audience among and beyond queer viewers and festivalgoers. I could feel myself brace a little at this logic, long familiar with the notion that culture counts only when dominant groups pay attention and can imagine themselves as the intended audience. I remembered critics' accounts of Harvey Fierstein's *Torch Song Trilogy* (1988, directed by Paul Bogart) as less "gay" than a universal story of attachment and loss.

Torch Song not gay? Only as not gay as *Brokeback Mountain*. Fierstein (unlike Ledger and Gyllenhaal) had protested. I wondered how Johnson might respond to Hofmann. Further into our conversation, however, I could hear Hofmann's thinking shift and flesh out. As a former actor who had noticed her opportunities diminish with age, Hofmann had refashioned herself as an independent producer on the edges of an industry in which, she plainly acknowledged, films by various classes of "outsiders" are "fucked":

Qualifying *Desert Motel* as a certain kind of movie and paying such attention to marketing it towards FTMs, queer cinema, and queer culture ... I think that's limiting. It is not just films about gay people or transgender people; it's films about black people, it's films about Asian people, it's films about women. They all suffer a marginalized or specialized existence in the commercial film and television marketplace. I mean, a perfect example is *Catwoman* (2004) with Halle Berry. ... Her performance was absolutely incredible. It was just out on the edge. It was ballsy—and I am not a Halle Berry fan. And I didn't think it was a great movie. It had lots of flaws, as all the super-hero movies do that make 50 gajillion dollars. The movie didn't make any money. It made not even as much money as it cost, I don't think, in the U.S. box office. I don't know how it did on a global level. But why? It is a fucking superhero movie. Everybody knows who Catwoman is. Because the superhero was a chick. ... They marketed it, and people didn't go. Men think it's a chick flick. Chicks don't consciously go out and support movies with chicks in them, if their guys don't want to go along. Whatever. My husband, I made him come. I said, "We are going to go see this movie. We are going to spend our money on the movie." We talked about it for a long time and he said, "You're right, I would never have gone to see that movie." . . . Anyway, there are hurdles to be overcome and I would say movies where the main characters or the subject matter covers gay themes have a more challenging time of it than *Catwoman*. And maybe a movie about life in the ghetto for black people doesn't have it as bad as a movie about Japanese internment camps. But to one degree or another, they're all fucked. . . . I think next, probably, the thing that will or should or could change will be Latino entertainers and then Asian. Don't even talk about people from the Middle East. I mean, they are fucked.

With a mixture of industry bravada and mercilessness and a vernacular of fuckedness reminiscent of the boys from *Entourage*, Hofmann renders the virtues of universal address in industrial terms (in which audiences share responsibility with producers for the state of things), not aesthetic ones. It is not an artistic or ideological failure but an "industrial reality" that queerness is "limiting" and "just a good story" is preferable, a reality Hofmann learned only too well as a female and, by movie standards, middle-aged actor in Los Angeles.

Johnson was less surprised and more encouraged than I was by Hofmann's wish that *Desert Motel* not be limited to queer festivals and audiences, in turn relating the film's meaningfulness and breadth of address to integrated production conditions on the set:

LIZA JOHNSON: Actually, I am flattered by what she says. I think her point is that discomfort, embarrassment, fear of unknown things, and the idea that gender is some deep shit . . . those things are not specifically queer ideas or feelings and I think that she is right that other people can relate to the film. And that was my experience of showing it in mixed audiences of not especially queer viewers. Absolutely my experience. And I also think that the film is about material that is much more familiar in queer culture, or a certain aspect of queer culture.

LISA HENDERSON: On the set, did it feel like people were on board, that they had the same idea of what they were doing?

LJ: Actually, I was shocked by how well that did work, considering. . . . I mean, you were there. You saw the diversity of experience of the members of cast and crew, right? And we were depending on the good faith of more than one community, right? There were all those AFI film worker people who were not getting a high day rate and there were all those friends of mine and the FTM guys—those people were mostly queer. People who had really different economic experiences in the world, people with different racialized experiences in the world, people who really had a whole lot of different ways of living in this country were all in one place working on one story. And it was really surprising to me how people got on board with that. . . . I also think that perhaps because the film does have explicitly queer content it wasn't like those things were underground. We were talking about "what does this moment of discomfort *look* like?" In order to do the acting with Candice, we had to talk about all kinds of things that, if the story had been somehow less queer, you could not talk about. And if they were not talked about, they could be more problematic.

Having spoken individually with Hofmann and Johnson (several months after production and several weeks apart), my guarded responses to Hofmann's judgment of the virtues of universal (versus queer) address began to shift. Not all such assertions are born of flattening or ideological indifference; some, like Hofmann's, are born of the conscious sting of exclusion in commercial filmmaking followed by strategic reentry. They exist alongside Johnson's wish to see an explicit queer sensibility from off the beaten track of commercial visibility, and to see it recognized for exploring what dominant culture naturalizes and denies: the pleasures, aggressions, and anxieties of gendered embodiment. That recognition was an accomplishment of the film itself and also, as Johnson points out, of rehearsal and production practices.

Reframed in these terms, the relay politics of *Desert Motel* surface more persuasively, as both a film to be screened for a range of festival audiences and as a queer project that had drawn collaborators from many contexts and sent them home one queer story richer. For both Hofmann and Johnson, moreover, *Desert Motel*'s mobility would heighten the chances for future filmmaking, queer and not. I could not be certain of the comparative political worth of trusting or refusing such relay equations, but I could no longer be certain that they meant losses to queer culture.

As *Desert Motel*'s casting director, Lipson was further inside queer scenes and vernaculars than was Hofmann, having been involved in lesbian relationships and lesbian communities in Los Angeles. Gayness, Lipson acknowledged, was still a matter of disclosure in Hollywood casting; if you were hiring an actor to play a gay character (in contrast, say, to a Jewish character), that had to be acknowledged early on, in casting calls and conversations with agents. All casting calls describe characters, but not all characteristics are considered career risks for actors. Lipson was not surprised, then, when two fairly well-established television actors whom she contacted through her professional networks turned down the role of Leslie, despite the potential value of a boutique project that might help an actor display a greater range than a prime-time television character. To make the career risk of playing a lesbian pay off (regardless of the actor's sexual orientation), the filmmaker would need to be higher profile or the budget bigger. A small production of a queer story by newcomers did not add up to hiring known actors and thus to the cachet or capital that "so-and-so playing a lesbian" might bring to *Desert Motel*. This stage of the casting process was a reminder of the limits of relay value in the movement from commercial (television) to queer (short), even as some feature productions bring career-making queer or transgender roles to such nonqueer actors as Cillian Murphy (*Breakfast on Pluto* [2005]), Philip Seymour Hoffman (*Capote* [2005]), Hilary Swank (*Boys Don't Cry* [1999]), Felicity Huffman (*Transamerica* [2005]), Jake Gyllenhaal and Heath Ledger (*Brokeback Mountain* [2005]), or Colin Firth (*A Single Man* [2009]).

For Lipson, *Desert Motel* was, however, a good first move out of television and into film, and out of staff status and into the role of casting director. Recruited by Hofmann, Lipson greeted *Desert Motel* as an opportunity to learn new character types and vernaculars, to encounter a new population of performers for a film whose FTM characters would be played by FTM actors, and, especially, to assume a creative rather than administrative role in working with a filmmaker new to narrative production who did not already have an established relationship with a casting director. As career peers, Lipson and Johnson would develop together; whether they would become (or want to become) Baz Luhrmann and Ronna Kress remained to be seen, but Lipson loved Johnson's script for *Desert Motel* and believed that between the story and Johnson's track record, she stood to learn a lot. Key measures of professional success in casting are recognition as a creative contributor on a given project and, later, distinction as a signature casting director. Working with Johnson on *Desert Motel* would be a step toward a casting career that might, ideally, come to look like that of Avy Kaufman, proprietor of her own New York firm and responsible for casting a wide range of recent, aesthetically distinguished independent features, among them *A Solitary Man* (2010), *The Lovely Bones* (2009), *American Gangster* (2007), *Children of Men* (2006), *Brokeback Mountain* (2005), and *Capote* (2005).

In casting *Desert Motel*, Johnson and Lipson posted an open call on Breakdown Services, an online network of casting calls routinely screened by agents and, unofficially, by actors who are not yet represented.

Lipson acknowledged how rare—and thus how interesting—it would be to encounter *Desert Motel*'s characters and story line in an open call. The casting itself, she said, "came down to a look," recognizable to Lipson in part through her earlier involvement in lesbian scenes, but primarily through her conversations and work with Johnson. "Leslie," said the casting call, "is in her early to mid-twenties. Caucasian. An attractive young lesbian on a trip with her girlfriend to the desert, Leslie has a sharp sense of humor and an aggressive personality. She is charming and charismatic and loving, yet at times needy, with a domineering streak that may come from her own insecurities. *Lead actor must be comfortable with partial nudity that is dramatically motivated, non-gratuitous.*" Candice Hussain's headshot, said Lipson, "definitely caught my eye": "The woman in the picture caught all of our eyes. She looks heavier in the picture, and she looks butchier than she really is. And the great thing about Candice is how she is so feminine and beautiful and how she really transformed herself into the athletic, kind of daddy figure that she played. . . . When she actually came in, we learned she'd borrowed clothes from a friend. She had practiced . . . she was imitating a friend of hers who is a lesbian."

In an earlier conversation on the set, Hussain herself acknowledged that the considerable opportunity for rehearsal that Johnson had provided—unusual for a small production—made a big difference in developing her character. They had worked on scenes, thrift shopped together for Leslie's clothing, and hung out in lesbian bars watching and soaking up the vibe. Hussain had also been very moved by Swank's performance in *Boys Don't Cry* and by the story that had circulated about Swank's audition with director Kimberly Peirce—her swaggering, smiling arrival in character as Brandon Teena. Hussain called *Boys Don't Cry* and Swank "amazing."

Thus, casting *Desert Motel* was a process of typification and countertypification, in which remarkable stories of lesbian and transgender characterization and actorly transformation across sexual and gender lines had circulated in the culture at large and had landed on the set of *Desert Motel*, less as exemplars to be mimicked than as arbiters of dramatic possibility. In limited contexts, in other words, it has become an actor's and casting director's job to understand queer characterization. This does not mean that everyone will do it well, that the implications of nonqueer actors "acting queer" (and feminine actors acting butch) as the ultimate dramatic challenge aren't suspect, or that the commonplace occurrence in film and elsewhere of queer and nonqueer actors "acting straight" is popularly recognized as performance (it isn't). But the ground of professional practice in acting and casting has shifted in a queer direction, in part through the participation of people like Lipson and

Etheridge, who had long migrated in and out of queer scenes, and like Hussain, a newcomer with a professional stake in queer recognition.

Anchoring Queer Relay

The sociability of filmmaking—its demand for small multitudes of workers and viewers—means that queer film will inevitably encounter its outside. As film, queerness cannot stay underground for long. Exposed, it oxidizes, transforms, and generates expected and unintended energy. Its very sociability is the ground for queer class renewal.

Imagining the relay runners of queer cultural production and the cultural and conceptual repertoires they embody and mobilize helps me resist the handy but illusory *fixatifs* of critique in the split universe of crossover. Relay thus contributes to the project of forming—as capaciously and with as little loss as possible—new subjectivities and alliances as filmmakers, critics, viewers, and cultural citizens. Relay does not ignore or even seek to disrupt the pleasure or safety of queer separation, voluntarily achieved, nor does it correct repression. But it is where and how most of us live—and need to live—most of the time. As Rich (2006a) observed with urgency and recognition in a Frameline Festival keynote address, we still need our queer venues, film festivals like Frameline and MIX, say, not just our (or their) *Brokeback Mountain*. And we need them not only for the films themselves—work that might otherwise never see the dark of the theater—but for our queer interpretations of that work and our particular enfolding of cultural forms into queer living. *Desert Motel*'s queer relay, as transparent as I hope it is, does not displace or threaten queer self-preservation but enables us to fathom political possibilities on reconfigured ground, rather than retilling old cultural hierarchies of art versus commerce and reproducing the taste politics and cultural exclusions those hierarchies bring with them in the name of true queerness. Relay is a historicizing concept for a changing cultural economy, a world not accounted for by an anachronistic calculus in which the expressive ambitions of lesbian and other outsider cultural producers are suspect, whether for selling out to industry ambition or holding on to queer cultural autonomy. Suspicion is punitive and paralyzing; relay looks for movement and repair.

For her part, in July 2006, Johnson had tentatively accepted a limited contract to screen *Desert Motel* on LOGO, the new gay and lesbian basic-cable outlet owned and operated by MTV. If LOGO had offered errors and omissions insurance to Johnson and, as producer, to Hofmann, the deal would have put *Desert Motel* exclusively in the LOGO rotation for one year and might have paid the musicians, but it would not have begun to recoup the modest, below-value costs of making the film.[13] As it turned out, Johnson and Hofmann decided that they couldn't afford LOGO's terms, and the contract was never signed. The LOGO negotiation was thus a reminder that queer cultural labor remains exploited because even an outlet innovation such as LOGO relies for much of its programming on festival work made on spec and sold cheap, not on commissioned series or in-house production. *Desert Motel*'s queer relay, then, is not evidence against industrial exploitation and its economic hierarchies, and the LOGO bid reels in the romantic character of relay as a mode of narrating labor. But without losing sight of that condition, relay remains the barely sung space of queer and other forms of outsider cultural production, challenging the commercial repressive hypothesis and inviting solidarity across people, places, and practices. It is neither commercial core nor sexual-political and aesthetic edge but, instead, the traversal of both and the ground of new times.

6

Plausible Optimism

Outside the Complaint

In a universe structured in hierarchy and represented through narratives of recovery and enfranchisement, what is the place of fantasy, and which fantasies do we trust? Those questions may seem suspect, coming from a critic, since critique leads us away from fantasy (as wishful thinking or flights of fancy) to attach futures to the long labor of ideological exposure and justice. A less romantic version of the question, one that respects a critic's conventional expertise, might ask about culture's role in making future worlds, including a world of queer solidarity across class lines.

But something is lost as soon as I think about the question that way. There is lightness in flight and wish, an antiprogrammatic disposition and an energy worth holding onto—culture not only as form but as a range of feelings that exceeds the distrust typically assigned to critique. If religious fantasies of deliverance (or liberation theology, protest rock, science fiction, or sexual scene-making) tell us anything, it is that fantasy gives futures feeling and form in the present, making it possible to imagine alternatives and to see what is already sustaining. It makes thought about futures more open—less driven or tethering or like hedging a bet than a real-time form of creativity. And as *Me and You and Everyone We Know* (chapter 3) pictures it, heartening fantasy needn't be an image of ease or wealth so much as one of regard—of observation, humor, and trust. In the end, it is the text that fantasizes and the critic who reads. But in reading, the critic gives over a piece of her absorption to feeling and imagination.

This chapter thus reads with and against two films from the contemporary canon of queer cinema for such workable fantasies, in the spirit of extracting a feeling of solidarity from queer-class trauma and hierarchy. The films are *Brokeback Mountain* (2005) and *By Hook or By Crook* (2001), the first an indie blockbuster by the standards of the second.[1] *By Hook* is Silas "Flipper" Howard and Harry Dodge's nearly-no-budget, San Francisco, urban trans buddy heist movie, suffused with the histories of feeling such an inventory connotes, explicit in its homage to *Midnight Cowboy* (1969), and yet with world-making energy neither captured nor released by its generic and canonical referents. The relationship form that interests me most in this comparison is not romance or sex (though both have a role), but queer friendship, and the critic who moves me to think in these terms is Lauren Berlant.

In *The Female Complaint* (2008), Berlant offers vital resources for thinking about the relationship of feeling and future, though hers is a study of feeling and past. Berlant gives form to what she calls the "complaint genre" in women's popular writing (and later film adaptations), arguing that the genre took root in the 1830s and persists in the present, even in such monumental feminist texts as Carolyn Kay Steedman's *Landscape for a Good Woman* (1986). The female-complaint genre repeats a story of women's disappointment and suffering in intimate and public life, usually at the hands of men. In complaint narratives, women repeatedly make bad attachments—mostly (though not only) to men—not because they are gluttons for punishment but because in the practice and promise of attachment lies affective and thus real life, however chronically unrealized the promise may be. The complaint story and the modern culture that so reliably reproduces it are thus marked by serial bargaining with social arrangements likely to lead to women's disappointment: patriarchy, heteronormative love, political alienation, and a life of emotional exposure and nonreciprocity.

Berlant (2008) does not identify the female complaint to expose women's neurosis and its cultural expression, but to accomplish something more consciously political: to recognize acts of supremacy in white, bourgeois women's psychic appropriation of the pain of racial and economic others, and also to recognize in the history of women's narratives of bad attachment the value and political potential of publicness. The complaint narrative, Berlant argues, signifies desire for the social. Women's intimate public is not political per se, if by "political" we mean structural maneuvering for resource control or contest in the electoral arena. It is instead *juxtapolitical* (8): it runs alongside the political as a sensibility and a narrative of need that distrusts official politics as a source of fulfillment. Indeed, women's intimate public distances itself from politics as a domain of antagonism and loss, in favor of the public life of feeling as a place not of thriving but of stop-loss. It is not a revolutionary story about changing the world but about surviving it, of not being defeated. The female complaint is, in other words, the story produced over and over again against the threat of the attrition of life in modern capital. In its misrecognition of others' suffering, it is also a part of the damage capital does.

In theorizing the female complaint and its social percussiveness, Berlant (2008) illuminates the conditions of culture and politics in modern America. Women's intimate public is cultivated, she argues, against the incoherence of political subjectivity and the contradictions endemic to belonging to a mass public, where the feeling of belonging itself—however abstracted, fantasized, and rooted in too-small pleasures—is as much as one can organize one's self to want. With Berlant (1997), I would add that political publics themselves bear the imprint of the complaint genre, where official and counterhegemonic politics are animated by desire, attachment, and affirmation as often as by recognition, redistribution, or a fuller enfranchisement (even where the language of justice is in play). These are not simple oppositions, however, and part of the force of Berlant's analysis lies in disentangling the "jumbles" and continuities among politics, sentiment, and bargaining (Berlant 2008, 22), where other authors demand opposition between what can be counted as politics and what must, instead, be described (and demoted) as something else. We witness such assertions of distinction and value in the opposition of redistribution and recognition (terms, I argued in chapter 4, that I would rather pair than separate), in the distinction between critique and emotion, overthrow and subversion, and, as a superordinate antagonism, between social transformation and survival. For many authors in cultural studies, there is no significant politics in survival and its everyday gestures; for others, including me, there is no politics without them.

Berlant's analysis in *The Female Complaint* contends with the historical record of sentimental fantasy by engaging it deeply, opening it up, aerating it, deconstructing its regressions and drawing from the persistence of dissatisfaction it narrates an escape route in another direction, away from the "closed shop of sentimental fantasy" (2008, 31). "The unfinished business of sentimentality," Berlant writes, "mostly profits people other than the ones it solicits to do more business. But it also teaches that endings can be made into openings" (ibid.). Such openings are not made easily, however; nor are they readily sustained by commercial narratives of individual (but universalized) triumph—the sentimental expression of transformation. Still, Berlant finds places to go. Having devoted a chapter to Edna Ferber's and Jerome Kern's novel and musical versions of *Show Boat* (1936) as critical examples of the female complaint genre, in her closing chapter captivatingly titled "Overture/Aperture," Berlant looks beyond the female complaint to an amalgamation of avant-garde form and popular feeling in Rick Schmidt's *Showboat 1988: The Remake* (1977).

As Berlant (2008) acknowledges, the original *Show Boat* is an unlikely target for "reviving optimism" about dismantling white supremacy and its liberalism. "But," she writes,

> Schmidt's return to *Show Boat* takes up the classic narrative's reparative
> motive to propel ordinary people to assume the being-such of the iconic

and the important. It brackets the race and sexual politics we have examined, foregrounding class struggle at the heart of mass fantasy. Ed, the protagonist, opines, "I want a film that comes out of America; a film America gives to itself instead of buying it prefab from Hollywood; I want to give the means of production, the production of images, back to the people." He thinks that *Show Boat* is the great vehicle for this return of the means of image production because, after all, "the greatest song in the American musical culture is sung by a stevedore" (Paul Robeson as "Jo" singing "Ol' Man River"). (275–76)

In Schmidt's work, Berlant finds an opening, a new fantasy to return to in a broad gesture of cultural refashioning.

Showboat 1988 stages auditions for a "gonzo remake" (Berlant 2008, 274) overseen by Ed, an aging librarian diagnosed with terminal cancer and a self-appointed impresario who wishes for "'a sidewalk *Show Boat*' in which any nobody could become that thing, a somebody-citizen who takes up public space and has a star-sized impact, for a moment" (276). Audition hopefuls include a punk performer of "Ol' Man River" enraged by structural suffering and corporate homogenization; lesbians in shared pants singing vaudeville; and a run of tap-dancers, among them a man in a turtle suit and a woman in a nun's habit who dances with her dog and strips while she taps. The film intercuts footage of actual auditions for an intended *Show Boat* remake that never came to be and dazzling images of 1970s black gay disco icon Sylvester, who sings *Can't Help Lovin' Dat Man* with the lyrics blocked on the track in response to "MGM's restrictions on Schmidt's use of the libretto" (277). Throughout *Showboat 1988*, a comical honking noise replaces fragments from the original lyrics, whose occurrence in the film MGM considered copyright infringement.

I read Berlant's description of *Showboat 1988: The Remake* in giddy and chastened surprise that such a work has existed for more than thirty years. I was anxious to know where, in its gestures, Berlant would locate sympathy and alterity to the female complaint and the limits of its fantasy. In her aperture at the close of *The Female Complaint,* she reveals the power of her critique by imagining—and finding—the complaint's outside in *Showboat 1988*'s vibrant gestures of reimagining, gestures that "reanimate" rather than trash "the sentimental tradition because its death or attrition would be a tragic blow to the collective life drive" (276).

In Berlant's reading, Schmidt's film embodies the political potential of form, in contrast to familiar claims about the value of historicism over (mere) formalism. Form, writes Berlant, is not simply a window on the ideological world and thus a second-string instantiation of the real, but a distillation and provocation of affect, in an analysis in which affect is an essential resource for "living otherwise" (265). The aspiration to normativity that female-complaint texts offer and extract from their beholders cannot simply be described as a disciplinary regime or ideological function. It is also a feeling, held by social actors who wish "an unshearable suturing to their social world" (266). Their wish is *summonsed* by conventional gestures and objects, but it does not inhere in them. What if that feeling were possible in relation to something else? And what kinds of something else do formal shifts make viscerally apprehensible? Critical change happens in the direction of the "something else," not by reducing feeling or diminishing the sociable aspiration to connect. What else might we connect to?

Change, in other words, is in the new form and object of attachment and not, as so many ideology critics and aesthetes argue, in contempt for the affective register of sentimentality. This is why *Showboat 1988*'s "reanimation" of the sentimental tradition is a part of and not apart from its critical project: through formal gestures, it sutures longing for inclusion to a new cast of characters and to new openings, not to romantic wish fulfillment or liberal fantasies of integration. "An opening," Berlant writes, "is not phrased in the genre of a full-bodied promise of a better future, but appears in any potentially transformative scene to which one can return" (272). To change, we need new places, images, and possibilities to come back to. Longing articulated to form thus "provides a sense of the better worldness that would exist if only real life would step up to the plate. Affect is formalism *avant la lettre*" (268). "This is the political," Berlant writes, "not politics: this is affect production, not management" (277).

"Political, not politics" distills for me the beautiful, energetic genie out of the bottle of criticism that is Berlant's work in *The Female Complaint*, itself a new precedent, part of a welcome new accretion against the lead weight of conventional criticism and generic theorizing about politics and culture, and a critical goldmine for animating fantasies of queer solidarity. Indeed, reading *The Female Complaint* provokes in me the feeling of buoyant unmooring—of detachment and release—I imagine in watching *Showboat 1988: The Remake*, which I haven't seen. I say that with conviction, however, because Berlant's gestures enable me to articulate the politics of form and affect in work I *have* seen and thus to argue for the dramatically different political possibilities enabled by recent queer class texts. In the spirit of still grander political possibility, I would add that Berlant's analysis of form in cinematic genre goes a long way toward opening up genre, affect and futurity in everyday life. *The Female Complaint*, in other words, addresses melodramatic novels and films, but it also speaks to and about the female complainers I have known and been. I would equally like my critique to address the queer class canon and its political possibilities, but also critics and theirs and, most ambitiously, to address future queer class living that I and others might do.

I like *Brokeback Mountain*. As a relay writer committed to the multivocality of cultural forms, I am not here to disparage its grandeur. But as important a film as I consider it to be, worth mining beyond my defensive reading of heterosexual anxiety in its marketing and publicity, I fear that it cuts political culture off at the impasse of disappointment, victimization, and repetition, not unlike the female complaint Berlant describes. In its text and the story of its production, *By Hook or By Crook*, in contrast, offers openings, new precedents, reparative possibilities. These are the resources I want to explore, accrete, return to—the ones with which I want to close *Love and Money*.

By Hook or By Crook (2001)

By Hook or By Crook is about Shy (Howard), Valentine (Dodge), and Billie (Stanya Kahn), three vulnerable and wildly creative characters, irresistible in their psychic and aesthetic potency and their collective gift for friendship, a gift both intuitive and hard-won. Shy grew up in small-town Kansas, the site of his favorite memory—decked out in Superman costume, diving from the porch steps into his father's arms—rendered early in the film in grainy Super 8 and recurring at key moments later on. In Shy's present life as a young adult, the image signifies both loss and relief. His father has died (his mother left after he was born) and their modest house is about to be repossessed by the bank. That's the loss. For the audience, though, there is relief in knowing that Shy has been loved. It isn't clear that's enough to sustain him (we are not loved once, then done), but, with his tender butch swagger, his muscle, angularity, and resourcefulness, he has something to go on, some feeling, some memory worth returning to. Possessed by a youthful ambition to go to the city and learn to rob stores (to steal retail capital, not customers' money, as reported on a recent television news item), he puts on a natty used suit and his dad's old brogues, sets fire to the house he can no longer occupy, and sets out for San Francisco.

It's a rough ride—not enough food, not enough sleep, little reason to believe his butch body will be safe despite the threadbare suit that styles and shields him. But so go all transitions for Shy: they are not brazen leaps of faith to the other side, but rocky, hard-scrabble gestures in time and space. Maybe things will get better in the city's bright light, maybe they won't. "Are you a boy or a girl?" some children ask Shy as he awakes on a city stoop, hugging his briefcase. "Both," he says.

Homeless at night, Shy encounters Valentine in an empty lot at a chain-link fence near the waterfront, being beaten up by a man who is young but still older, taller, blonder, and better-dressed than Val. Shy recognizes a john attack on a street kid and comes to Val's rescue, kicking his attacker in the crotch and hustling Val out. Val's appreciation surfaces quickly, a grateful, believing smile breaking through his bloodied face. Val isn't your average young person; too openhearted, too poetic in his language, too here-and-now while embodying some other time and place, a wish, maybe, a freaky, wrenching buoyancy at odds with trauma and bleak circumstance.

Shy and Val go for coffee and crullers as Val's treat, with a stop at the diner pay phone for Val to check the directory, dial a number, and ask the person at the other end if she'd had a baby on May 31, 1966. No. He is an adoptee, born a girl, looking for his birth mother. Shy watches Val scrape hardened sugar from the dented cap of the shaker with a table knife and repeat his artful but illegible hand gestures. "Are you okay?" he asks him. "Yeah, I'm fine." Val's response doesn't explain anything, but it does tell Shy what he needs to know—that Val is familiar to himself. They leave the diner for a bar. "Thanks for the donuts man," says Shy. "Ah, no problem; come on, I'll buy you a drink, I got sixty-three bucks left."

Shy and Val arrive at the famed Lexington Club in San Francisco's Mission district, home for years to gender queer young people and older forebearers. Val steps onto the dance floor and Shy steals his wallet. "Sometimes," Shy says in voiceover, "you do the wrong thing for the right reason. I'm afraid this was one of those times." It is a reddish night, save for the fluorescence of the bodega where Shy buys a plastic pistol. Val heads home, feeding a wiry little dog behind a neighborhood fence on his way. "You're beautiful, Max," he tells the dog, "I'll come back again, okay?"

Home, for Val, is with Billie, a leggy, edgy, warmhearted fem with cascading hair, platform shoes, vintage nylon print dresses, a wacky demeanor off the map of convention, and a cooing affection for Val. We learn later that Billie, like many fem characters, is also protective and fierce, a skilled city dweller with fewer illusions than those suggested by the small, funky artscapes of her kitchen and attic bedroom.

The house itself is a little hard to fathom, a room, really, fragmented by low-budget filmmaking in which interior scenes are lit and shot quickly and cover only so much space. The kitchen lightbulbs are red and the macaroni and cheese decorated with multicolored chocolate sprinkles, an unlikely combination save as modest, childhood comfort foods. There is no doorbell.

Shy and Valentine at Billie's.

Billie awakes, *By Hook or By Crook* © 2001 Steakhaus Productions and NGB Inc.

A flimsy glass pane in the front door makes it easy to talk through, but instead Billie has rigged that other childhood staple: two cans, one inside and one out, connected by string. Even when Billie and Val can see through the window who is at the front door, Val commands the caller to "use the cans!" The house is safe space in a universe of aggression, shielded inside by love, sex, food, and acceptance, and outside by a mission-control network of low-tech gimmicks and overgrown vines. It is a tree house or secret fort, but still the place of real life carved out of the uninhabitable expense of San Francisco. Val and Billie's lovemaking in the red-lit kitchen is deep and tender, seated in a chair, Billie facing Val and straddling his lap, rising and lowering in a slow grind that roots them in the present. For Val, it is a soft landing after a hard night, feathered again by Shy's arrival with the stolen wallet. "You forgot this at the bar," he tells Val. "I had to borrow some money from you, but I'll pay you back this afternoon."

Shy, Val, and Billie are a sweet, raggedy crew of accomplices in small-time crime. Shy and Val grift in a tool warehouse, convincing a clerk that the boxed-up saw they just lifted off the shelf was in fact bought earlier but is the wrong kind and needs to be returned for a refund or they'll be reprimanded by their construction boss. They practice pulling their plastic guns in the mirror, but the only bodega holdup Shy attempts is foiled by an irate woman clerk who gives Shy a you've-got-to-be-kidding stare then slaps him, and he retreats. It is a protective blow to his fragile masculinity; he is a survivalist who discovers he can't harden after all, and there will be grace for him in that.

As would-be felons, the three succeed most dramatically in holding up a vending machine, dousing the change slot with Super Squirters to short its electronic safe and watching the jackpot of quarters spit and flow. It isn't a livelihood, but it's a small success and a turnaround in their makeshift life. As friends, their biggest success comes when Shy and Billie take Val out of the state hospital to which he is committed after a neighbor (owner of the dog Max) reports their hot-wire car theft to the police. Billie is less wacky now than mortally fearful. "He has priors," she tells Shy, a newcomer—no priors—to the urban police department released after his interrogation. After several days, Shy arrives at the hospital, rouses Val (groggy with Thorazine), and takes him out of the ranging, understaffed facility.

During Val's hospitalization, Shy called every number under Val's birth mother's name in the Bay Area phone books. He found her. Val remains deeply anxious that she won't like him—"I mean, look at me!"—but the three head to a bleak ward of bungalows on the city's outskirts and take Max with them. We don't know the upshot of the reunion, because the film closes on a grainy freeze frame of this motley, good-faith, chosen threesome (plus Max)—out of the car, uncertain what they'll find, transformed by friendship. It is a happy moment, survival moving toward something less harsh, not the stuck or near-end-point of harshness itself.

By Hook or By Crook was shot by Ann T. Rosetti, best known for her lyrical, transporting, black-and-white images and cadences in *Go Fish* (1994). Directed by Rose Troche, *Go Fish* was a breakthrough, a feature-length lesbian romantic comedy both classical and anticanonical in its scene and evocations. In the 1990s, it too made vibrant use of communal, no-budget production through poetic discontinuities, aestheticized grain, newcomer faces, creative archness, and a lightness of heart alongside queer rage (Henderson 1999). As was so often true in the early days of "new queer cinema," *Go Fish* was produced in stops and starts, its production team gathering resources, shooting a little, taking the unfinished project on the queer festival circuit, and slowly priming an audience for the film's theatrical release in 1994, distributed by Samuel Goldwyn. It was a relay project par excellence, if with different scope and transit points than *Desert Motel*.

The look and the making of *By Hook or By Crook* reveal some of the cultural traces and visual markers of *Go Fish*, this time as a communally produced breakout feature about trans and gender queer characters, beloved by its festival, theatrical, DVD, and download audiences (Rich 2006b). Like *Go Fish*, *By Hook or By Crook*'s piecemeal fund-raising and rock-bottom production conditions are aesthetically maximized. Shot in color on mini-DV by a creative, accomplished, semiprofessional crew in more than sixty Bay Area locations (a range, Howard and Dodge acknowledge, born of inexperience),[2] the image does not have the rich saturations and textures enabled by film stock, painstaking lighting setups, and more time in fewer locations, but its look and feel are no less affecting for that. The film stands as an alternative more than a challenge to the claim that "feeling costs money." It is an outlaw story rooted in writing and performance by Howard, Dodge, and Kahn, and rendered in a mixed, swirling style of colorful low-contrast, warehouse backdrops, cloistered and underlit interiors, spiky, refracted sunsets into the lens, a discordant, thrashing, and melodic original score, and spectacular, layered expanses of urban rooftops—the sites of toy gun play, tough-guy rehearsal, psychic disclosure, and streaming, poetic talk from Val. As a speaker Val is manic, readable as crazy were Shy and Billie not so openhearted nor so needful themselves of a little tenderness.

By Hook or By Crook is a beautiful film, especially for its affinities among queer scene, queer story, found joy, and pulsing spatiotemporal energy. Its improvisatory feel is both real and make-believe, given three scripts written over two years by Howard and Dodge before they settled on something they wanted to shoot.[3] From 1991 to 2001, Howard was singer and lead guitarist in the queer punk band Tribe 8, and Dodge is a well-known performance artist in San Francisco. Together, they founded and ran Red Dora's Bearded Lady Café and Truckstop, a famed San Francisco performance space in the Mission. Dialogue for Billie was written by actor Stanya Kahn, herself a revered avant-gardiste in off-mainstream Bay Area poetry and performance. Scenes from the film's wrap party, included on the DVD, feature producer Annie Imhoff holding up a digital video cartridge and growling "64 fucking hours of footage." It is a proud, exhausted expression, one I recognize only too well from the close of a long labor of backbreaking love and drama, of shooting in cold, wet exteriors and cramped, hot interiors, of not enough food, almost no pay, and still less sleep for days on end.

Sixty-four hours for a ninety-minute film means a shooting ratio of 40:1 and a monumental task of postproduction shaping. It is the cheaper end of the process, where editors Silas, Dodge, and five colleagues sequestered themselves with computers in a nonspecialized room (in an apartment block that burned down the night they locked picture) to build story, character, rhythm, momentum, and counterpoint from a huge archive of digital material. The more expensive option is to shoot and process film stock; in independent production, the ratio stands to be much lower due to cost—consider Johnson's 10:1 on *Desert Motel*—but the processing, preproduction, and well-populated shooting expenses for polished production values are, minute for minute, much higher.

Two years of script writing and sixty-four hours of digital video: not expressions of youthful stamina and reckless good luck but a long process structured in gangliness and emerging from a deep network of creative contributors, however informal the connections were or how coolly outside official culture in Northern California. Do-or-die production practices *are* visible in the image (and narrated in publicity with gallows energy), but at the service of a gentle sense in the film itself of Shy and Val coming to love each other, and of Shy, Val, and Billie making deep and hand-crafted solidarities from threadbare resources. From the film itself and the story of its production, we glean pieces of a new fantasy of friendship and survival.

By Hook or By Crook does not leave out the deprivation in Shy's, Valentine's, or Billie's lives. They do not have what they need. They are not well nourished on crullers and macaroni with sprinkles. Their lives are by definition insecure, made so by a common condition of border living between youth and adulthood, with few to no resources coming to them from an older generation. As loving as Shy's father was, he didn't own his house and thus it provided no coverage for Shy when his father died. And as brightly as Shy and Valentine inhabit their variant genders, they are targets, a condition made clear at their arrest and at their first encounter, as Val was beaten, and as their dialogue about Val's childhood expresses. He was institutionalized, he tells Shy, at thirteen, in "a nice place in the country, where all I had to do is learn how normal people act . . . I'd only wear boys' clothes." "Just for that?" Shy responds, countering the historic register of pathology with matter-of-fact surprise and acceptance. As butches who vary their pronouns by context (Val is "she," for example, when Shy is conning the tool warehouse clerk), they have adjusted and are most at ease in environments, like the Lex, equally adjusted or at least hospitable. Police interrogations and hospitals aren't among them; there Val's poetry, gender, poverty, and street ways mark him for heightened surveillance and control.

Nor are Shy, Valentine, and Billie cut out for conventional employment; they are young, and it isn't clear they've been to school. As characters, they inhabit an economic gray zone of theft and found resources, lightened by genre fantasies of social accountability. *By Hook or By Crook* is a heist film, but not everyone's money is fair game and the trio's greatest take comes from a vending machine off-shift. Shy tells Val that he is "tired of being poor."

It is also hard to witness Shy's, Val's, and Billie's exhaustion. They live frenetically, signaled by Val's speech but also by a restless camera, an often thrashing score, and by constant movement from one place to another—planning, scheming, unable to stay for long (in Shy's case, in a single-room occupancy hotel), but still trying to clean up and make things homey. Motion in the film signifies survival as much as youth, energy, or erotic intensity. *By Hook or By Crook* is full of conversation and heart-to-heart exposition between Val and Shy, but there isn't a lot of rest.

Were *By Hook or By Crook* a documentary, it would bear continuities with other documentary accounts of young people, especially young queers, abandoned by adult guidance and resources. This is not to suggest that things would be fine if only parents were around. For Shy, they would be a lot better, but young queers like Val leave home in disproportionate numbers to escape abuses there. The adult world of accumulation, greed, and social control represses where it might assist, were it to live up to its own rhetoric of opportunity and family value.

Shy and Val are not quite like Rosetta and Igor, the child leads, respectively, of the Dardenne brothers' films *Rosetta* (1999) and *La Promesse* (1996), who, in a trick of utopian near-normativity, aspire to become average workers at an unlivable wage in the aboveground economy of new Europe (Berlant 2007). But Shy and Val share something with Rosetta and Igor, as poor, dispossessed young people in a volatile world of work and exploitation, set, in Shy and Val's case, in a criminally expensive urban scene in San Francisco, famed for its alternative enclaves but successful at turning even them into the amenities of privilege.

Still, it is helpful to consider Shy, Val, Igor, and Rosetta together, since the comparison reveals quite different character frameworks in response to poverty and exploitation. None responds to deprivation amid wealth with rage. *By Hook or By Crook*, instead, offers friendship and hope, where the new realism of *Rosetta* and *La Promesse* is less hopeful (though not enraged), more observational about the social fraying it narrates and the costs to young characters of bargaining in a world where they can't win even the limited resources they wish for: reliable attachment and steady, underpaid work (Berlant 2007). For Igor, though, there is change: he leaves his cruel and exploitative father in favor of a brusque and uncertain new friendship with an African immigrant woman, whose husband's worksite death Igor's father has made Igor conceal. As Igor leaves, despite his father's promise that he'll do right by him after all, we, the audience, pray that Igor sees through his father's manipulations and keeps going. A future without his father is uncertain; a future with him will be dehumanizing, more of the same.

The contrast between the Dardennes' approach and Howard and Dodge's is instructive, since a familiar way to make sense of it is through an appeal to U.S. and European cinematic tradition, the former notoriously optimistic, its optimism rooted in the singular protagonist; the latter famously bleak, its bleakness rooted in images of structural oppression. Such a comparison frames the optimism of *By Hook or By Crook* as a wish—appealing but insubstantial by the standards of social change. But that very framing provokes me to take an alternate analytic route through a more precise question of affect—can the image and feeling of queer, working-class hope be politically substantial?—and through another comparison, this one with a U.S. melodrama par excellence of queer class relations, *Brokeback Mountain*. *Brokeback* can stand as an illuminating third case, whose insertion interrupts the worn opposition between optimism and bleakness and its cultural-political homology in self- vs. social determination (self-reliance is optimistic, social dependency and determination are bleak). Through form and genre, *Rosetta* and *La Promesse* feel to me politically more solid, more *true* than *By Hook or By Crook* as stories of insecurity and deprivation in neoliberal times. But that is itself a conventional response, one that the new comparison to *Brokeback Mountain* might recalibrate, enabling us to see *By Hook or By Crook*, in its hopefulness, as a politically attuned fantasy of friendship on the social, cultural, and psychic edge.

Inside the Complaint: *Brokeback Mountain* (2005)

Brokeback Mountain is the story of Ennis del Mar (Heath Ledger) and Jack Twist (Jake Gyllenhaal), migrant range and rodeo cowboys looking for work in the Wyoming sheep herd of 1963. Sequestered for a season on Brokeback Mountain, one cowboy setting up camp and the other watching the herd and fending off wolves, Jack and Ennis discover a powerful attraction to each other, articulated through roughhousing, camaraderie, dependency under harsh conditions, and eventually through sex. Jack is expressive and less undone by his feelings than is Ennis, who is closed and fearful but still compelled and thus all the more anxious. At the end of the season, they come down off Brokeback and go their separate ways, Ennis returning to marry Alma Beers (Michele Williams) and have two daughters with her, Jack rejoining the Texas rodeo circuit, where he meets and marries Lureen Newsome (Ann Hathaway), a competitive barrel rider and the daughter of a prosperous farm-equipment dealer. They, too, have a son, though the *longue durée* of family life does little to diminish Jack and Ennis's attraction; for the next twenty years, they orchestrate returns to Brokeback every few months. In one early reunion, when Jack arrives at Ennis and Alma's apartment over a laundromat, Alma catches the two men in a throw-down kiss, backed into the exterior wall of their little building, Ennis's hands forcefully holding Jack's face and torso. Through anger and frustration, she tolerates their affair, but only just, until the marriage finally falls apart and Ennis moves to the edge of town, seasonally employed and living in a bare-bones trailer. Jack's life is plusher and more secure on account of Lureen's family money; though he and Lureen are openly distant from each other, they stay married.

After years of trysts and disappointments, Ennis's most recent postcard to Jack—terse, plain, its handwriting rough, just a few words to ask about the next fishing trip—is returned, stamped *deceased*. Shaken, Ennis calls Lureen and discovers that Jack died in a freak accident, hit in the head at the side of a road by an exploding tire he was trying to fix. Lureen is detached, suspicious of Ennis, and unconvincing; Ennis pictures an assault on Jack as he listens to her, knowing that Jack (unlike Ennis) would take public sexual chances and thus expose himself to thugs. The film doesn't tell us whether we are to receive images of Jack being beaten as truth or as Ennis's imagination, but that doesn't trouble our belief. The murder of gay men is familiar enough, and plausibility slides into resolution.

Lureen tells Ennis that Jack's ashes are with his parents, and how Jack always said that when he died he wanted his ashes taken to Brokeback. "Brokeback Mountain, he said it was his favorite place." Ennis's face begins to break. "Get in touch with his folks, about the ashes," says Lureen. Ennis goes to Lightning Flat, Texas, the parched territory of Jack's family home and his grim Pentecostal upbringing. Jack's father is cold, suspicious, and laconic in his insults and insinuations, but his mother invites Ennis to go upstairs to Jack's old bedroom, "if you want to." There, Ennis finds Jack's boots, jacket, and the shirts each had worn that first season on Brokeback, bloodied by their roughhousing. Ennis is quietly startled by the shirt he thought he had lost, but that Jack had safeguarded all those years. He takes the shirts downstairs, and Jack's mother gives him a plain paper bag to put them in. Jack's father rejects Ennis's offer to take the ashes to Brokeback. "We'll bury him in the family plot," he declares, having already said that Jack thought he was too good for his own family. Ennis returns to his trailer home in Wyoming, toasts his oldest daughter Alma Jr.'s plan to marry, and sustains his memory of Jack with the two shirts hung in his flimsy trailer closet, one inside the other, a Brokeback postcard tacked up near the hook.

Brokeback Mountain is grand, even where the worlds in which it is set are sparse. Streams of sheep are funneled by wooded terrain across blue-gray and green landscapes, under big skies of gold light. Social environments are dressed down to heighten the feel of the interactions taking place; spectacular vocals recorded for the track are sometimes barely used in the background (fragments of Emmylou Harris's "A Love That Will Never Grow Old" are heard on Jack's tinny truck radio, for example), while tonally lush, nondiegetic themes from solo guitar and orchestra connote simplicity and depth. Fidelity to cowboy practice was heightened, the DVD extras tell us, by a cowboy boot camp preceding the long production period in Alberta, Canada, where Ledger and Gyllenhaal learned to wield axes, handle riding gear, and control wriggling, muscular sheep, and where Hathaway learned barrel racing to complement her stunt double for close-ups. "Fidelity" is a key term in the production stories: fidelity to time, place, and character and especially to the emotional tone and "power" of E. Annie Proulx's short story, on which Diana Ossana and Larry McMurtry based their script. Nestled into accounts of production fidelity are cautiously forthright comments, from the actors and from director Ang Lee, about the importance and awkwardness of filming Jack and Ennis's sexual encounters, even as *Brokeback Mountain* itself is promoted as a story about love "as a force of nature."

For all its press, *Brokeback Mountain* is almost never described as a class text—surprising to me, given its reliance on exploited cowboy labor as the scene of queer encounter between Ennis and Jack. I have discovered the occasional expression of relief, for example, on Dave Cullen's *Ultimate Brokeback Guide* on the web (n.d.),[4] that *Brokeback Mountain* offers an image of gay men different from the wealthy urban types on *Will & Grace*, and screenwriter Diana Ossana is quoted in production notes as explaining the story in general class terms:

> Ennis and Jack are very poor country boys. Because of the difficulty of where they've grown up, it's always about survival for them; not just financially, but physically, with the snow and the wind and the rain and the harsh landscape. Brokeback Mountain is very removed from the rest of the

world and the rest of life. It's private up there, there's no intrusion, and they feel comfortable. When they come down off Brokeback and they're back in their small towns, everything closes in on them again.

Ossana's remarks are quoted by Joanne Laurier (2006) in her review of *Brokeback Mountain* on the World Socialist Web Site, and here, not surprisingly, the question of working-class portrayal surfaces in basic, descriptive terms:

> While *Brokeback Mountain* is not without weaknesses—it is relatively predictable and overall lacks complexity—the film is sincere and has an appreciably angry tone. Lee has done a credible job representing working class types and depicting their problems. Ennis's wife Alma (Michelle Williams) is well played. Both Ledger and Gyllenhaal give fine performances, although at times Ledger's emotional inflexibility strains. In his depiction of Ennis's pinched, tightly wound affection for his children, Ledger strikes a realistic note.
>
> A certain richness and multiplicity, however, is never quite attained in the characterizations. Working class life is more imagined from afar, as if through a looking glass, than presented with a deep degree of understanding, and, therefore, dynamism. As commendable as it is that Lee portrays ordinary people with sensitivity, he still falls somewhat short. The question arises: If Ennis is so utterly incapable of emotional articulation, why does Jack fall so hard for him? The years between 1963 and 1983 saw many changes that would inevitably have worked upon the protagonists with consequences not envisioned by the filmmakers.

I don't disagree with Laurier on the question of working-class portrayal: unlike many working-class characters in contemporary U.S. film, we do see Jack, Ennis, and Alma doing difficult and underpaid jobs. Jack and Ennis are at a particular disadvantage as seasonal laborers required to bend grazing laws on behalf of a cruel foreman, who, having surveilled their Brokeback roughhousing at a distance, will not rehire them and threatens them with exposure. "You boys sure found a way to make the time pass up there," he tells Jack. "Twist, you guys wasn't gettin' paid to leave the dogs babysit the sheep while you stem the rose. Now get the hell out of my trailer."

Alma, for her part, is a young, disappointed mother married to a handsome, intense, but uncommunicative and economically stuck husband. He does appear to love his daughters (this is more apparent later on, when Alma Jr. becomes a teenager), but that doesn't stop him from dumping them at Alma's grocery store workplace to topple product displays in the middle of her shift, while he responds with irrepressible excitement to an invitation from Jack (all the while telling Alma he needs to hit the road for work "cause the heifers are calving"). Alma has already witnessed Jack and Ennis's kiss, which makes the real source of his excitement and abandonment especially painful. Alma protests, is unheard, and is left in a state of barely controlled anger and grief to apologize to her shift manager for her daughters' chaotic arrival.

Jack's and Ennis's class locations, while communicated most powerfully by the form of their labor, are also looped into their story of queer attachment through the affect of shame, as is so often the case in popular working-class and queer portrayal in narrative fiction film. One evening, for example, after a bad round of bronco riding, where Jack is thrown early in the ride and is spared a bull charge by a skilled rodeo clown, Jack offers his coworker a drink at the bar. "I'd like to buy Jimbo here a beer," he says, toasting him as "the best damn rodeo clown I've ever worked with." His appreciation is overdrawn, to save face and to cover his tentative cruise on the rodeo bar circuit. But "Jimbo" rejects Jack as a rider, a drinker, a rodeo compatriot, and a potential sexual encounter. "No thanks, cowboy," he tells Jack. "If I let every rodeo hand I'd pulled a bull off buy me liquor I'd've been an alcoholic a long time ago. Pullin' bulls off of you buckaroos is just my job, so save your money for your next entry fee, cowboy."

Laurier's call for deeper working-class portrayals makes sense. But she also asks a question about Jack and Ennis's relationship that expresses a psychic and cultural flatness. She asks: "If Ennis is so utterly incapable of emotional articulation, why does Jack fall so hard for him?" She then goes on to question the kinds of sex-class bargaining both men do, and claims that social changes from 1963 to 1983 would have intervened, inevitably.

All things considered, Laurier's question isn't a bad one: Why *does* Jack fall so hard? Why do *any* of us—people, let alone characters—fall for others who are emotionally unavailable to them? The question is answerable through the lens of bad attachment and the persistence of the complaint narrative, which, in *Brokeback Mountain,* moves to a queer story about male characters attuned to a primarily female (and heterosexual) audience. Cassie (Linda Cardellini)—a waitress with whom Ennis is briefly involved late in the story—sees Ennis in a Greyhound diner when she arrives there with the nice-enough guy she started dating after Ennis disappeared. She turns to Ennis, sitting in a booth, and asks him what happened, why he never answered her calls and letters. "I don't get you Ennis del Mar," she tells him, her face crumbling. "Guess I was no fun anyway," he responds. "Ennis," she says in disbelief, "girls don't fall in love with *fun.*"

Nor do boys, though, in fact, Ennis and Jack had the most fun of their lives—the most physical, verbal, and emotional pleasure—on Brokeback. It is precisely knowing how it can feel to be with Ennis and wishing that it might feel that way more often that keeps Jack (and Cassie) coming back. I had to wonder, then, as I read Laurier's incredulity, whether she had ever found herself in a bad or mixed attachment, and whether she expects stories of bad attachment in film melodrama, by some standards the key to the genre and to many fans' interest. Bad attachments, in Berlant's terms, are those that mainly have the drive of attachment to commend them; they provide something—the promise of connection, the maintenance (if not fulfillment) of that wish for "an unshearable suturing" to a social world (Berlant 2008, 266). But they are, finally, routes to the attrition of life, not to thriving.

People and characters, however, do not choose attachments in a simple way, as if from a menu of conscious possibility, nor are bad attachments only bad, nor do we always abandon those we may recognize as diminishing. Rosetta does not leave her exploitative, dishonest mother, nor—at the outset (until he finds the possibility of another family, however unlikely)—does Igor leave his violent father. Even as both recognize their parents' failures and inverted dependencies, they stay—they are children—and hope for transformation, eking warmth out of their situation one quiet prayer in bed or one fleeting and unstable friendship at a time.

Nor does Jack leave Ennis, or Ennis, Jack. Ennis scrapes by on seasonal labor, trying to meet child-support payments (where once he'd "have just quit") and reminding Jack that he's forgotten what it's like to be broke all the time. It is a stiff and familiar bargain, stuck between an economic rock and a romantic hard place. Jack, for his part, tolerates the abuse and contempt of his father-in-law (with one triumphant moment of refusal at Thanksgiving, where he asserts his rightful, because patriarchal, place at the head of the table—and the family—over his father-in-law *and* his wife). Ennis is correct: Jack *has* forgotten what it's like to be broke all the time. His image of the future is entrepreneurial—a small sheep farm where they'll be left alone—but he can't leave Lureen without Ennis and so he stays—tolerating, cruising, bargaining, finally dying by means that heighten rather than diminish Lureen's suspicion and disappointment as his wife.

Alma, for her part, leaves Ennis because her girls are at risk, because the image of Jack and Ennis's kiss at the house makes the limits of Jack's love for her bracingly clear, and because she wishes for a marriage that will enable some measure of upward mobility, a marriage she indeed finds. But she never quite abandons her anger or disappointment and thus her attachment to Ennis, who, compared to her respectable but anodyne new husband, remains

Jack's frustration, last trip to Brokeback.

Ennis crumbles after fighting with Jack, *Brokeback Mountain* © 2005 Focus Features LLC.

the more attractive if impossible target of her love. Cassie, meanwhile, has no choice in her separation from Ennis; he passively disappears from her life and she remains drawn by his fleeting presence and her own grief and incomprehension.

What is at stake in *Brokeback Mountain*'s narrative of attachment that can be understood in queer class terms? The commercial viability and success of the film are not queerly specified: "Love is a Force of Nature" might serve as a tag line for any number of romantic melodramas, even as it liberally argues that gay love is born, not made. There is, though, the *frisson* and commercial attraction of this particular genre variant, making sexually explicit what other cowboy movies have sustained as "merely" homosocial, and thus arguing for sexual queerness in the roots of cowboy culture, the American West, and Western genres (Rich 2005). All things considered, that is no small feat. Beyond the limits of Ennis and Jack's relationship, moreover, *Brokeback Mountain* signifies both its characters' and the culture's attachment to romantic love as the measure of human capacity and even as the solution to class stuckness—through transcendence, not pooled resources. It is a queer articulation of an endlessly topped-off stream of cultural returns to the drama of love's unfulfilled promise.

This form of repetition is, arguably, itself a bad or at least costly attachment: not because romantic love is insufficient as a measure of human capacity after all (it is, but that doesn't change its hold as fantasy or form), but because such a cultural return—repeatedly dressed in grandeur, money, celebrity, the deep imprint of prestige cinema, the deep sincerity of those involved in the making of the film, and the deep gratitude of many who saw it and recognized pieces of their story or at least *how their story feels*—offers us nowhere else to go, no new attachments, no new pairings of affect and social form. Some of us are grateful for queer recognition through the molten but still leaden glow of hardship romance, as the dominant popular account of love and as melodrama's anchor for ideological narratives of bad attachment.[5] In its genre bravery, then, *Brokeback Mountain* re-welcomes queer history to an old message less brave than perversely consoling: we love us when we're suffering. It is a conclusion that makes Laurier's skeptical question—why *does* Jack fall so hard?—politically rich, richer than Laurier herself conveys.

Plausible Optimism

Consider such a conclusion against the ending of *By Hook or By Crook*: we love us at our most alive and our most solidary, our most transformed by friendship and the contingent emergence of trust amid social misrecognition and deprivation. Trust is not a bourgeois skill in *By Hook*, neither a luxury nor the entitlement of those whose securities make it easy to come by. We love us at our most viscerally and aesthetically buoyant—our movement quirky, energetic, and a little all over the place in contrast to *Brokeback*'s solemn march toward the predictability of death. We love our queer scenes and their communal productions and performances. "We've always hoped," said Howard in a publicity interview, "[that] this project would reflect the creativity and actual valor of the community of people we came from. And I think

Val (with dog Max), Billie, and Shy on their way to meet Val's birth mother.

Closing freeze frame, *By Hook or By Crook* © 2001 Steakhaus Productions and NGB, Inc.

it does. From the get-go this movie had its roots in our extended family of weirdos in San Francisco" (quoted in Halberstam 2005, 94).

We love the possibility those scenes offer of being somebody but not standing for everybody (Berlant 2008, 277), of remaking social space one tree fort of a crummy rental at a time. There is room in this story of transformative friendship for romantic love and familial reconnection—the film ends, recall, with Billie, Shy, and dog Max taking Val to see his birth mother. Neither romance nor family is vanquished as the condition of radical difference, though they are remixed as two forms of love among others. It is also impossible to predict beyond the film's close how Val's encounter will go, save that he will not be on his own. In its grainy group freeze frame, the film signals that uncertainty and the importance of hard-won companionship in surviving it.

What difference might it have made had Jack and Ennis changed through friendship and class recognition, not romantic seclusion? That, too, is a familiar enough story of the 1960s and 1970s—sexual friendships between men sustained amid functional, heterosexual marriages and repression. They are socially imperfect relationships by the standards of honesty and freedom, but, more to my point, they lower, not raise, melodramatic value in narratives of doomed attachment. Once reserved for cross-class and interracial loves, such stories are now A-listed and green-lighted for queer ones, for queer attachments that are still, tellingly, set *within* class and racial categories. Here *Brokeback Mountain* shares class and racial foreclosure with *Boys Don't Cry* and with the relationships among leads in *By Hook or by Crook*.

I am not antiromantic. Indeed it is my romance with romance that compels me to consider why such a devastating narrative as *Brokeback Mountain* holds so much apparent cultural promise. There are practical reasons that explain it, in a relay universe where a producer like James Schamus has moved from the edges of the new queer cinema to the edges of industrial clout, bringing big budgets to gay stories, if not without effort, turmoil, and delay (Rich 2007). But there are questions of fantasy and resonance, too, and an opportunity for détente, not repulsion, between romance and a more broadly conceived solidarity, including in queer class terms. If films and other popular narratives recognize and enfranchise our feelings, distill our wishes and impulses and attach them to worlds and outcomes, why not link a desire for connection to a world of solidarities and specificities rather than to melodramas of generalized disappointment? This is not a bid to be happy, feel forward, or ransom the present to the future, none of which *By Hook or By Crook* signals.[6] Nor is it a utopian wish. It is an appeal to what I am calling *plausible optimism* as a renewed fantasy of queer possibility, a fantasy rooted not in some reductive idea about a queer gift for friendship but in the historic practice of friendship in modern queer life.

"Plausible optimism" extracts a quality of possibility from the psychosocial dialectic that Berlant (2006, 21) crystallized as *cruel optimism*:

"Cruel optimism" names a relation of attachment to compromised conditions of possibility. What is cruel about these attachments, and not merely inconvenient or tragic, is that the subjects who have *x* in their lives might not well endure the loss of their object or scene of desire, even though its presence threatens their well-being, because whatever the *content* of the attachment, the continuity of the form of it provides something of the continuity of the subject's sense of what it means to keep on living on and to look forward to being in the world.

We need even our bad objects—or feel we do—because without them as signs of attachment, we cannot recognize ourselves or imagine how to survive.

Berlant (2006) theorizes cruel optimism through three literary texts—an untitled poem by John Ashbery, "Exchange Value," a short story by Charles Johnson, and Geoff Ryman's novel *Was*. She looks to characters' responses to small and big changes and the impasses they provoke, "three episodes of the suspension of the reproduction of habituated or normative life" (23). Sometimes the changes are for the better, or so they seem, but that doesn't make them changes characters can use. In "Exchange Value" (Johnson 1994), for example, Cooter and Loftis are African American brothers living hand to mouth on Chicago's South Side. They enter the home of their deceased neighbor Miss Bailey and are shocked to discover, contrary to their own lives and their presumption about hers, that she possessed great wealth, inherited from her employer. They take the things and the cash, revel in them, catalogue them, but have no way of using them to improve their circumstance. Loftis's response, like Miss Bailey's, is to hoard, since to buy something is the loss of power to buy something else, to become "panicky about depletion, and locked now in the past because every purchase, you know, has to be a poor buy: a loss of life" (37–38).[7] Unlike Loftis, brother Cooter refuses his parents' commitment to labor and deprivation in the interest of a better future. They died in middle age of overwork and obesity, and thus it was a future they never lived long enough to enjoy. Rejecting such a diminished mode of living, Cooter takes Miss Bailey's cash to the foreign land of downtown Chicago with the intent of living large, of seeing what living large feels like. But rather than transcendence, he discovers there that he is ill-equipped to use the money to make his life better:

> He doesn't have a clue how to spend the money happily and realizes sickeningly that money cannot make you feel like you belong if you do not already feel that way. He buys ugly, badly made, expensive clothes. He eats meat till he gets sick. He takes cabs everywhere. When he gets home, his brother's gone psychotic. Loftis has built an elaborate trap, a vault to protect the money. He yells at Cooter for spending, because the only power is in hoarding (Berlant 2006, 30).

Work to the bone or hoard; both are cruel in form, in the ruin they bring about, and in the permanent withholding of the reward promised to poor people in exchange for their embodied labor. But in Johnson's story, the interruption of either means the coming of death, because the conditions that make working and hoarding the means to life continue to exert their pressure, even with the onslaught of cash. "Cooter sees that there is no way out now, no living as if not in a relation to death, which is figured in all of the potential loss that precedes it" (Berlant 2006, 31). Cash and things bring madness, not relief, a ruinous loss of a subjectivity formed in deprivation that cannot be re-formed in provision.

What, then, do we need to re-form ourselves, to detach from bad objects like overwork, hoarding, or doomed romance, when all bring few pleasures and cultivate attrition while promising reward? A culture of capital accumulation offers little to go on, save that people get rich or die trying, and indeed some do get rich and less wealthy others claim the rewards of privilege in exchange for our labor. But not most, and even for privileged subjects (those in the historical narratives of *The Female Complaint*, for example, or employed critics such as myself), detachment remains a threat when the conditions of life as they know it demand the presence of familiar bad objects—people, practices, forms of relating—in order to exist into the future. In such an equation, privilege also comes to mean a relative abundance of good attachments and the relative confidence, born of footing and other securities, to see the bad ones and let them go. In queer life, privilege in that form is elusive, too.

Still, Berlant finds an expression of such footing and acceptance in Ashbery's untitled poem, a work she describes as a "send-up of suburban monotony" (Berlant 2006, 25), of living the "decaffeinated good life."[8] But it is a send-up suspended by a humane impasse and its penetration:

> . . . He came up to me.
> It was all as it had been,
> except for the weight of the present,
> that scuttled the pact we made with heaven.
> In truth there was no cause for rejoicing,
> nor need to turn around, either.
> We were lost just by standing,
> listening to the hum of the wires overhead.

That scuttled the pact, Berlant reads, not to be gay. One character regards the other, lost there, but not stricken. Says Berlant of the poem's narrator:

I am not the subject of a hymn but of a hum, the thing that resonates around me, which might be heaven or bees or desire or electric wires, but whatever it is it involves being in proximity to someone and in becoming lost there, in a hum not where "we" stood but all around, not in the mapped space of drives and driving, but a space that is lost. Queerness substitutes itself for religious affect's space of reverence: in the end, life is at the best imaginable of impasses. What intersubjectivity there is has no content but is made in the simultaneity of listening. . . . Life has been seized, as Badiou would say, by an event that demands fidelity. (25)

It is a glorious reading, the delicate, critical exposure of a quality of feeling in Ashbery's poem, that instant of queer attraction and suspension that might undo people, but doesn't.

As accountable to Marx as she is to Badiou, however, Berlant reads Ashbery's rendering of fidelity to the impasse—the change in conditions of attachment—through the lens of political economy. *For whom*, she asks, does this impasse open things up, rather than destabilizing and exploding its subjects, as the discovery of Miss Bailey's cash drives Loftis into psychosis? Who speaks this poem? "A confident person," someone with "the chops for improvising unknowing while others run out of breath, not humming but hoarding . . ." (26–27): "He finds possibility in a moment of suspension and requires neither the logic of the market to secure his value nor the intimate recognition of anything municipally normal or domestic to assure that he has boundaries. He can hold a nonspace without being meaningful. This does not seem to threaten him" (26). Does confidence belong, then, only to the bourgeois denizens and readers of *The New Yorker*? I don't think Berlant would put the question that way, but in her pressing on from Ashbery to Johnson to the tale of Dorothy Gael in Ryman's *Was*, there is a Left critic's drive to bleakness in recognizing the cruelest of optimisms—the least hope for detachment and thriving—outside the bourgeois precincts of the decaffeinated life. Dorothy Gael's creativity, her survivalist fantasizing, "makes a wall of post-traumatic noise, as she has been abandoned by her parents, raped and shamed by her Uncle Henry Gulch, and shunned by other children for being big, fat, and ineloquent" (Berlant 2006, 32). Dorothy Gael, in other words, is neither confident nor bourgeois, and neither were Cooter and Loftis. Does that leave her, or them, or other nonbourgeois subjects ineligible for a transformative experience of the impasse? Are they doomed by the loss of familiar conditions, no matter how diminishing?

My claim is no, and *By Hook or By Crook* is my queer-class counterplot. Shy takes Val into his own battered psychic and social world; he stands with

Val at the impasse of deep uncertainty, recognition and modes of being at once resonant—like butchness—and dissonant, like delirium or mania. Shy is not desperate; he is needful. Val, too, is needful and has something to offer: the welcome and protection of the fort, his gifts for language and friendship, his gentleness in a universe whose harshness he knows well, his capacity for love and solidarity. Shy was primed in childhood for a return to love (where, in other stories, he'd have been primed for desperation and bad attachments by his mother's abandonment). There is reason to have faith in the trust narrated there, to rise with the film's hitching of its loopy energy, bargain-basement production, and rich formal expansion to the gift of good friendship in hard places and to a narrative of re-subjectivation, where old lives and earlier modes of living are lost in death and so must be detached by arson and forward motion. *By Hook or By Crook* is, in other words, a story of good attachment in harsh circumstances, a fantasy of queer-class friendship, sexual love, and self-made family as the means to thriving. It is a common enough story in queer history, but a rare one in contemporary queer narrative. In Berlant's terms, *By Hook or By Crook*, like *Showboat 1988* (1977) and *Me and You and Everyone We Know* (2005), offers queer-class opening.

These stories—the complaint's, Jack's, Ennis's, Ashbery's, Johnson's, Cooter's, Loftis's, Ryman's, Dorothy's, Shy's, Val's, Billie's, Igor's, Rosetta's, Schmidt's, Lee's, Howard's, Dodge's, Berlant's, and mine—are not infrastructures. They are not the state, the wage, the union, the economic practice or apparatus, and thus they are not the means of redistribution as we familiarly imagine them. But reading them releases juxtapolitical affects and energies to be returned to and accrued against the tide of political depression. At their most promising—*Showboat 1988*'s claiming the stage for everyday citizens, Ashbery's humane impasse, *By Hook or by Crook*'s politically attuned trust in friendship, that other context for an "unshearable suturing"—they express a social form of queerness that it is never too late to rekindle against the class protectionism that has come to define gay enfranchisement. Accumulation can only protect accumulators. Love and solidarity have a broader, plausible, more optimistic reach.

Conclusion: A Cultural Politics of Love and Solidarity

Room to Move

The period since World War II is very telling when it comes to the story of changes in cumulative income growth in the United States. According to Larry M. Bartels (2008), Princeton professor of public and international affairs, the postwar period is not one of uniform upward distribution, where growth is concentrated at the top of the heap; instead, from 1947 to 1974, incomes grew in the lowest (the 20th) percentile by 97.5 percent, in the 60th percentile by 97.6 percent, and in the 95th percentile by 89.1 percent. Contrast the similarity of these rates with those in the same percentiles from 1974 to 2005: in the 20th, growth was a devastating 10.3 percent, in the 80th it was 42.9 percent, and in the 95th it was 62.9 percent. Rates of growth in this second period were slower overall than in the first, but that's not the real story: the relative egalitarianism in income growth (not salaries or wages) in the first period is replaced by deep upward concentration in the second, when the rich got exponentially richer at the expense of the poor.[1] As Bartels additionally points out, none of these census data reflect income growth for the superrich top 1 or 2 percent of income earners in the United States. From 1945 to 1974, top real incomes in the 95th, 99th, 99.5th, 99.9th, and 99.99th percentiles are fairly close; between 1975 and 2005, however, the 99.9th and 99.99th percentile groups break away in a dramatic pattern of income expansion. "What is most striking," says Bartels, "is that, even at this elevated income level, income growth over the past 25 years has accelerated with every additional step up the economic ladder. For example, while the real income of the taxpayers at the 99th percentile doubled between 1981 and 2005, the real income of taxpayers at the 99.9th percentile nearly tripled, and the real income of taxpayers at the 99.99th percentile—a hyper-rich stratum comprising about 13,000 taxpayers—increased *five*fold" (2008, 11).

The source of the big difference between periods came as a surprise to me when I read Bartels's analysis. Escalating economic inequality is in large measure a political outcome; it matters who is in power in Washington. Democratic administrations are more likely—*much* more likely—than Republican ones to favor policies that redistribute. Says Bartels: "Bush era tax cuts, estate tax repeal, and the eroding minimum wage shed light on both the political causes and the political consequences of escalating economic inequality in contemporary America" (2008, 5).

As a political observer, I am in the habit of presuming bipartisan strip-mining when it comes to the economic well-being—or fate—of working people in the United States, the presumption that both Republicans and Democrats serve corporate lobbyists first and working people, especially poor ones, last or not at all. Bartels's analysis makes apparent the limits of that political presumption, without concluding that policies introduced by Democratic administrations always favor redistribution. Clearly they don't. Still, since World War II, "[o]n average, the real incomes of middle-class families have grown twice as fast under Democrats as they have under Republicans, while the real incomes of working poor families have grown *six times* as fast under Democrats as they have under Republicans. . . . [A] great deal of economic inequality in the contemporary United States is specifically attributable to the policies and priorities of Republican presidents" (Bartels 2008, 3).

If we accept Bartels's analysis, since the mid-1970s we have lived through a stretch of politically ensured wealth expansion for the superrich that would make nineteenth-century robber barons blush, a period Bartels calls "the new gilded age." Under pressure of Republican policymaking, from Reaganite trickle-down to Bush's tax heaven for the very wealthy (and such Democratic cooperation as punitive welfare reform in 1996), the rich got richer and the poor got poorer, and each passing policy has made it harder, or next to impossible, for poor and working people even to begin to catch up to the less harsh version of their place at or near the bottom of the economic ladder. In the wake of the 2008 bank bailout and again with the surge of Tea Party aggression, unions and wage activists are tarred with accusations of self-interest and of politicking away America's future for representing workers' rights to make a living wage. Working poor people and those at the income edges of the middle class play a running shell game in which, mainly, they lose, and in which winning means keeping your nose barely above water. Meanwhile, hyperwealthy people compete for who can pay the most for a cocktail. One story comes from London in 2008, where "a bar announces that it is offering the most expensive cocktail in the world: £35,000. That buys you a shot of cognac, half a bottle of champagne, a diamond ring, and the attentions of two security guards to protect you for the rest of the evening" (Lanchester 2008).

Responding to greed with astonishment, however, doesn't go very far; it is true that some people live to amass more than they and everyone they've ever known—together—could possibly spend on a version of the good life that most of us couldn't dream up at gunpoint. The socialization of loss on Wall Street through tax-financed bailouts, moreover, has done little to stem greed as first principle in the finance sector, and nothing, yet, to change income tax policy.[2] But my impulse to start with Bartels in concluding *Love and Money* is not simply to reassert indignation. It is to remind myself, first, that thirty years of queer politics and culture in the United States have taken shape amid socially and politically crippling economic policy and a national culture of hyperaccumulation; second, that the market fundamentalism that underwrote such rates and forms of accumulation is—as I write—in tatters (even as capitalism itself is not), though its effects will long be felt; and, third, as Bartels's analysis of party policy tells us, it matters who does politics and how. Together, these are reminders that now is a critical time to rethink queer formation as a class project that can challenge wealth and class arrival as measures of legitimacy and liberation. The tatter phase does not make us an egalitarian nation overnight. But the state of the market nation does mean that it's a good time to take stock of our queer future and the terms in which we want to cast it.

My wish, in saying this, is not to be moralistic or scolding. That is hard to avoid, however, when cultural politics and criticism have lost track of a language of accountability to class hierarchy rooted in wealth. Take me, for example. Writing in 2011, I am an employed, fifty-three-year-old, tenured academic with no dependents. I own outright a faded car, a faded retirement account, my domestic stuff, and my education. I have never expected an inheritance, though I may receive one, nor do I have to financially support aging parents or other relatives. At different points, I have bought plane tickets and visited places at great distances from where I live, and I feel rich in experience in this and other ways. I have rented the same 750-square-foot apartment in Northampton, Massachusetts, for seventeen years, in part because I have never saved a cash down payment, though colleagues with similar salaries in the same period have, nor have I shared expenses, or received family gifts or academic housing and mortgage benefits. But it's also because my landlords are sweethearts who have my back and whose generosity and big windows have given me every reason to stay. I downsized without ever having upsized; financially and otherwise, it has been an agreeably low-maintenance arrangement.

Despite what *feels*, then, like modest professional security in a state university system at permanent budgetary war with its legislature, I am in the *80th percentile* on the *New York Times* class-o-meter, which considers income and wealth and scales its outcomes in 2005 dollars.[3] With a promotional salary increase (which I knew to expect with the publication of *Love and*

Money), I land firmly in the top quintile of income earners and owners of wealth in the United States, even (or especially) as the *Times* scale is adjusted to current economic measures. As Bartels points out, the range in that top quarter is obscene. Still, by the standards of wealth and cultural participation, I am in the top 20 percent of citizens in one of the wealthiest nations on the planet. Thus I, and many others like me, have room to move in forming common cause with others, including queer others, who are struggling well below the 80th percentile. There isn't a lot of free time or a multidirectional, contemporary practice of queer-class trust across gender, racial, ethnic, and political difference, which means it isn't easy to do. And lots of us do it with and for those closest to us—friends and family members in the four-fifths of the U.S. population who can't count on personal resources like mine. But it is essential; *Love and Money* has been my way of building this conclusion in the context of class and queer studies.

Cultural contributions to developing common cause are often indirect, even while the political importance of cultural formation is clear. As critic and fieldworker in cultural production, I have opinions, analyses, and my own political activity, but I do not have a program for intervention into the harsh contexts of social injustice and maldistribution, for queers or non-queers, whether in health care, taxation, public education, worker's rights, policing, immigration, or incarceration. All have local, national, and transnational coordinates and advocacy organizations, where people participate in ways shaped by those organizations and their allied movements.

In most of those contexts, we find profound and complex interactions among queerness, class, other roots of social hierarchy, and the operations of repression or privilege. The contemporary prison industrial complex, for example, is rooted in private enterprise and designed to capture—as units of revenue—as many people as bureaucratically possible. Prison is harsh for prisoners, unfairly high proportions of whom (given categories of conviction, federal sentencing practices, and long histories of economic racism) are inmates of color. For those who are of color and transgendered, the harshness intensifies: there are few institutional requirements to recognize or accommodate variant gender identity in prison. In addition to treacherously inadequate health care and access to hormone treatments, transgender people are thus at heightened risk of violence from other inmates and prison personnel.[4] With high rates of employment discrimination among transgender people (Badgett et al. 2007, 7), high rates of unemployment in official sectors, and frequent work (especially for young people) in the unofficial economies of prostitution and street drugs, vulnerability to repeated arrest and incarceration goes up, and with it repeated exposure to the cruel and unusual conditions of imprisonment in a setting that systematically misrecognizes gender-identity expression. That's why grassroots organizations like the Sylvia Rivera Law Project in New York City undertake legal intervention for low-income, transgender people in New York's municipal and state prison systems. Sylvia Rivera's attorneys (many of whom are transgender) are prepared to address the conditions of gender expression, poverty, race, and youth discrimination in prison, and to work with a Prisoner Advisory Committee of some fifty currently incarcerated transgender people.[5] The Project thus offers a model of both remedies to injustice at multiple social intersections, and of the long labor and development such remedies require.

As a cultural critic, I can support the Sylvia Rivera Law Project, teach the commentary and legal scholarship of the attorneys who work or have worked there, and thus introduce noninmate populations of students and others to the densely woven social conditions that make life for young, low-income, transgender people of color unjust, and especially harsh for those who are incarcerated. I can also introduce students to a more general model of analysis and action that recognizes fundamental mediations among sex, gender, race, class, age, social enfranchisement, and loss. That is my work as teacher and citizen. Here it is worth recognizing the difference between queer politics, on the one hand, and radical or progressive queers doing political work, on the other. Such work may or may not address queer questions or may redress matters of sexual hierarchy in relation to other kinds of injustice, like police profiling, the inaccessibility of health care, or double standards in immigration policy.[6] But in my own cultural scholarship, I can also offer a hopefully spirited ideological alternative to class ascendance as the myopic measure of queer accomplishment, to queer bashing as evidence of Left rigor, and to the *queer* distrust of *gay* culture in articulating political priorities and forming practical interventions as workers, lovers, leaders, and friends. Exploring the relations of queerness and class in representation and everyday cultural practice, and keeping in mind Berlant's analysis of political affect, *Love and Money* was written to find new conditions of queer class attachment. It has moved from trauma and the class markers of queer worth (chapters 1 and 2) to observation, recognition, relay, and optimism (chapters 3, 4, 5, and 6) to offer, I hope, ground for the cultivation and accrual of new points of return for queer and class others.

Weak Theory and Democratic Culture

More than fifty years ago, at the close of *Culture and Society, 1780–1950*, Raymond Williams (1958) argued that democratic culture is society's tending ground, the place where society grows, where people develop as communities and subjects. Such development is a necessarily collective project, Williams said, notwithstanding the bourgeois history of the promotion of the individual. That promotion is also collectively accomplished to enfranchise some at the expense of many. Writing from the depth of the Cold War, Williams offered a language of class that I would like to reintroduce to queer politics, in the spirit of class recognition and repair and in the name of the democratic culture he favored. "We live in almost overwhelming danger, at a peak of our apparent control," Williams observed. He continued:

> We react to the danger by attempting to take control, yet still we have to unlearn, as the price of survival, the inherent dominative mode. The struggle for democracy is the pattern of this revaluation, yet much that passes as democratic is allied, in spirit, with the practice of its open enemies. It is as if, in fear or vision, we are now all determined to lay our hands on life and force it into our own image, and it is then no good to dispute on the merits of rival images. . . . We project our old images into the future, and take hold of ourselves and others to force energy towards that substantiation. We do this as conservatives, trying to prolong old forms; we do this as socialists, trying to prescribe the new man. A large part of contemporary resistance to certain kinds of change, which are obviously useful in themselves, amounts to an inarticulate distrust of this effort at domination. (336)

Williams is critical of both bourgeois privilege and state socialism as reactive modes of domination. His critique shares a tenor and an invitation to ideological opening with Sedgwick's (2003) reparative mode of criticism and J. K. Gibson-Graham's (2006) "weak" theorizing of the economy. Strong theory, Gibson-Graham argues, has "an embracing reach and a reduced, clarified field of meaning" (4) in which outcomes are mostly known before practical conditions are explored: a field in which "social experiments are already co-opted and thus doomed to fail or to reinforce dominance," or in which "the world economy will be transformed by an international revolutionary movement rather than through the disorganized proliferation of local projects" (8). "Weak" theory, in contrast,

> can be undertaken with a reparative motive that welcomes surprise, entertains hope, makes connection, tolerates coexistence and offers care for the new. As the impulse to judge or discredit other theoretical agendas arises, one can practice making room for others, imagining a terrain on which

the success of one project need not come at the expense of another. Producing such spaciousness is particularly useful for a project of rethinking economy, where the problem is the scarcity rather than the inconsistency of economic concepts.[7]

As I have acknowledged, in the course of writing Love and Money I was moved by Gibson-Graham's formulations, as well as Sedgwick's; producing spaciousness and avoiding conceptual foreclosure have been valuable to me for rethinking culture on new ground, for finding a new mood and a new theoretical point of entry, and thus for rethinking queer class cultural politics. If culture is where society *tends to* its formation, where it cultivates its future in the most creative and "unplannable" ways (Williams 1958, 336), and if democratic culture is a "struggle for the recognition of equality of being" (337), then a democratic queer cultural politics stands to gain considerable breadth and to return considerable value from the openness and practice of weak theory.

In Love and Money, I have undertaken the weak theorizing of queerness and class in the name of a politics of love and solidarity, the first term gathering the practices of love in many forms—sexual, filial, romantic, avocational, communal, platonic, and intimate—and the second signifying bonds of witness, regard, and support rather than the clenched fists of "common action" (Williams 1958, 334). I do not oppose action in common—on the contrary— but I resist the clenched version of solidarity in parsing queer class encounters, since the key terms of the encounter—"queerness" and "class"—are mobile and permeable, even when they provoke domination or stuckness and are otherwise harsh in their effects.

To unclench the fists of queerness and class and find new conditions of solidarity, Love and Money offers three resolutions and a gesture. The first resolution is to challenge the claim that there is no discourse of class in the United States. The second is to broaden both the Marxist and liberal definitions of social class to better recognize class's cultural formation and expression. The third is to tolerate—for good analytic reasons—the conflation of class and status. The gesture, finally, is to draw upon both the history of queer friendship and the future of queer becoming to change queer class solidarity in the present.

First, to question rather than repeat the claim that there is no discourse of class in the United States: I hope the work presented in Love and Money and the approaches I have taken to reading queerness for class (as social hierarchy, sexual value, and aesthetic taste) enable us to give that claim a rest. For those whose experience leaves them to feel class hierarchy most pointedly, it is hard *not* to imagine and respond to the world through a class lens. That is not a failure of definition; it is the acute success of recognition, the knowledge—sometimes articulate, other times haunting—that one is being judged, dominated, and diminished, including within queer contexts, even or perhaps especially in the course of actions that may be masked by idealism or benevolence (Williams 1958, 337).

Second, *Love and Money* challenges Marxist and liberal empirical traditions as offering the only weight-bearing definitions of class. This means class as defined by a group's relation to the means of production as owners or wage workers, or combining occupation, education, income, and wealth in a multivariate measure of class or socioeconomic status. In both, class cultures become the expressions and productions of different class fractions. But, returning to Williams (and despite my devotion to Bourdieu), no cultural instance is uniquely the work of one class or fraction. Cultural history is, perforce, the mixing and melding of forms across the most permeable of social and historical boundaries, where what was once the cultural expression of privilege, say, later becomes the standard form or the insider satire of nondominant groups (Williams 1958, 322–23).

It has not been my goal to set aside class as relation to the means of production or as multivariate measure. With Ortner, I use and reconfigure both terms, harnessing contemporary instabilities of economic position and privilege to variable forms of social power and vulnerability, as well as to cultural practices closely calibrated to and by those hierarchical forms. Where, I have asked, do we see social hierarchy culturally expressed, and how have old idioms of class expression been renewed in and by queer representation? How, finally, has queer culture confused, toppled, and enriched class expression?

Third, these alternative formulations have sometimes asked that we let stand the conflation of social class (by the standards of the Marxist definition) and social status. Here, as my third conclusion, I would extend that move to claim that status *is* a register for the enactment of social power, that it is quite reasonably experienced by many as the root of domination (see Lillian Rubin 1992). Members of professional-managerial groups, such as employed civil servants and college professors, may not own the means of production, but the conditions of our lives and our work enable forms of pleasure and decision making about others that those who are excluded and decided about experience as class hierarchy. By now, the conflation of status and class is not to be dismissed as so much folk theoretical confusion but contended with as a deeply social conflation whose registers oppress or enliven everyday life. It makes me cringe to remember, as a nineteen-year-old and later, my enthusiasm for newly learned Marxist concepts, accompanied by rooting out everyone else's (including my parents') hopeless muddle about the distinction between status and class. In a universe where gender and race stagger all kinds of distributions, where sexuality vilifies and valorizes, where age, language, and embodiment can cost you your survival, and where those without the objects of a secure or pleasurable life work cheek-by-jowl with the heartily endowed (those others, for example, in the 80th percentile of U.S. economic and educational resources), status-class conflation is experientially wise, not conceptually sloppy.

Love and Money asks us to recognize that experiential wisdom as an essentially social effect. Mindful status-class conflation does confuse the matter of constituency—*who* is recognized in the process of queer class recognition?—and thus requires of the Marxist and Liberal empirical traditions that they recognize each other's terms in their own. But that very confusion tells us that while class boundaries are unstable, the practice and the project of class hierarchy have not gone away. Class history also reminds us, however, that absent the mood to dominate, the persistence of hierarchy does not make it impossible to imagine or practice queer solidarity across class lines. Here, in my concluding gesture, the insight that draws me the most comes from queer radical historian and philosopher Michel Foucault.

Return to Friendship

> Another thing to distrust is the tendency to relate the question of homosexuality to the problem of "Who am I?" and "What is the secret of my desire?" Perhaps it would be better to ask oneself, "What relations, through homosexuality, can be established, invented, multiplied, and modulated?" The problem is not to discover in oneself the truth of one's sex, but, rather, to use one's sexuality henceforth to arrive at a multiplicity of relationships. And, no doubt, that's the real reason why homosexuality is not a form of desire but something desirable. Therefore, we have to work at becoming homosexuals and not be obstinate in recognizing that we are. The development toward which the problem of homosexuality tends is the one of friendship. —Michel Foucault 1981/1997, 135–36

In his short and beloved interview with *Le Gai Pied* in 1981, "Friendship as a Way of Life," Foucault reflects on friendship among men as a deeper threat to the social order than gay sex. The fleeting sexual encounter in a semipublic night provokes vice squads and morality tales and has unfairly cost people their safety and liberties. But, says Foucault, the unease it generates is limited or only part of the story, since "it responds to a reassuring canon of beauty," and it "cancels everything that can be troubling in affection, tenderness, friendship, fidelity, camaraderie, and companionship, things that our rather sanitized society can't allow a place for without fearing the formation of new alliances and the tying together of unforeseen lines of force" (136). Homosexuality, Foucault says at the end of the interview, is a chance to make "a truly unavoidable challenge of the question: What can be played?" (140).

What *can* be played? I am slow to accept Foucault's ranking of the threats of friendship versus sex, as though tenderness and fidelity (to community sexual practice, say) are absent from the latter. But friendship is socially demanding, and especially sweet when it is neither presumed nor supported by social codes or dispositions in common. Thus the question of what can be played is a critical historical question, one to be posed and re-posed with changes in conditions that queers and other nondominant subjects do not control. *Love and Money* asks whether it is possible to play the card of love and solidarity across queer-class lines as a means of challenging, together, the conditions of social hierarchy we are now in, rather than waiting until conditions are more favorable and thus the solidarities less risky. As every history of urban queer experience I've read makes clear, sexual, racial, and class mixing in the name of a new or alternate sociality has a long and broad provenance.[8] These are not accounts of untroubled or unexploitative urban scenes, though the troubles and exploitations they document are wrought from multiple points on the class spectrum. But as accounts, they test the contemporary assertion of queer, class, and racial segregation in the United States, a universe of upmarket, same-sex married homonormatives over here, and something else (antirelational, queer radical communalists, maybe, or masculine Left revolutionaries) over there. I have had truck and sympathy with these distinctions, but as they entrench foundational political oppositions, their energies and ascendancies have cooled. In my conspicuous middle age, I am drawn more to the warm, to relay living and boundary crossing rather than upward movement as the route to securing a queer future, to multiplicities of friendship in combination or company with the obdurate affections of family or romance, and to the generous possibility that queerness remains a state of becoming. "We have to work at becoming homosexuals," says Foucault (1997, 136). "Queerness," writes José Esteban Muñoz, "is not yet here" (2009, 1). What can be played?

In *Cruising Utopia*, Muñoz (2009) finds himself defending his choice of German Idealist Ernst Bloch, author of *The Principle of Hope* (1995), to theorize queer utopianism as his—Muñoz's—reparative gesture (15). In the contemporary mood of queer negativity, "anti-relationality,"[9] and pessimism, he argues, there is little fortune for utopian thinking as an essential political element, whether for sustaining the queer present or imagining a queer future. Muñoz recognizes the importance of strong critiques of the current terms of queer futurity, critiques such as Lee Edelman's (2004), which caution queers against normative drives—like reproduction—in making that future at the expense of what is queer in the present. But Muñoz wants that future (11) and so do I. Writing especially to the conditions of queers of color, a future rooted in relationality is, for Muñoz, something people want and cannot afford to set aside. I would add that we cannot dismiss a future of relational queerness except at the expense of queer class solidarity, too. We need the big tent.

As critic and cultural theorist, Muñoz looks to the history of queer cultural production for traces and energies of the utopian imagination. Early in *Cruising Utopia*, for example, he reads a passage from *Chelsea Girls* (1994), lesbian author Eileen Myles's memoir of "coming into queer consciousness in the 1960s and 70s" (Muñoz 2009, 13). He finds there an acute utopian expression; better, he finds a *performative* of that project, expression that enacts or provokes, through image and feeling, a piece of the universe it describes. Late in her memoir, says Muñoz, the young Myles "has become part-time caretaker [at New York's Chelsea Hotel] for the great queer voice of the New York School of poetry—James Schuyler" (13). Myles writes:

> You had to stay silent for a very long time some days. He was like music, Jimmy was, and you had to be like music too to be with him, but understand in his room he was conductor. He directed the yellow air in room 625. It was marvelous to be around. It was huge and impassive. What emerged in the silence was a strong picture, more akin to a child or a beautiful animal. (Myles 1994, 274; quoted in Muñoz 2009, 13)

Muñoz notes that "Myles is paid to take care of Schuyler" (14), who is very ill. "On the level of political economy," Muñoz continues,

> this relationship is easy to account for. But if we think of [Samuel] Delany's championing of interclass contact within a service economy and the affective surplus it offers, the passage opens up quite beautifully. . . . The relationality is not about simple positivity or affirmation. It is filled with all sorts of bad feelings, moments of silence and brittleness. But beyond the void that stands between the two poets, there is something else, a surplus

that is manifest in the complexity of their moments of contact. Through quotidian service-economy interactions of care and simple conversation the solitary scene of an old man and his young assistant is transformed. . . . This is the music that is Jimmy, this is the music of Eileen, this is the hum of their contact. (14)

There's that hum again, the one Berlant heard in Ashbery's poem ("I am not the subject of a hymn but of a hum, that thing that resonates around me"), the one that captures the humane impasse, a moment where the conditions of attachment change and people could lose their moorings, but don't.

Muñoz observes of Myles's passage: "its tone lights the way to the reparative" (2009, 15). There's that illumination again, the one I saw in Miranda July's work, the one that sustains a responsiveness that is hard to hold onto in these mean times.

I did not undertake *Love and Money* to close on the claim that poetry will light our way. But like Muñoz, I am a student and scholar of cultural production in part because the cultural is where queers and other outsiders have found and made, and can find and make, transformative resonances and conditions in the present. This is not to say that people will behave like poems or characters, or that critics can read the zeitgeist from cultural works and predict the social future. It is to argue that we need culture to find the feelings that enable us to act, and to act differently than we have.[10] For Muñoz, that means cruising utopia. For Raymond Williams, it meant challenging the mood to dominate in the interest of a future democratic culture. For Berlant, amid her radical skepticism, it means holding on to the wish for social suturing and finding new objects of attachment that enable us to thrive. For Gibson-Graham, it means retooling our theoretical dispositions enough to see and use the progressive adaptations already in the making, rather than theorizing them away in the name of their never being enough, and replacing them instead with a revolutionary wish. For Allan Bérubé, it meant retracing the steps of his queer, working-class intellectual formation and offering up those traces to others, for whom the unlikely combinations of his life present both hope and map. For Miranda July, it means breathing, watching, and moving gently so as not to topple vulnerable efforts at change and reconstruction, and using art like her car, to get to the next place. For Dorothy Allison and her readers, it means recognition and class relay, but not at the cost of squelching the real social differences that make and unmake people's survival. For queer independent filmmakers, it means getting and making work where you can and drawing resources from every quarter to reimagine the world and take others with you. For Shy, Valentine, and Billie, it means trusting your friends. For Eve Kosofsky Sedgwick, it meant repair and survival. For me, it means love and solidarity. But that is just a place to start.

NOTES

1. See Hennessy (2000) for the most sustained, contemporary treatment of sexuality, labor, and capital.
2. Lauren Berlant, personal communication, 2003.
3. The Human Rights Campaign describes this exclusion as a "one-time" exception to its principle of inclusive antidiscrimination legislation, adopted when leadership in the U.S. House of Representatives informed HRC in 2007 that there were not enough votes to pass a bill inclusive of gender identity. For HRC Board policy on the Employment Non-Discrimination Act (ENDA), see http://www.hrc.org/issues/workplace/12346.htm (accessed July 28, 2010). For a chart documenting the years elapsed between city, county, and state inclusion of sexual orientation and gender-identity expression as protected categories, see data from the National Gay and Lesbian Task Force, http://www.thetaskforce.org/downloads/reports/fact_sheets/years_ passed_gie_so_7_07.pdf (accessed July 28, 2010). The Task Force calculates an average of 14.5 years between the protection of sexual orientation and gender identity among the 103 jurisdictions that included both as of 2007.
4. For historical monographs that speak to class relations in lesbian and gay communities and populations, see, e.g., Kennedy and Davis (1993), Chauncey (1994), Johnson (2004), and Houlbrook (2006). Also, Badgett et al. (2007, iii) note that recent data on lesbian incomes are less clear. "In some studies, [lesbians] earn more than heterosexual women but less than heterosexual or gay men."
5. Another post- (or now pre-) election task is to block the refrain, among elite liberals and conservatives, against "crass" candidates and their constituencies, a refrain reinvigorated during the 2010 midterm elections. In 2008, Sarah Palin was irresistible to comics and critics alike for being a misinformed spendthrift, and, more recently, Christine O'Donnell, Tea Party primary winner (defeating the Republican incumbent from Delaware in 2010), was rousted for her history of debt and unemployment. Neither Palin's politics nor O'Donnell's especially distinguished them from their elite party *confrères* among Republicans, but they were easy targets as barely educated figures for conservative politicos like Karl Rove, progressive pundits like Rachel Maddow and Jon Stewart, and celebrity anchors like Katie Couric. It was a relief, for example, to read Jonathan Raban's scathing account (2008) of Palin's gubernatorial politics in Alaska, a piece rich in political exposure and devoid of class baiting. I recall many 2008 election-season conversations with academic colleagues from working- and mixed-class backgrounds;

we cringed at the mockery of political candidates without college educations (or those who'd worked their way through nonelite institutions) or with a history of bad debt or near foreclosure on a mortgage, as though that didn't include the overwhelming majority of the U.S. electorate who might find it easy to sympathize with those circumstances and to discover a sense of political representation in those who'd survived them. As Glenn Greenwald (2010) points out, Tea Partiers are a lot like most Republicans in their xenophobic and militaristic views, but unlike Republican or Democratic elites in their tastes, cultural practices, speech, and unwillingness to play by the rules of discretion about politically objectionable intentions like military invasion. Progressive critics would do well to follow Greenwald's lead, skip reaction-inducing cheap shots about "white trash," and focus instead on political critique and popular challenges to dominant Republican and Tea Party aggression.

6. In August 2010, federal district court judge Vaughn Walker ruled that Prop 8 was unconstitutional. As of this writing, activists expect the judge's decision to be appealed up to the U.S. Supreme Court, and it remains uncertain whether the ruling will reinstate California's same-sex marriage rights while appeals move through the court system. See Hunter (2010).

7. I discuss the recognition-redistribution debates again in chapter 4. See chapter 4, note 1, for citations.

8. *Bowers v. Hardwick*, 478 U.S. 186 (1986); *Lawrence v. Texas*, 000 U.S. 02-102 (2003).

NOTES TO CHAPTER 1: THE CLASS CHARACTER OF *BOY'S DON'T CRY*

1. For the most comprehensive critical treatment of the Brandon Teena archive, see Halberstam (2005).

2. My description of Brandon's sexed body comes largely from Prosser (1998), though to call Brandon "female-bodied" sets aside the ways in which his masculinity was indeed felt in and written on his body. Prosser, however, locates material embodiment more centrally in chemical and surgical transsexuality. His discussion of Venus Xtravaganza (45–50), a preoperative transsexual woman featured in Jennie Livingston's *Paris Is Burning* (1990), also addresses relations between Xtravaganza's corporeal materiality and the social materialism of her class position (50).

3. Parts of the sheriff's recordings were adapted into the script of *Boys Don't Cry*. Original excerpts had been used earlier in the documentary film *The Brandon Teena Story* (1998), written and directed by Muska and Olafsdottir.

4. For example, when the sheriff in *Boys Don't Cry* suggests to Lana and her mother that everyone will be better off if Brandon just leaves town following his "alleged rape" by John and Tom, Lana quickly responds that everyone would be better off in fact if the sheriff were to lock up John and Tom. It is a wise response, which expresses what characters and the audience know but what Lana and others are powerless to resist—that John and Tom are violently out of control.

5. The phrase "condescending glamorizing" comes from Munt (2000, 12). In North America, with a few religious exceptions, poverty is most noble in the eyes of those who are not (or are no longer) poor. With the pain and corrosion of poverty set aside, a poor background can make for noble material indeed if a person moves into a position of status and authority, for example, in cabinet and Supreme Court confirmation hearings. In truth, I think there is human nobility in surviving poverty and millions of people routinely do it in the United States without ever becoming cabinet ministers or Supreme Court justices. But when popular discourses are not condemning poverty as a personal rather than social failure, they redeem it with attributions of noble modesty. Such an equation says little about poverty or inequality, though much about the representational authority of privilege.

6. Brandon is also exposed for car theft and bad checks, but he is punished for gender fraud, not check fraud. The criminal proceedings lead to his exposure, however, and justify the accusation that he brought his fate on himself as a liar. But here, too, the lie that counts is the judged disparity between his "female" morphology and masculine gender identification.

NOTES TO CHAPTER 2: QUEER VISIBILITY AND SOCIAL CLASS

1. *Lawrence v. Texas*, 000 U.S. 02-102 (2003); *Goodridge v. Dept. of Public Health*, 798 N.E.2d 941 (Mass. 2003).

2. Since 2002, same-sex marriage has been legally recognized in six states, including New Hampshire, Vermont, Massachusetts, Connecticut, Iowa, and the District of Columbia. In California, same-sex marriage was recognized in 2008 and rescinded later that year by ballot Proposition 8. See Introduction, n. 5, this volume.

3. The only regular black character on the program, Bette's half-sister Kit, played by Pam Grier, is a cabaret singer and recovering alcoholic, whose depth of understanding comes at the cost of a difficult and mismanaged life. Grier delivers the show's most sentient and multidimensional performance. I couldn't help but wonder, however, if the racial coding of her character doesn't frustrate her as an actor. The white characters are no less predictable, but their numbers mask the reduction in contrast to Kit's racial singling-out among leads.

4. Bill Cosby's funny, flawed, but finally wise doctor/father character on *The Cosby Show* (1984–92).

5. In Season 4 of *Six Feet Under* (2004), David acquires his own volatile cross to bear after being the victim of a carjacking and a torturous, sexualized attack. In the wake of his trauma, he partly conceals the depth of its effect on him and tries to function as well as possible, but is provocative and physically assaults strangers, one of whom will later seek half a million dollars in restitution. It is a chilling development, and arguably homophobic, as the rendering of the attack makes dangerous precisely the gay male sexual ethos the program had, until then, recognized as legitimate. In this same season, moreover, Keith continued to

exercise dubious judgment, including engaging in a fleeting tryst with Celeste, the out-of-control pop star he shadows as security guard, who immediately fires him for taking up her offer of sex and—to boot—"cheating" (Celeste's designation, not Keith's) on his struggling lover. Some fans argued that *Six Feet Under* jumped the shark in 2004, especially with its gay characters—depleting the series of its contradictions and social critique and going over the top with characters' traumas and troubled lives.

6. On the butch-fem relationship in *Set It Off*, see Keeling (2007), especially chapter 6, "What's Up With That? She Don't Talk?"
7. Mari Castañeda, personal communication, 2010.

NOTES TO CHAPTER 4: RECOGNITION

1. See Fraser (1996; 1997a; 1997b; 2000). For responses, see Butler (1997), Smith (2001), and O'Kane (2002).
2. As I discuss later in this chapter, first-person narration of family abuse and trauma is often the object of recognition and emotional realism that links Allison readers across class.
3. In addition to Allison's writing, this chapter draws from five public readings and lectures that she gave between 1999 and 2001 in San Francisco, Emeryville, CA, Boston, and Philadelphia; from an archive of reviews and interviews in print; from other documents produced about her, such as the short 1996 film by Tina DiFeliciantonio and Jane C. Wagner, *Two or Three Things But Nothing for Sure*; from other texts based on her writing, such as the Showtime feature film *Bastard Out of Carolina* directed by Anjelica Huston (1996) and Kate Ryan's play *Cavedweller* (2003); from an interview I conducted with Allison in 2001 about writing, reading, and social class; from an online exchange between Allison and readers at Previewport.com in 2002; and from ten recorded interviews with readers contacted through Allison's talks and performances.
4. Sennett and Cobb (1972) introduced the phrase "hidden injuries of class" forty years ago (1972).
5. I return in detail to Berlant's work on affect, repetition, and thriving (or not) in chapter 6, "Plausible Optimism."
6. MacDonald has since added *Easter Rising: A Memoir of Roots and Rebellion* (2006).
7. Hereafter, all live quotes are excerpted from recordings of the events referred to or from interviews with Allison and readers. An ellipsis in the text signifies a speaker's pause. An ellipsis in parentheses signifies material removed, though I have preserved the speaker's sequence.
8. See Willis (1977) for a sustained discussion of class mobility through compliance at school, as expressed by manners and the acceptance of authority (among the attributes Willis's "lads" were deemed not to possess).
9. See, for example, the "Conclusion" in Williams (1958) for a discussion of class mobility and the maintenance—and loss—of working-class community.

10. To quote Liza Doolittle in *My Fair Lady*, the difference between a flower girl and a duchess is not the way that she behaves but the way she is treated (quoted in Walkerdine 1997, 26).

11. See Steedman (1994) and Walkerdine (1997) for pointed critiques of the avoidance of psyche and psychology in cultural studies of social class.

12. See Felski (2000) on the structuring ambivalence of lower-middle-class identity.

13. See Willis (1977). Bettie (2003) has updated and relocated Willis's work to class life in the United States with a field study that attends closely to class, gender, and ethnic subject formation in the everyday culture of white and Chicana girls in a public high school in California's Central Valley.

14. For a lyrical memoir on the contradictions and concealments of "genteel poverty," see Brownworth (1997).

15. For insight on Thompson's intellectual legacy in contemporary cultural studies of social class, see Kaplan (2000).

16. Borrowing from theories of drama, cultural studies treats such linkages as the foundation of "emotional realism," an expressive possibility that relies on feeling, not empirical resemblance, to produce identification between text and reader; see Ang (1982).

17. Though it is not something Joanna expressed, for many Southern readers "modesty" is code for white respectability and distance from blackness and especially black poverty.

18. Cf. Gibson-Graham (2006, xxv–xxvi) on such transformations in alternative economic communities.

19. I have, on the other hand, spoken with academic critics of Allison's writing who take this position. Also, see Felski (2000) for a discussion of lower-middle-class identity as enabling much of the shame but little of the pride of working-class status. See Ortner (1991) for a discussion of ethnographic work on class difference and a contrasting literary analysis of the displacement of class hostility onto (hetero)sexual and gendered idioms in Philip Roth's *Goodbye Columbus* and *Portnoy's Complaint*. See Skeggs (2004) for a critique of who is included (and who is excluded) from rituals of recognition. For Skeggs, those who suffer most from deprivation and class hostility are least likely to benefit from a politics of recognition. I agree, where such a politics is detached from redistribution. The experience of class "escapees" could be argued to have accomplished that detachment, if in a painfully incomplete way (for individuals but not their families and networks). Still, this chapter asks whether there are contexts of class recognition and misrecognition (the answer by now is yes), considering their significance against the grain of the assertion that a politics of recognition leaves class out.

20. This is not true, however, of Allison's writing, which is marked by a sociological as well as literary imagination, by Allison's training in anthropology, and by a conscious Left politics that seeks to identify the dehumanizing conditions of existence that make her characters' lives and mistakes comprehensibly human without absolving them of accountability. Such a critical perspective is what attracts many

of Allison's readers. For a theoretical argument about how and why global capitalism effaces class injustice, see O'Kane (2002).

21. On memories of a conflicted working-class Jewish childhood in 1960s Brookline, Massachusetts, see Rich (1998).

22. For an important account of cross-class encounters in underpaid service labor, see Ehrenreich (2001).

23. For a prescient critique of productivity as the basis of social value, see Jonathan Cobb's "Afterword" in Sennett and Cobb (1972). See also chapter 3 in Bledstein (1976) for a historical account of the place of productivity in the culture of professionalism in the United States.

24. See Sender (2003) for an account of desexualization as the route to respectability in the formation of an upscale gay market and of the enfranchisement such a market is argued to bring gay people as a historically reviled class.

NOTES TO CHAPTER 5: QUEER RELAY

1. See, e.g., Green (2005).

2. On Waters, see Tinkcom (2002, 155–88); on Zamora and Basquiat, see Muñoz (1999, 37–56, 143–60); on drag kinging and *Austin Powers*, see Halberstam (2005, 125–51).

3. Halberstam does not theorize relay but uses the term in passing to refer to "relays between subculture and avant-garde."

4. Matthew Soar, personal communication, August 2005.

5. On the "speaker's benefit," see Foucault (1986, 6); on affect and libidinal investment in theorizing, see Gibson-Graham (2006, 1–21).

6. For an especially rich example of cultural analysis that follows a formal fragment through multiple articulations over historical time and geographic space, see Feld (1996) on the movement of a traditional Cameroonian flute sound from ethnomusicological field recording to U.S. jazz improvisation to Madonna hit to Neutrogena advertising soundtrack.

7. All quotes from production personnel are drawn from on-set and pre- and post-production interviews I conducted in Los Angeles and New York between 2004 and 2007.

8. When a casting director is herself cast in a film, she runs the risk of alienating actors and their representatives, especially those actors who had auditioned for the part. Mandy.com posts announcements for freelance employment in the film industry.

9. I spoke with Codikow about this outcome, but she had not corresponded directly with Johnson and could not comment. At the filmmakers' request, I did not contact Panavision.

10. Synchronous-sound filmmaking, with open microphones on the set, microphone booms close to frame's edge, and digital sound recorders calibrated to the camera, introduces multiple technical variables in production, from performance, dialogue, continuity, and blocking camera (and mic) movement in relation to actors,

to focus, exposure, recording, and shooting speed, artificial and natural light, extraneous exterior sound, slating (coordinated picture and sound identification on image and sound tracks), and the consistency of electrical supply, among many others. Sync crews are bigger, and sync setups (where each element of a take is planned, blocked, lit, mic'ed, and rehearsed) are much more time-consuming than scenes without sound. The room for error and uncertainty increases, and usually more takes per scene are required over scenes without sound. The ratio (of footage shot to footage used in the final film) typically goes up with sync, likewise with narrative continuity, where contiguous shots in the film must match, even though they may have been shot days apart. Ambitious small films like *Desert Motel*, with high production values; interiors and exteriors; day, night, and underwater shooting; tight schedules; and modest budgets (for location time, personnel, film stock, and processing) are thus among the most demanding projects to pull off.

11. The Director's Guild of America is one of Outfest's venues.

12. Although I do not quote them here, additional interviews with Stacy Codikow and Shari Frilot, a filmmaker and Sundance Film Festival programmer, contributed to this discussion and its reworking in Table 1.

13. Errors and omissions is an insurance policy to cover potential lawsuits for copyright infringement. As it turns out, Johnson mounted *Desert Motel*—for free—on John Cameron Mitchell's *Shortbus* website (www.shortbusthemovie.com/fvideo. html), a project she describes as "on the side of stigmaphilia and community" but that remains an expensive commercial enterprise by *Desert Motel* standards. Still, she said, it made more sense to be on *Shortbus* for free, with less risk of errors and omissions lawsuits, than underpaid at LOGO, as layered (and, I would add, as expressive of her relay position) as that preference might seem. Immediately after *Desert Motel*, Johnson went on to make the short (and not queer) film *South of Ten* (2006), a poetic hybrid of fiction and documentary form about a group of citizens making do on the Mississippi Gulf Coast after Hurricane Katrina. *South of Ten* was selected to open the New York Film Festival at Lincoln Center in September 2006, preceding Stephen Frears's *The Queen* (Liza Johnson, personal communication, July 2006 and December 2007).

NOTES TO CHAPTER 6: PLAUSIBLE OPTIMISM

1. *By Hook or By Crook* is distributed on DVD by Wolfe Video, a revered San Francisco firm devoted to "mainstreaming" queer independent cinema. I first encountered *By Hook or By Crook* in Halberstam (2005).

2. See the interview with Howard and Dodge conducted for the Sundance Channel and included as a DVD extra.

3. Howard and Dodge, interview.

4. http://www.davecullen.com/brokeback/.

5. The relative absence of melodrama distinguishes *Rosetta*, *La Promesse*, and *By Hook or By Crook* from *Brokeback Mountain* more than bleakness distinguishes the Dardenne films from the optimism of *By Hook or By Crook*.

6. "Feel forward" responds to Love's (2007) fond exploration and reclamation of queer ambivalence and bad feeling in *Feeling Backward: Loss and the Politics of Queer History*; "ransoming the present" responds to Edelman's protest call, in *No Future: Queer Theory and the Death Drive* (2004), against rooting queer futurity in homonormativity.

7. Quoted in Berlant (2006, 30).

8. The "decaffeinated" good life is Slavoj Žižek's phrase, quoted in Berlant (2006), 24. Ashbery's poem appeared in Larissa MacFarquhar, "Present Waking Life: Becoming John Ashbery," *The New Yorker*, November 7, 2005, 88, cited in Berlant (2006), 23. It appears as "Ignorance of the Law Is No Excuse," in *Notes from the Air: Selected Later Poems* (New York: HarperCollins 2007), 329. Used with permission.

NOTES TO THE CONCLUSION

1. See Figure 1.2, "Cumulative Income Growth by Income Percentile, 1947–1974 and 1974–2005," in Bartels (2008, 9).

2. Bush-era income tax cuts were due to end December 31, 2010. In the run-up to the 2008 election, Obama pledged to return the top marginal income tax rate from 35 percent to 39.6 percent, with corresponding changes in lower income brackets. (See Herszenhorn 2010.) It hasn't happened.

3. The class-o-meter is an interactive graphic embedded in the *Times* series "How Class Works" (2005). The graphic uses a reader's input to determine where the reader fits in a multivariate profile of class in the United States that combines occupation, education, income, and wealth. See http://www.nytimes.com/packages/html/national/. 20050515_CLASS_GRAPHIC/index_01.html (accessed July 14, 2010).

4. The risk of violence is especially true for MTF inmates identified as male on birth documents and incarcerated with nontrans men.

5. See http://srlp.org/areas/criminal_justice (accessed July 20, 2010).

6. The distinction between queer politics and queers doing politics is simple, but it was clarified for me by Margaret Cerullo in a panel presentation titled "LGBT Life Over the Past 25 Years: Politics," honoring the 25th Anniversary of the Stonewall Center at the University of Massachusetts Amherst, December 1, 2010. Also, in most instances, I mean "citizen" in the broad sense of participatory belonging rather than the legal sense of being a born or naturalized citizen of a particular country.

7. Weak theory does not undermine the possibility of institutional or macrolevel economic analyses and remedies, though macrolevel chauvinism may undermine weak theorizing. Increases in state income tax rates, for example, might be pursued (as they recently were in Oregon) alongside community barter programs as concrete means of redistribution in a solidarity economy. On the Oregon tax ballots, see Yardley (2010).

8. For examples, see Newton (1972, 1995), Kennedy and Davis (1993), Chauncey (1994), Stein (2000), Johnson (2004), Houlbrook (2006), and Heap (2009).

9. "Anti-relationality" is a term derived from Bersani (1995) to signify a queerness that cannot be located in idealist communitarianism. It is, by some measures, a rigorous purist ethic and, by others, including Muñoz's (2009), one too committed to negativity in its resistance to the social contingency of sexuality (10–11).

10. As I write, a mixed group of activists is protesting the hyperaccumulation of wealth, finance industry deregulation, private profit amid socialized bailout, and criminal entitlement in the banking industry. Their banner, Occupy Wall Street, stretches across the country and to many centers around the world, and one of their slogans—We Are the 99%—advocates solidarity among people across the income spectrum who share their rage at corporate government and planned poverty. I visited New York City's Occupy Wall Street location in Zuccotti Park in October 2011, and, like others, was moved by the forms of expertise, creativity, democratic self-organization, and stamina activists drew upon to sustain themselves and inspire others over the course of weeks, in the face of immense hostility from police, City Hall, and an abundance of hecklers. I encountered one particularly belligerent, self-described millionaire during my visit, who was confused by my solidarity with activists. "You look like an RB," he told me. "An RB?" "A rich bitch, Miss Suede Jacket." I acknowledged my position in the professional managerial class and my talent for consignment shopping. "You fucking hypocrite, what the hell are you doing here?" he asked. This was his most revealing pronouncement. A hypocrite is someone who appears (correctly) to enjoy relative security and who expresses her solidarity with poor and working people and those on the frayed edges of the middle class who oppose obscene maldistributions of wealth. I wondered what had become of the idea, familiar in my 1970s Canadian upbringing, that security feels best when others have what they need. I speculated that the millionaire who had introduced me to "RB" was riddled with hostility born of guilt. Probably not. He had his and everyone else could just "get a job." In contrast, "We are the 99%" is a demanding and beautiful call to solidarity, a challenge to thirty-five years of government-sponsored I've-Got-Mine–You're-On-Your-Own.

REFERENCES

Allison, Dorothy. 1988. *Trash: Stories by Dorothy Allison*. Ithaca, NY: Firebrand; 2nd ed. New York: Plume, 2002.

———. 1991. *The Women Who Hate Me: Poetry, 1980–1990*. Ithaca, NY: Firebrand.

———. 1993. *Bastard Out of Carolina*. New York: Dutton.

———. 1994a. *Skin: Talking About Sex, Class, and Literature*. Ithaca, NY: Firebrand.

———. 1994b. *Two or Three Things I Know for Sure*. New York: Dutton.

———. 1998. *Cavedweller*. New York: Dutton.

Ang, Ien. 1982. *Watching Dallas: Soap Opera and the Melodramatic Imagination*. London: Methuen.

Appadurai, Arjun. 2002. Deep Democracy: Urban Governmentality and the Horizon of Politics. *Public Culture* 14: 21–47.

Ashbery, John. 2007. "Ignorance of the Law Is No Excuse," *Notes from the Air: Selected Later Poems*. New York: HarperCollins, 329.

Badgett, M. V. Lee. 2003. *Money, Myths, and Change: The Economic Lives of Lesbians and Gay Men*. Chicago: University of Chicago Press.

Badgett, M. V. Lee, Holning Lau, Brad Sears, and Deborah Ho. 2007. Bias in the Workplace: Consistent Evidence of Sexual Orientation and Gender Identity Discrimination. Report of the Williams Institute, University of California, Los Angeles. Accessed July 23, 2010. http://www.law.ucla.edu/WilliamsInstitute/publications/Bias%20in%20the%20 Workplace.pdf.

Bartels, Larry M. 2008.*Unequal Democracy: The Political Economy of the New Gilded Age*. Princeton: Princeton University Press.

Berlant, Laurent. 1997. *The Queen of America Goes to Washington City: Essays on Sex and Citizenship*. Durham, NC: Duke University Press.

———. 2006. Cruel Optimism. *differences: A Journal of Feminist Cultural Studies* 17, no. 3: 20–36.

———. 2007. Nearly Utopian, Nearly Normal: Post-Fordist Affect in *La Promesse* and *Rosetta*. *Public Culture* 19: 273–301.

———. 2008. *The Female Complaint: The Unfinished Business of Sentimentality in American Culture*. Durham, NC: Duke University Press.

Bersani, Leo. 1995. *Homos*. Cambridge, MA: Harvard University Press.

Bérubé, Allan. 1997. Intellectual Desire. In *Queerly Classed: Gay Men and Lesbians Write About Class*, ed. Susan Raffo, 43–66. Boston: South End Press.

Bettie, Julie. 2003. *Women without Class: Girls, Race, and Identity*. Berkeley: University of California Press.

Bledstein, Burton J. 1976. *The Culture of Professionalism.* New York: W. W. Norton.

Bloch, Ernst. 1995. *The Principle of Hope.* Translated by Neville Plaice, Stephen Plaice, and Paul Knight. 3 vols. Cambridge, MA: MIT Press.

Bourdieu, Pierre. 1984. *Distinction: A Social Critique of the Judgment of Taste.* Translated by Richard Nice. Cambridge, MA: Harvard University Press.

Brooks, David. 1997. New-Class Nuptials. *City Journal* 7, no. 3 (Summer), http://www.city-journal.org/html/7_3_urbanities-new_class.html.

Brownworth, Victoria A. 1997. Life in the Passing Lane: Exposing the Class Closet. In *Queerly Classed: Gay Men and Lesbians Write About Class,* ed. Susan Raffo, 67–78. Boston: South End Press.

Bryan-Wilson, Julia. 2004. Some Kind of Grace: An Interview with Miranda July. *Camera Obscura* 55: 180–97.

Butler, Judith. 1997. Merely Cultural. *Social Text* 52/53: 265–77.

Chauncey, George. 1994. *Gay New York: Gender, Urban Culture, and the Making of the Gay Male World, 1890–1940.* New York: Basic Books.

Cvetkovich, Ann. 2003. *An Archive of Feelings: Trauma, Sexuality, and Lesbian Public Cultures.* Durham, NC: Duke University Press.

Duggan, Lisa. 2003. *The Twilight of Equality? Neoliberalism, Cultural Politics, and the Attack on Democracy.* Boston: Beacon Press.

Dyer, Richard. 1979. In Defense of Disco. *Gay Left* 8: 19–23.

Edelman, Lee. 2004. *No Future: Queer Theory and the Death Drive.* Durham, NC: Duke University Press.

Ehrenreich, Barbara. 2001. *Nickel and Dimed: On (Not) Getting By in America.* New York: Metropolitan Books.

Eng, David L., Judith Halberstam, and José Esteban Muñoz, eds. 2005.What's Queer About Queer Studies Now? Special issue, *Social Text* 23, nos. 3–4.

Feld, Steven. 1996. Pygmy POP: A Genealogy of Schizophonic Mimesis. *Yearbook of Traditional Music* 28: 1–35.

Felski, Rita. 2000. Nothing to Declare: Identity, Shame, and the Lower Middle Class. *PMLA Journal* 115: 33–45.

Ferguson, Roderick A. 2004. *Aberrations in Black: Toward a Queer of Color Critique.* Minneapolis: University of Minnesota Press.

Field, Nicola. 1995.*Over the Rainbow: Money, Class, and Homophobia.* London: Pluto Press.

Foucault, Michel. 1986. *The History of Sexuality: Volume 1, An Introduction.* New York: Pantheon.

———. 1981/1997. Friendship as a Way of Life. In *Ethics: Subjectivity and Truth.* Vol. 1 of *Essential Works of Michel Foucault, 1954–1984*, ed. Paul Rabinow, 135–40. New York: New Press.

Fraser, Nancy. 1996. Social Justice in the Age of Identity Politics: Redistribution, Recognition, and Participation. The Tanner Lectures on Human Values, Stanford University, Palo Alto. http://www.tannerlectures.utah.edu/lectures/ documents/ Fraser98.pdf.

———. 1997a. *Justice Interruptus*. New York: Routledge.

———. 1997b. Heterosexism, Misrecognition, and Capitalism: A Response to Judith Butler. *Social Text* 52–53: 279–89.

———. 2000. Rethinking Recognition. *New Left Review* 3 (May–June): 107–20.

Freeman, Elizabeth. 2002. *The Wedding Complex: Forms of Belonging in Modern American Culture*. Durham, NC: Duke University Press.

Gamson, Joshua. 1998. *Freaks Talk Back: Tabloid Talk Shows and Sexual Nonconformity*. Chicago: University of Chicago Press.

Gibson-Graham, J. K. 2006. *A Post Capitalist Politics*. Minneapolis: University of Minnesota Press.

Gibson-Graham, J. K., S. A. Resnick, and R. D. Wolff. 2000. Introduction: Class in a Poststructuralist Frame. In *Class and Its Others*, ed. Gibson-Graham, Resnick, and Wolff, 1–22. Minneapolis: University of Minnesota Press.

Green, Jesse. 2005. Who's Afraid of Sarah Schulman? *New York Times*, October 23.

Greenwald, Glenn. 2010. The misguided reaction to Tea Party Candidates. *Salon*, September 16. Accessed November 2, 2010. http://www.salon.com/news/opinion/glenn_greenwald/2010/09/16/tea_party/index.html.

Grindstaff, Laura. 2002. *The Money Shot: Trash, Class, and the Making of a TV Talk Show*. Chicago: University of Chicago Press.

Gross, Larry. 2001. *Up from Invisibility: Lesbians, Gay Men, and the Media in America*. New York: Columbia University Press.

Halberstam, Judith. 2001, February 10. The Brandon Teena Archives. Lecture presented at John Sims Center for the Arts, San Francisco.

———. 2005. *In a Queer Time and Place: Transgender Bodies, Subcultural Lives*. New York: New York University Press.

Hall, Stuart. 1982. The Rediscovery of Ideology: Return of the Repressed in Media Studies. In *Culture, Society and the Media*, ed. Michael Gurevitch, Tony Bennett, James Curran, and Janet Woollacott, 56–90. London: Methuen.

Heap, Chad. 2009. *Slumming: Sexual and Racial Encounters in American Nightlife, 1885–1940*. Chicago: University of Chicago Press.

Hemphill, Essex. 1995. *In Living Color*: Toms, Coons, Mammies, Faggots, and Bucks. In *Out in Culture: Gay, Lesbian, and Queer Essays on Popular Culture*, ed. Alexander Doty and Corey K. Creekmur, 389–403. Durham, NC: Duke University Press.

Henderson, Lisa. 1999. Simple Pleasures: Lesbian Community and *Go Fish*. *Signs: Journal of Women in Culture and Society* 25: 37–64.

———. 2000. Queer Communication Studies. In *Communication Yearbook*. Vol. 24, ed. William Gudykunst, 465–85. Thousand Oaks, CA: Sage.

Hennessy, Rosemary. 2000. *Profit and Pleasure: Sexual Identities in Late Capitalism*. New York: Routledge.

Herszenhorn, David. 2010. Next Big Battle in Washington: Bush's Tax Cuts. *New York Times*, July 24. Accessed July 25, 2010. http://www.nytimes.com/2010/07/25/us/politics/25tax.html?_r=1&scp=1&sq=Bush%20tax%20cuts&st=cse.

Horowitz, Eli. 2005. Interview with Miranda July: Performance Artist and Filmmaker. *The Believer,* June. Accessed August 10, 2008. http://www.believermag.com/exclusives/ ?read=interview_july.

Houlbrook, Matt. 2006. *Queer London: Perils and Pleasures in the Sexual Metropolis, 1918–1957.* Chicago: University of Chicago Press.

Hunter, Nan D. 2010. Proposition 8 Ruling Stresses Stigma of Gay Marriage Ban. *The Guardian*, August 5. Accessed August 5, 2010. http://www.guardian.co.uk/world/ 2010/aug/05/proposition–8-california-gay-rights.

Ingraham, Chrys. 1999. *White Weddings: Romancing Heterosexuality in Popular Culture.* New York: Routledge.

Johanson, Mary Ann. 2005. *Me and You and Everyone We Know* (review). July 13. Accessed August 10, 2008. http://www.flickfilosopher.com/blog/2005/07/me_and_ you_and_everyone_we_kno.html

Johnson, Charles. 1994. Exchange Value. In *The Sorcerer's Apprentice: Tales and Conjurations.* New York: Plume.

Johnson, David K. 2004. *The Lavender Scare: The Cold War Persecution of Gays and Lesbians in the Federal Government.* Chicago: Chicago University Press.

July, Miranda. 2007. *No One Belongs Here More Than You.* New York: Scribner.

Kaplan, Cora. 2000. Millennial Class. In "Re-reading Class," ed. Cora Kaplan, special issue, *PMLA Journal* 115, no. 1: 9–19.

Keeling, Kara. 2007. *The Witch's Flight: The Cinematic, the Black Femme, and the Image of Common Sense.* Durham, NC: Duke University Press.

Kennedy, Elizabeth Lapovsky, and Madeline D. Davis. 1993. *Boots of Leather, Slippers of Gold: The History of a Lesbian Community.* New York: Penguin.

Kipnis, Laura. 1999. Disgust and Desire: *Hustler* Magazine. In *Bound and Gagged: Pornography and the Politics of Fantasy in America,* 122–60. Durham, NC: Duke University Press.

———. 2003. *Against Love: A Polemic.* New York: Pantheon.

Lanchester, John. 2008. Cityphilia. *London Review of Books* 30, no. 1 (January 3): 9–12. Accessed July 22, 2010. http://www.lrb.co.uk/v30/n01/john-lanchester/ cityphilia.

Laurier, Joanne, and David Walsh. 2006. Two Recent Films: *Brokeback Mountain* and *Walk the Line.* Review of *Brokeback Mountain,* by Ang Lee, and *Walk the Line,* by James Mangold. World Socialist Web Site, January 5. Accessed April 28, 2008. www. wsws.org/articles/2006/jan2006/film-j05.shtml.

Lipsitz, George. 1997. Class and Consciousness: Teaching about Social Class in Public Universities. In *Class Issues: Pedagogy, Cultural Studies, and the Public Sphere,* ed. Amitava Kumar, 9–21. New York: New York University Press.

Lorde, Audre. 1984. Poetry Is Not a Luxury. In *Sister Outsider: Essays and Speeches,* 36–39. Freedom, CA: Crossing Press.

Lotz, Amanda D. 2004. Textual (Im)possibilities in the U.S. Post-network Era: Negotiating Production and Promotion Processes on Lifetime's *Any Day Now. Critical Studies in Media Communication* 21: 22–43.

Love, Heather. 2007. *Feeling Backward: Loss and the Politics of Queer History.* Cambridge, MA: Harvard University Press.

MacDonald, Dwight. 1957. A Theory of Mass Culture. In *Mass Culture: The Popular Arts in America,* ed. Bernard Rosenberg and David Manning White, 59–73. Glencoe, IL: Free Press.

MacDonald, Michael Patrick. 1999. *All Souls: A Family Story from Southie.* Boston: Beacon Press.

———. 2006. *Easter Rising: A Memoir of Roots and Rebellion.* Boston and New York: Houghton Mifflin.

McElya, Micki. 2001. Trashing the Presidency: Race, Class, and the Clinton/Lewinsky Affair. In *Our Monica, Ourselves: The Clinton Affair and the National Interest,* ed. Lauren Berlant and Lisa Duggan, 156–74. New York: New York University Press.

Morton, Donald. 1996. *The Material Queer: A LesBiGay Cultural Studies Reader.* Boulder, CO: Westview Press.

Muñoz, José Esteban. 1999. *Disidentifications: Queers of Color and the Performance of Politics.* Minneapolis: University of Minnesota Press.

———. 2009. *Cruising Utopia: The Then and There of Queer Futurity.* New York: New York University Press.

Munt, Sally. 2000. Introduction. In *Cultural Studies and the Working Class: Subject to Change,* ed. Sally Munt, 1–19. London and New York: Cassell.

Murphy, Kevin P., Jason Ruiz, and David Serlin. 2008. Editors' Introduction, in "Queer Futures," ed. Kevin P. Murphy, Jason Ruiz, and David Serling, special issue, *Radical History Review* 100: 1–9.

Myles, Eileen. 1994. *Chelsea Girls.* New York: Black Sparrow Press.

Nardi, Peter K. 1999. *Gay Men's Friendships: Invincible Communities.* Chicago: University of Chicago Press.

Newton, Esther. 1972. *Mother Camp: Female Impersonators in America.* Chicago: University of Chicago Press.

———. 1995. *Cherry Grove, Fire Island: Sixty Years in America's First Gay and Lesbian Town.* New York: Beacon Press.

O'Kane, John. 2002. Capital, Culture, and Socioeconomic Justice. *Rethinking Marxism* 14, no. 2 (Summer): 1–23.

Ortner, Sherry B. 1991. Reading America: Preliminary Notes on Class and Culture. In *Recapturing Anthropology: Working in the Present,* ed. Richard G. Fox, 163–89. Santa Fe: School of American Research.

———. 2003. *New Jersey Dreaming: Capital, Culture, and the Class of '58.* Durham, NC: Duke University Press.

Penn, Liz (Dana Stevens), *Look at Me*: Vive le Juicebomb! *High Sign*, April 21, 2005, www.thehighsign.net/archives/review/look_at_me.html.

Prosser, Jay. 1998. *Second Skins: The Body Narratives of Transsexuality.* New York: Columbia University Press.

Raban, Jonathan. 2008. Cut, Kill, Dig, Drill. *London Review of Books* 30, no. 9 (October 9): 7–10.

Radway, Janice. 1991 (1984). *Reading the Romance: Women, Patriarchy, and Popular Literature*. Chapel Hill: University of North Carolina Press.

Rich, B. Ruby. 1998. Preface: Jews Without Books. In *Chick Flicks: Theories and Memories of the Feminist Film Movement*, xv–xix. Durham, NC: Duke University Press.

———. 2005. Hello Cowboy. *The Guardian*, September 23. Accessed October 23, 2012. www.guardian.co.uk/film/2005/sep/23/3?INTCMP=SRCH

———. 2006a. The Q-Word, the Post-*Brokeback* Landscape, Queer Normativity, and the Genderation Gap. Keynote address at the Persistent Vision Conference, San Francisco, June 19–22.

———. 2006b. The New Homosexual Film Festivals. *GLQ* 12: 620–25.

———. 2007. Brokering *Brokeback*: Jokes, Backlashes, and Other Anxieties. *Film Quarterly* 60, no. 3: 44–48.

Rose, Jennie. 2004. "The Last Refuge of Democracy: A Talk with B. Ruby Rich," *Green Cine*, May 7. Accessed August 20, 2008. www.greencine.com/article?action=view&articleID=119&pageID=227.

Rubin, Gayle S. 1984/1993. "Thinking Sex: Notes for a Radical Theory of the Politics of Sexuality." In *The Lesbian and Gay Studies Reader,* ed. Henry Abelove, Michele Aine Barale, and David M. Halperin, 3–44. New York: Routledge.

Rubin, Lillian B. 1992. *Worlds of Pain: Life in the Working-Class Family*. 2nd ed. New York: Basic Books/HarperCollins.

Rymon, Geoff. 1992. *Was*. New York: Alfred A. Knopf.

Scott, A. O. 2005. *Me and You and Everyone We Know* (2004). *New York Times*, June 17. Accessed August 10, 2008. http://movies.nytimes.com/2005/06/17/movies/17mira.html?_r=1.

Scott, James C. 1990. *Domination and the Arts of Resistance: Hidden Transcripts*. New Haven: Yale University Press.

Sedgwick, Eve Kosofsky. 2003. "Paranoid Reading and Reparative Reading, or, You're So Paranoid, You Probably Think This Essay Is About You." In *Touching Feeling: Affect, Pedagogy, Performativity*, 23–53. Durham, NC: Duke University Press.

Sender, Katherine. 2003. "Sex Sells: Sex, Taste, and Class in Commercial Gay and Lesbian Media." *GLQ: A Journal of Gay and Lesbian Studies* 9, no. 3: 1–31.

———. 2004. *Business, Not Politics: The Making of the Gay Market*. New York: Columbia University Press.

Sennett, Richard, and Jonathan Cobb. 1972. *The Hidden Injuries of Class*. New York: Alfred A. Knopf.

Shaviro, Steven. 2005. *Me and You and Everyone We Know*. August 10. Accessed August 10, 2008. http://www.shaviro.com/Blog/?s=Miranda+July

Skeggs, Beverly. 2000. The Appearance of Class: Challenges in Gay Space. In *Cultural Studies and the Working Class: Subject to Change*, ed. Sally Munt, 129–51. London: Cassell.

———. 2004. *Class, Self, Culture*. London: Routledge.

Smith, Anna Marie. 2001. "Missing Poststructuralism, Missing Foucault: Butler and Fraser on Capitalism and the Regulation of Sexuality." *Social Text* 67: 103–25.

Stallybrass, Peter, and Allon White. 1986. *The Politics and Poetics of Transgression.* Ithaca, NY: Cornell University Press.

Steedman, Carolyn Kay. 1994. *Landscape for a Good Woman: The Story of Two Lives.* New Brunswick, NJ: Rutgers University Press.

Stein, Mark. 2000. *City of Sisterly and Brotherly Loves: Lesbian and Gay Philadelphia, 1945–1972.* Chicago: University of Chicago Press.

Stevens, Hampton. 2010. *Modern Family* and *The Middle*: A Tale of Two Series. *TheAtlantic.com*, March 17. Accessed November 2, 2010. http://www.theatlantic.com/culture/archive/2010/03/modern-family-and-the-middle-a-tale-of-2-series/37582/.

Tinkcom, Matthew. 2002. *Working Like a Homosexual: Camp, Capital, Cinema.* Durham, NC: Duke University Press.

Tucker, Scott. 1997. There's No Place Like Home: Straight Supremacy, Queer Resistance, and Equality of Kinship. In *The Queer Question: Essays on Desire and Democracy*, 202–47. Boston: South End Press.

Walkerdine, Valerie. 1997. *Daddy's Girl: Young Girls and Popular Culture.* Cambridge, MA: Harvard University Press.

Walters, Suzanna. 2001. *All the Rage: The Story of Gay Visibility in America.* Chicago: University of Chicago Press.

Warner, Michael. 1999. *The Trouble with Normal: Sex, Politics, and the Ethics of Queer Life.* New York: Free Press.

White, Patricia, and others. 1999. Queer Publicity: A Dossier on Lesbian and Gay Film Festivals. *GLQ* 5: 73–93.

Williams, Raymond. 1958. *Culture and Society, 1780–1950.* New York: Columbia University Press.

———. 1961. *The Long Revolution.* London: Chatto and Windus.

Willis, Paul. 1977. *Learning to Labour: How Working Class Kids Get Working Class Jobs.* Farnborough, Hants, UK: Saxon House.

Willse, Craig, and Dean Spade. 2005. "Freedom in a Regulatory State? Lawrence, Marriage, and Biopolitics." *Widener Law Review* 307: 309–29.

Woods, James D. 1993. *The Corporate Closet: The Professional Lives of Gay Men in America.* New York: Free Press.

Yardley, William. 2010. "Voters in Oregon Approve Tax Increases." *New York Times*, January 27. Accessed July 23, 2010. http://www.nytimes.com/2010/01/28/us/28oregon.html?_r=1&ref=oregon.

FILMS

Anderson, Jane, Martha Coolidge, and Anne Heche, directors. 2000. *If These Walls Could Talk II*. New York: HBO.

Apatow, Judd, director. 2005. *The 40-Year-Old Virgin*. Universal City, CA: Universal Pictures.

Bigelow, Kathryn, director. 1991. *Point Break*. Tokyo: JVC Entertainment Networks.

Bogart, Paul, director. 1988. *Torch Song Trilogy*. New York: New Line Cinema.

Brest, Martin, director. 1984. *Beverly Hills Cop*. Los Angeles: Paramount Pictures.

Caouette, Jonathan, writer/director. 2003. *Tarnation*. Documentary. New York: Wellspring.

Cuarón, Alfonso, director. 2006. *Children of Men*. Universal City, CA: Universal Pictures.

Dardenne, Jean-Pierre, and Luc Dardenne, directors. 1996. *La Promesse*. Strasbourg: Eurimages.

———. 1999. *Rosetta*. Paris: ARP Selection.

Dietch, Donna, director. 1985. *Desert Hearts*. Los Angeles: Desert Hearts Productions.

DiFeliciantonio, Tina, and Jane C. Wagner, directors. 1996. *Two or Three Things but Nothing for Sure*. Documentary short. New York: Naked Eye Productions.

Dodge, Harriet, and Silas Howard, writers/directors. 2001. *By Hook or By Crook*. Los Angeles: Steakhaus Productions.

Duthie, Karen, director. 2004. *100% Woman*. Documentary. Vancouver, BC: Artemis Dreams Productions.

Ephron, Nora, writer/director. 2005. *Julie and Julia*. New York: Columbia Pictures.

Ford, Tom, director. 2009. *A Single Man*. Los Angeles: Artina Films.

Fears, Stephen, director. 2006. *The Queen*. Italy: BIM Distribuzione.

Gray, F. Gary, director. 1996. *Set It Off*. New York: New Line Cinema.

Guest, Christopher, director. 2000. *Best in Show*. Beverly Hills: Castle Rock Entertainment.

———. 2003. *A Mighty Wind*. Beverly Hills: Castle Rock Entertainment.

Hardwicke, Catherine, writer/director. 2003. *Thirteen*. Los Angeles: Fox Searchlight Pictures.

Herman-Wurmfeld, Charles, director. 2001. *Kissing Jessica Stein*. Los Angeles: Fox Searchlight Pictures.

Huston, Anjelica, director. 1996. *Bastard Out of Carolina*. New York: Showtime Networks.

Ichaso, Leon, director. 1985. *Crossover Dreams*. New York: CF Inc.

Jackson, Peter, director. 2009. *The Lovely Bones*. Los Angeles: Dreamworks SKG.

Jaoui, Agnes, director. 2004. *Look at Me*. Paris: Les Films A4.

Johnson, Liza, writer/director. 2005. *Desert Motel*. Los Angeles: 5 Aces Productions.

———. 2006. *South of Ten*. Documentary. Saltwater Pictures.

Jordan, Neil, writer/director. 1992. *The Crying Game*. London: Palace Pictures and Channel 4.

———, director. 2005. *Breakfast on Pluto*. London: Pathé Pictures International.

July, Miranda, writer/director. 2005. *Me and You and Everyone We Know*. New York: IFC Films.

King, Michael Patrick, director. 2008. *Sex and the City*. Los Angeles: New Line Cinema.

Koppelman, Brian, and David Levien, directors. 2010. *A Solitary Man*. Los Angeles: Millennium Films.

Lee, Ang, director. 2005. *Brokeback Mountain*. Calgary, Canada: Alberta Film Entertainment.

Livingston, Jennie, director. 1990. *Paris Is Burning*. New York: Miramax Productions.

McKay, Adam, director. 2000. *Talladega Nights: The Ballad of Ricky Bobby*. New York: Columbia Pictures.

Miller, Bennett, director. 2005. *Capote*. New York: A Line Pictures.

Muska, Susan, and Greta Olafsdottir, directors. 1998. *The Brandon Teena Story*. Documentary. New York: Bless Bless Productions.

Peirce, Kimberly, writer/director. 1999. *Boys Don't Cry*. Los Angeles: Fox Searchlight Pictures.

Pierson, Frank, director. 2003. *A Soldier's Girl*. Los Angeles: Bachrach/ Gottlieb Productions.

Pitof [Jean-Christophe Comar], director. 2004. *Catwoman*. Burbank, CA, and New York: Warner Bros. Pictures.

Reynolds, Kevin, director. 1995. *Waterworld*. Universal City: Universal Pictures.

Roach, Jay, director. 1997. *Austin Powers: International Man of Mystery*. Beverly Hills: Capella International.

Schlesinger, John, director. 1969. *Midnight Cowboy*. New York: Florin Productions.

Schmidt, Rick, director. 1977. *Showboat 1988: The Remake*.

Scott, Ridley, director. 2007. *American Gangster*. Universal City, CA: Universal Pictures.

Troche, Rose, writer/director. 1995. *Go Fish*. New York: Can I Watch Pictures.

Tucker, Duncan, writer/director. 2005. *Transamerica*. Toronto, Ontario: Belladonna Productions.

Wain, David, director. 2008. *Role Models*. Universal City, CA: Universal Pictures.

Waters, John, writer/director. 1988. *Hairspray*. New York: New Line Cinema.

———. 1994. *Serial Mom*. Lauderdale Lakes, FL: Polar Entertainment Corporation.

———. 2004. *A Dirty Shame*. New York: This Is That Productions.

Whale, James, director. 1936. *Show Boat*. Universal City, CA: Universal Pictures.

TELEVISION PROGRAMS

Brothers and Sisters
Curb Your Enthusiasm
Ellen
Entourage
Friday Night Lights
Gay Weddings
George Lopez
Glee
Home Improvement
How I Met Your Mother
In Living Color
Modern Family
My Wife and Kids
Queer as Folk
Queer Eye for the Straight Guy
Roseanne
Saturday Night Live
Sex and the City
Six Feet Under
The Bernie Mac Show
The Cosby Show
The Golden Girls
The Hughleys
The L Word
The Middle
The Prime Time Emmy Awards (2010)
Ugly Betty
Will & Grace

ABOUT THE AUTHOR

Lisa Henderson is Professor of Communication and Chair of the Department of Communication at the University of Massachusetts Amherst. She is also a founding member of the Lesbian, Gay, Bisexual and Transgender Studies Interest Group of the International Communication Association, and in 2011 received the Roy F. Aarons Award of the Association for Education in Journalism and Mass Communication for Outstanding Contribution to GLBT Education and Research.